Phra Farang

Peter Robinson became a Buddhist monk at the age of forty-five. As Phra Peter Pannapadipo, he founded the Students' Education Trust – a charity to help impoverished students and novice monks continue their higher education. Monks cannot earn money or directly fundraise, so after ten years Phra Peter temporarily disrobed from the monkhood to establish SET as a Foundation in Thailand.

ALSO BY PHRA PETER PANNAPADIPO

Little Angels

PHRA FARANG

PHRA PETER PANNAPADIPO

arrow books

First published in the United Kingdom by Arrow Books in 2005

13

This edition first published in 1997 by Post Books,
the publishing arm of the *Bangkok Post*

Arrow Books
The Random House Group Limited
20 Vauxhall Bridge Road, London, SW1V 2SA

Random House Australia (Pty) Limited
20 Alfred Street, Milsons Point, Sydney,
New South Wales 2061, Australia

Random House New Zealand Limited
18 Poland Road, Glenfield
Auckland 10, New Zealand

Random House (Pty) Limited
Endulini, 5a Jubilee Road, Parktown 2193, South Africa

The Random House Group Limited Reg. No. 954009

www.randomhouse.co.uk

A CIP catalogue record for this book
is available from the British Library

Penguin Random House is committed to a sustainable future for
our business, our readers and our planet. This book is made from
Forest Stewardship Council® certified paper.

ISBN 978-0-09-948447-9

Typeset by Palimpsest Book Production Limited
Polmont, Stirlingshire

Printed and bound in Great Britain by Clays Ltd, Elcograf S.p.A.

Intro

*N*AMO: Homage. Homage to the Buddha. The first word of a longer salutation at the beginning of every Buddhist service. But for me, *Namo* means more than paying homage to the Buddha himself. It is also homage to the supreme effort he made to reach Enlightenment; to the sacrifices he made in renouncing his family and princely lifestyle, and to the pain and suffering he endured as an ascetic before he discovered 'The Middle Way'. It is homage to the selfless devotion of forty-five years of his life to teaching what he discovered; teaching all people, regardless of creed or social status. It is homage to *what* he taught – the *Dhamma*; a shining beacon of wisdom that has drawn men and women for more than 2,500 years and lit the path to lead them from suffering. And it is homage to the *Sangha*; the community of monks and nuns which has devoted itself to follow what he taught, and which has preserved and practised the teaching for so many centuries, thus helping countless others along that difficult path.

1

Sometimes, when I am full of confidence, I picture the word with an exclamation mark: *Namo*! Proclaim it loudly throughout the world for the benefit of all mankind! But at other times, times of doubt in my strength and ability to follow, to know and to live what the Buddha taught, there is a question mark: *Namo*? Then my mind may be full of uncertainty that no amount of inward-looking seems to answer.

I have chanted *Namo* with dozens of other monks in the most magnificent temples, kneeling on polished marble floors before golden, jewel-encrusted images of staggering beauty, glittering in the light of huge candles and crystal chandeliers. Sometimes, then, it has been just a word, its own beauty seemingly diminished by the awesome but insignificant grandeur.

But also, late at night, sometimes feeling miserably lost and full of doubt, I have knelt alone on the dusty, wooden floor of a simple little temple in Thailand's remote countryside, before a cobweb-festooned image gleaming dully in the light of a single candle. Then, my voice choked with emotion, I have whispered *Namo* and bowed low before something so overwhelmingly vast and beautiful, it is almost beyond comprehension. And my heart and mind have been uplifted and my strength has returned.

Namo Tassa Bhagavato Arahato Samma Sambuddhassa.
Homage to the Exalted One, Perfectly Enlightened by Himself.

1

The first question most people ask me when we meet is, 'Why did you become a Buddhist monk?' I think they expect my answer to reveal some personal inadequacy or character flaw, a dreadful tragedy in my past, or some other dark secret. If that had been the case, I'd have joined the Foreign Legion. Becoming a Buddhist monk was not, for me, the result of running away from some personal darkness but rather of progressing towards a great light.

I don't believe there was any one specific reason why I decided to ordain. I believe everything that ever happened to me, everything I ever did – good, bad or indifferent – led in some small way to my decision. It just happened, fortuitously, that I reached a point in my life, at exactly the right moment for me, when all my circumstances came together, came right, to enable me to view my old life more objectively and to see an alternative and more worthwhile way of living.

I don't often bother looking back at the past but when

I do I can see that a lot of my life before I ordained was a waste of precious time. Although I certainly seemed to enjoy it then, at least superficially, with hindsight it wasn't even very interesting, not in any profound way. Like a lot of people, probably most people, I was motivated almost entirely by the baser senses and threw most of my time away on cheap thrills, trying to gratify every little whim and craving in an almost desperate effort to give my life some apparent meaning.

My parents were vaguely Christian so I suppose I was too, in an equally vague way. I went to Sunday School as a child, to christenings, weddings and funerals, and all the family attended services at the local church at Easter and Christmas. But somehow, religion just seemed to drift out of my life. By the time I was about sixteen, 'Church of England' had become something to write on official forms in the space for 'Religion'. As a pre-teenager at Sunday School I was quite happy to embrace the child's traditional idea of 'God' but by the time I entered my teens I started having something of a struggle with the whole concept. I suppose a vague idea of 'God' in some form or other remained at the back of my mind but I found it increasingly difficult to accept such a concept intellectually, let alone spiritually. Although I lived my life in a reasonably moral way, I was quite happy to shelve the whole issue of religion and didn't identify with any particular teaching. It all seemed a bit irrelevant to my life at that time and became even less relevant as I got older.

In my twenties and thirties I had fun, lots of it, in

all the usual ways. I was young, reasonably well educated, reasonably affluent and very, very confident. I knew who I was, what I was and where I was going. There were ups and downs, of course, but I was a survivor; I believed I knew how to play this game called Life.

I was just about forty years old when I started to re-evaluate my life. I had consciously made re-evaluations at other times too, of course, but they had been based on seeking change and improvement within the parameters of my existing lifestyle, rather than changing the whole way I viewed life and my role within it.

In all the previous years, I had tried to live my life to the full, or what I then thought of as 'full'. My lifestyle was neither extreme nor excessive, neither dishonest nor immoral, but I ducked and dived, wheeled and dealed my way through it, always seeking some new experience, some new thing to make it seem worthwhile. At the time I never questioned whether any of it was genuinely worthwhile or not. I was usually having fun, or at least managed to convince myself that I was, and I was far too busy to question its validity. As long as I had a heart full of dreams and a pocket full of money and could buy some transient happiness or new exciting experience, that was all that seemed to matter. The idea of 'spiritual satisfaction' never really entered my head.

I worked hard, usually in my own businesses. Most were interesting, at least until they became routine and ceased to stimulate me, some were fun and a few seemed worthwhile. Usually they brought me sufficient money to be able to indulge myself. Sometimes I used my money wisely, occasionally generously, usually wastefully, to help me try to achieve happiness, or at least the ultimate 'good time'. I never found it, of course.

My life was not based solely on the pursuit of fleeting pleasures or material acquisition. I actively and at times successfully sought strong emotional and long-term attachments. But even within my close personal relationships, I sometimes sensed that something was missing. There was an incompleteness and my relationships never seemed quite as fulfilling as others claimed theirs to be. Perhaps there was some emotional inadequacy on my part but I believe I always gave as much as I could, living my relationships to the full, just as I did the rest of my life. It hardly matters now anyway.

My brother David was two years older than I. He lived in Paris and he *really* had money and knew how to enjoy it. He had worked most of the hours of the day for many years to build up a very successful business and he thoroughly deserved and enjoyed the material and sensual diversions his success provided. An apartment in Paris, a chateau in the countryside, a Ferrari, a yacht . . .

Without warning, he was dead at forty-two.

In retrospect it is a pity that, on my occasional visits to my brother's home, I never saw beyond his material success or superficial happiness. If I had, I think I would have earlier recognised the great underlying dissatisfaction from which he suffered, but covered up well, and

I might have been able to relate that to my own similar and equally futile materialistic ambitions.

I had already started to realise that my life didn't seem to be going anywhere in particular but my brother's sudden death was such a shock it prompted my re-evaluation to take on a new urgency. He and I were never really close and it wasn't so much the fact of his death that shook me but more the ending of his life and the apparent futility of everything he had achieved, experienced and acquired. All his success, material gains and future plans were suddenly without an iota of importance. Nor were mine.

I suppose most people ask themselves the 'why?' and 'what for?' questions at some dramatic point in their lives. Unfortunately, the questions frequently seem to have no obvious answers or solutions. Even if the answers are realised, they may seem too complex or frightening to acknowledge or act upon. I don't mean about death necessarily – it seems pointless to me to speculate or worry about that – I mean about Life and all its ramifications. Dying isn't difficult, it's living that can scare the hell out of us. I've never been frightened of life's ups and downs, its twists and turns, nor have I ever been frightened to actively seek to encourage change in myself. And that's what I decided to do, but I didn't really know in which direction I had to go.

By coincidence, at about that time I made my first trip to Thailand. It was the usual tourist package; a week in Bangkok, a week in Chiang Mai and a week on a beach somewhere. Not being one for lying on beaches,

I instead took the opportunity to visit many Buddhist monasteries; not just the big important ones on every tourist's agenda but also little out-of-the-way, ordinary working monasteries. I was immensely impressed by the feeling of tranquil purpose in some of them and made a point of talking at length with any English-speaking monks I could find.

I had only the most superficial understanding of Buddhism and much of what I thought I knew turned out to be quite wrong. I returned to England determined to find out more, though that was still mainly out of passing intellectual curiosity. Over the next few weeks I read as much as I could about Buddhism and then a telephone call to the Thai Embassy put me in touch with the Thai monastery in London: Wat Buddhapadipa in Wimbledon. *Wat* means monastery or temple and *Buddhapadipa* means 'Lamp, or Lights, of the Buddha'. Soon afterwards I made the first of many hundreds of visits to the monastery.

Although I claim my initial interest was mainly out of intellectual curiosity, I think I must subconsciously have known almost from the start that it might develop further than that. Before my first visit to Wat Buddhapadipa, on a Sunday, I had telephoned to check whether the monastery welcomed visitors. I'd spoken on the phone with a monk named Phra Khru Silananda, who told me I would be welcome and suggested I should ask for him when I arrived. Wat Buddhapadipa was about forty minutes' drive from my home and I parked outside. I sat in my car for about half an hour, trying to work out in my mind why I had come and whether this visit was really necessary. In all my life, I had never been any sort of soul searcher, tending to consider such people (unfairly, I know) as being slightly pathetic, like train spotters. Although I had never felt the need for spiritual guidance of any kind, I also felt I was now at a crossroads in my life and needed some direction. I wasn't grasping at straws but I was prepared to consider all the options, even those that seemed fairly wild. I sat in my car and mentally prevaricated but finally decided it wasn't necessary. I turned the car round and drove home and then, once back home, immediately turned round yet again and drove back to Wimbledon.

After all this uncertainty and to-ing and fro-ing, it was quite late by the time I actually entered the monastery and had a chat with Phra Khru Silananda. He wasn't at all what I expected and impressed me greatly with his genuine friendliness, humour and down-to-earth approach to my spiritual uncertainties. He didn't try to sell the idea of Buddhism to me at all. He suggested that I didn't need to make any sort of commitment but that it might be helpful for me to join the monastery's Sunday morning course about basic Buddhism and meditation, which I decided to do. After more than thirty years, it was back to Sunday School for me.

Through attending regular classes at the monastery, I learned first the basic principles of Buddhism, then something of the higher teaching and also made my first attempts at meditation. I was lucky enough to meet a Thai monk there, Phra Maha Laow, who became not only my guide on many spiritual matters but also a good friend. Some years later he arranged my ordination in Bangkok.

Whilst studying at Wat Buddhapadipa, I realised that Buddhism seemed to provide the answers to questions I didn't even realise I had been asking myself. Some of those unacknowledged questions and doubts had probably been lurking at the back of my mind for many years but now they were forced to the surface, to be examined and faced. The teaching answered them all or, through my developing meditation skills, I was able to discover the solutions for myself.

There are two main schools of Buddhism; *Theravada* (Doctrine of the Elders) and *Mahayana* (The Great Vehicle). Theravada is considered by its adherents to be the original, orthodox teaching, while Mahayana is a later development and includes several schools within itself, such as Zen (itself having numerous sects). The Theravada and Mahayana schools agree on the fundamental principles of Buddhism though there are differences of emphasis in some aspects of the teaching as well as many differences in outward form. Most Thais follow Theravada Buddhism.

Although all the monks at Wat Buddhapadipa were Thai, the teaching for Westerners was almost entirely free of the many Animist and Brahmanic traditions that have been absorbed into popular Thai Buddhism. Although I knew by then that the Buddhism I had observed in Thailand had been corrupted by those influences, at least at a superficial level, that didn't affect my decision to ordain in Thailand; at that time anyway it wasn't possible to ordain in England. I decided that I could be a Buddhist monk in Thailand but that I didn't have to be a Thai Buddhist monk. As things later turned out, that proved easier in theory than in practice.

I think I knew after only a few months of studying at Wat Buddhapadipa that I would probably ordain. The teaching of the Buddha seemed so absolutely right for me that I felt I would have been foolish not to follow it. Of course, I didn't have to ordain to follow the Buddha's teaching but I've always been one for throwing myself totally into everything I do. In this case, it wasn't just a matter of throwing myself into something but also of throwing something else out. All of it, all the garbage of my life: all my delusions, cravings and aversions, my stupid fixed ideas and all the conditioning that had built up in my head over so many years. Away with it all!

The decision to ordain wasn't a difficult one at all but it was to be nearly five years before all my circumstances came right to enable me to take that giant step. During those five years, I grew more and more close to life at the monastery and slowly started to withdraw from the pleasures of my old lifestyle. My once-a-week visit for Sunday morning classes soon turned into several visits each week, then I started staying overnight, until finally I decided to give up my spacious house in South East London and moved into the former gardener's tiny cottage in the monastery grounds.

By that time all my possessions had been disposed of, thrown away, given away or sold and I was left literally with hardly more than the clothes I stood up in. I'd spent most of my life acquiring nice things and surrounding myself with stuff, so it was initially quite difficult to give up these props. That's all they really were, even though every one had seemed essential for my comfort, happiness and wellbeing. However, I soon discovered that every time some thing left my life, my heart became a little less heavy and my mind became a little more free. When I moved into the monastery to live, I became an *Upasaka* and helper to the monastery whilst preparing for my own ordination.

As an Upasaka I followed the Eight Precepts. Most lay Buddhists follow the Five Precepts: not to cause harm to any living creature, to refrain from taking what is not given, to refrain from illicit sex, to refrain from false speech and refrain from taking drink or drugs which cloud the mind. Included in my Eight Precepts were additional rules that helped ease me towards my forthcoming life as a monk. I became celibate, could eat only before noon and then not again until the following dawn. I could not drink alcohol and had to live a very simple lifestyle without unnecessary luxuries and without entertainment. I wore simple white clothes without personal adornment and cut my hair very short.

I lived full-time at the monastery for about six months and they were very happy days for me. As each day passed, I drew further away from my old lifestyle and began to see it more objectively and dispassionately and began to understand how superficial much of it had been. I realised that most of the things I had enjoyed doing were done as much from habit as anything else and that they had never really given me any lasting satisfaction. I worked hard at the monastery, working in the grounds, doing maintenance work around the house, meeting visitors and helping to take care of the nine resident monks. In that time I learned a lot from the monks, just by observation, but there was a great deal more I would have to learn on my own.

At last, the long-anticipated day of my departure from England came. A little to my own surprise, there was no sense of sadness, no sense of loss, and no regrets – only a great feeling of relief.

I was leaving nothing of importance or value behind except a few good and very puzzled friends. I don't think I ever adequately explained my decision to them. One old friend had asked, 'Why on earth do you want to spend the rest of your life sitting cross-legged in a tropical forest, watching your navel?'

I couldn't really explain but I had no doubt I had made the right decision. I felt I had taken my first step on a new road. Quite where that road would eventually lead I had no idea.

2

Why *did* I want to spend the rest of my life 'watching my navel'? In general terms I was not so much different from most people, but few go to the extreme of following the path that I decided to tread. We all face much the same problems and mental suffering in life but frequently, I think, we try to find the answers in solutions that always eventually bring more of the same. Each of us would like our life to be without anguish, worry or suffering; to be fulfilled, to have meaning. We all want to be happy and content and we all want freedom.

Consciously or subconsciously, we all constantly strive to change or improve our personal, work and social environments to match our own but continuously evolving ideal of what constitutes happiness and freedom. Equally, we strive to remove ourselves from the things or situations that we dislike, which cause us unhappiness or which seem to limit our personal freedom. In doing so, we are frequently simply trying to find some temporary escape from our dissatisfaction with the way things are.

The pressures of modern society lead many to believe that the way to happiness and freedom is through the acquisition of material things, or through wealth, fame, power, status or the accumulation of experiences. But to me – now – that is confusing true happiness and freedom with superficial physical wellbeing and personal comfort. Our definition of happiness and freedom sometimes comes to mean the ability to fulfil our desires, to indulge ourselves, to do whatever we like within our financial and physical means and to avoid every situation we find unpleasant in any way. Often, fulfilling our desires is simply laying a veneer over an underlying unhappiness and dissatisfaction.

We crave for the situations and things that we believe make us happy. If we can't get them, we mentally suffer. When we have them, we crave for more. When we lose them, we suffer again. And we crave for release, for freedom, from those things or situations that make us unhappy. Our conditioned clinging, craving and aversion mentally delude us, becoming the basis for habitual and frequently unwise responses to the things, people and situations with which we come into contact.

Whether we acknowledge it or not, most of us are under subtle pressure to compete, to acquire, and to measure our spiritual worth by our temporal gains. We are often judged by our success or failure and may even come to judge ourselves by the same yardstick.

Some pressures are not so subtle. They assault the

senses from every hoarding, from television and radio, from every multi-coloured, flashing neon display. Bigger! Better! Newer! Try me! Buy me! And everything from washing powder to the latest model of car promises to make our lives more rewarding and more satisfying. The pressure never lets up and eventually we may come to accept that this is actually the path to happiness, contentment and freedom; that this is the meaning of life. We can become so busy achieving and acquiring that we shut off that part of our mind which might question whether this is really the best way to live our lives.

People do not necessarily crack under these subtle and not-so-subtle pressures, though I'm sure many do, but if we are lucky there may come a moment when some spark of sanity inside says 'stop!' When we look around ourselves, when we look within ourselves, we may see that this is all basically unsatisfactory and leads nowhere, certainly not to lasting happiness or true freedom. And then we may realise that we are no longer in harmony, either with ourselves or with the natural order of things. Then perhaps we begin to wonder what it's all about, where we are going wrong – where we are *going* – and start to search for some method to bring genuine meaning and understanding to our lives. It is at that point, I think, that many people turn to meditation.

For some, it may simply be a search for a way to relax more easily, not to worry so much or to be able to cope more efficiently. For others it may be a spiritual quest; a positive turning away from materialism, hedonism and society's false values to something more deeply satisfying. Others may seek a greater understanding, for a truth that goes even beyond religious teaching.

Few people seem to know very much about meditation. Most would probably believe it is a method of relaxation that can relieve both physical and mental stress. But sitting cross-legged and breathing deeply is not meditation. At best it is a relaxation therapy, at worst merely daydreaming. If that is what is sought and if it works for the individual, then there's nothing wrong with it. The body may be relaxed and the mind calmed for a short time but stress is only temporarily relieved while the practitioner is actually in 'meditation' and perhaps for a short time afterwards. Stress is only a symptom. To remove the dis-ease entirely one must go deeper and find the cause of the stress; one must go into genuine meditation.

Vipassana (Insight) meditation was realised and taught by the Buddha more than 2,500 years ago. It is true Buddhist meditation and can lead to the freeing of the mind from the craving, aversion, attachment and delusion which, the Buddha taught, are the cause of all mental suffering. It can clear the mind of all the mud that has built up in it from the moment of birth leaving it, in the words of Phra Ajahn Char, a famous Thai meditation teacher, 'Like a still forest pool'. Vipassana can lead ultimately to the arising of Insight-Wisdom; personal realisation of the true nature of life and the perfect peace and mental freedom that comes from that knowledge: *Nibbana*.

In Vipassana, Insight-Wisdom does not necessarily arise in a sudden flash all at once. There may be many lesser insights to be realised along the way. It takes time, patience and perseverance. The Buddha established his order of monks and nuns so that they could withdraw from the daily pressures of lay-life into an environment suitable for practising intensively. It doesn't follow that only monks or nuns can achieve the fullest benefits from practising meditation or from following the Buddha's teaching. As I had already begun to discover for myself from practising meditation as a beginner at Wat Buddhapadipa, with skilled guidance anybody can begin to uncover their Buddha nature and develop their potential as a human being.

The Buddha described his meditation system at great length and detail in the *Maha Satipatthana Sutta*: 'The Four Foundations of Mindfulness'. Many people may know that 'watching the breath' is a meditation technique but mindfulness of breathing is just one aspect of the system as a whole. The Sutta details fourteen ways of contemplating the body, from the simple act of breathing to meditating on the nature of corpses. The Sutta also details contemplation of feelings, the activities of the mind, and mental objects.

The Buddha said in the Sutta, 'This is the only way for the purification of beings, for the overcoming of sorrow and lamentation, for the destruction of suffering and grief, for reaching the right path, for the attainment of Nibbana.'

In Vipassana, the meditator opens up to everything

18

going on in the mind and body and does not deliberately exclude any thoughts, emotions or sensory perceptions that arise. The meditator does not dwell on them nor allow them to lead to daydreaming or to discursive or judgemental thinking. They are merely observed as they arise and pass away. The meditator does not attach to, or try to hold on to, any thought or emotion, even happy ones, but instead observes objectively and dispassionately without any sense of 'I' or 'my' or 'self' being involved. Freed of the I-concept, the mind in its pure state is not disturbed by feelings such as anger, jealousy or unhappiness. It is only the I-concept which gives these feelings life and makes them into '*my* anger', '*my* unhappiness'.

With practice, the meditator begins to look at everything in a new and more balanced way, unaffected by preferences, desires, craving or aversion, all of which lead to dissatisfaction and unhappiness of some degree or another. Eventually, the level of non-attachment to thoughts and emotions increases. From this state of equanimity, Insight-Wisdom can arise.

The Venerable Sayadaw U Janaka, a Burmese meditation master, explains Vipassana in this way: 'Vipassana or Insight meditation is, above all, experiential practice based on the systematic and balanced development of a precise and focused awareness. By observing one's moment-to-moment mind and body processes from a place of investigative attention, Insight arises into the true nature of life and experiences. Through the wisdom acquired by using Insight meditation, one is able to live more freely and relate to the world around with less clinging, fear and confusion. Thus one's life becomes increasingly directed by consideration, compassion and clarity.'

I had already practised Vipassana meditation for several years but for as long as I continued to live the lay-life, with all its pressures, distractions and sensual diversions, I knew I would never be able to progress beyond a fairly limited point. I wanted to try to go further; to reach towards the highest goals of Vipassana. It was only by dropping out of lay-life completely that I would have the opportunity.

There are many 'states of knowledge', or insights, to be realised as a result of practising Vipassana meditation. These are sometimes preceded or accompanied by strange physical sensations or mental visions. I spend a great deal of my time in meditation but, as a monk, never speak or write about my own experiences in any detail, even to other meditators. It's not particularly helpful to others to do so.

The meditation programme I had been following at Wat Buddhapadipa and which I was to continue to follow for several more years was that recommended in *The Path to Nibbana* by the late Chief Meditation Master of Thailand, the Venerable Phra Dhamma Theerarach Mahamuni. Until his death in 1988, the Master was head of Section 5 at Wat Mahadhatu in Bangkok, where many Westerners train in meditation. He guided many thousands of students along the sometimes difficult path of Vipassana meditation and his methods were followed at Wat Buddhapadipa. Many of the London-based monks had been personally trained by him.

The Path to Nibbana sets out a programme of Insight meditation exercises, including walking and sitting meditation, as well as 'mindfulness' exercises. It also offers a guide to the possible 'States of Insight Knowledge' to be realised. My own published meditation manual, *One Step at a Time*, is based on the Master's teaching, though simplified for beginners.

3

A s a monk I have attended hundreds of ordination ceremonies in Thailand. Unfortunately, the very first I attended was my own. If I had previously had the opportunity to witness the ceremony perhaps I wouldn't have been quite so nervous when my own big day came.

Phra Maha Laow spent many patient hours at Wat Buddhapadipa coaching me with the difficult Pali requests and responses that I had to make and even recorded the whole of the spoken ceremony onto cassette tape. From that, I phoneticised the Pali as closely as I could into English and then typed out my script, including the various movements I had to make: 'enter stage left, bow', that sort of thing.

It took me about six months to learn; a ridiculously long time compared with how quickly a Thai man can learn it. I don't think Phra Maha Laow ever understood why I felt I had to be word perfect or why I was so nervous about the ceremony. He kept telling me not to worry and that nobody expected me to get it one hundred per cent correct. If I managed sixty per cent, the senior officiating monk would be pleased, he said.

Phra Maha Laow is Thai and Thai men often view ordination quite differently from most Westerners. I don't necessarily mean that they take it less seriously, but as virtually every Thai man ordains at some time in his life (sometimes more than once) and as all his friends are likely to attend the ceremony, everybody eventually goes to so many ordinations that they become quite familiar with the procedure. The Pali language is also not so difficult for a Thai person, since many Thai words have their roots in Pali or Sanskrit and may even be exactly the same.

For a Westerner, however, everything about the ceremony is strange: the language in which it is conducted, the traditions involved, the robes the ordainee wears during the ceremony, the movements, the surroundings – all are unfamiliar and daunting.

I also felt that ordaining was the most important thing I had ever done in my life; perhaps another big difference between Thai and Western men. Even if a Thai man has only a superficial interest in Buddhism he will still usually ordain, perhaps for a few months or even only a few days, to 'make merit' for his parents. Despite their frequent indifference to their religion, Thai men may also find themselves under great social pressure to ordain, since a Thai man isn't really considered complete unless he has spent even a short time in the robes. Men of ordination age who haven't yet ordained are sometimes referred to as *khon dip* – unripe – and are usually expected to have ordained before they get married. I have even known of Thai Christians who have ordained for a short time because of these cultural and social pressures. Temporary ordination is such an accepted tradition in Thailand that all government departments and many private companies allow up to four months' ordination leave for their male employees.

Of course, many Thai men ordain for a period because they genuinely want to study what the Buddha taught. Afterwards they will return to their old jobs and lives, perhaps spiritually enriched by the experience and ready to apply what they have learned to their lives as laymen. A very few may enter the monkhood intending to stay for a short time but instead may spend the rest of their lives in the robes.

Although Thai men enter and leave the monkhood almost casually, I felt for me there would be no going back. I had given up everything to become a monk and the 'becoming' itself was such a major step that it was important to me to get it right.

Originally I had hoped to ordain at the London monastery as I then thought of it as my spiritual home. I knew all the monks and most of the lay supporters there, I was familiar with the various routines of the monastery and I felt comfortable in the environment. At that time though, it wasn't possible. Although the abbot of Wat Buddhapadipa was an *Upachaya* (a senior monk trained and authorised to conduct the ceremony), Wat Buddhapadipa is a missionary monastery and comes under the auspices of the Royal Thai Embassy in London, which makes it rather different from any other monastery.

Each year during the summer, about a dozen young Thai boys are temporarily ordained as novice monks and they live at the monastery for two weeks while studying the basics of Buddhism. Many of the boys were born in England or arrived in the country when they were very young. They may be more European than Thai in their cultural outlook. Some have never been to Thailand and cannot speak the language, so besides their religious training, the temporary ordination also helps them to understand something of their own cultural backgrounds. Not all the boys are willing participants in this, for even two weeks as a novice means having the head shaved. I have seen many young boys burst into tears at the first sight of the razor! That's very different from Thailand, where young boys traditionally ordain as novices for a day when a relative or friend dies, and shave their heads without a second thought.

Although young boys were sometimes dragged unwillingly into the Sangha, for adult men, European or Thai, ordination as a monk was not possible at that time. The abbot of Wat Buddhapadipa recommended that I should ordain at Wat Mahadhatu in Bangkok, since the London establishment is a branch of that famous monastery. Soon after I left England, both the abbot and the policy of Wat Buddhapadipa changed and ordination is now sometimes possible, though I think it is still a rare occurrence.

Wat Mahadhatu is a very old monastery. Its name means 'The Great Element' and it is home to Mahachulalongkorn University, one of two universities in Thailand specifically for monks. The university was opened in 1947 and although there can be many hundreds of monks living at Wat Mahadhatu during term time, the monastery still manages to retain a wonderful air of peacefulness, despite its huge size and location in one of Bangkok's busiest tourist areas.

Phra Maha Laow was already in Thailand at Wat Mahadhatu, his home temple, and I moved into Section 5 of the monastery about a week before my ordination. During that time, I had to be interviewed by the abbot to obtain his official consent to my ordination. Nobody, not even a Thai man, can simply walk into a monastery and be ordained. Forms have to be filled, guarantors found and backgrounds checked. These are obviously sensible precautions because otherwise the Sangha could degenerate into a refuge for all sorts of undesirables. I don't know if it was ever enforced, but at one time there was even talk of potential ordainees having to be tested for drug abuse, since this is an occasional problem in Thai monasteries, though usually amongst young men who have ordained for a very short time.

The abbot of Wat Mahadhatu, Phra Sumethadhibodi, is a very high-ranking monk indeed. At that time he was the religious governor of Bangkok Province and I was (and remain) more than a little in awe of him, but he was very kind to me at my interview. Surprisingly, he asked me why I hadn't ordained at Wat Buddhapadipa.

26

He said that he personally could see no reason why I should not have done so. Anyway, by that time I had fully adjusted to the idea of ordaining in Thailand rather than in England.

By coincidence, both the then abbot of Wat Buddhapadipa, and my meditation teacher, Phra Ajahn Amara Thera, were in Bangkok at that time. Phra Sumethadhibodi therefore appointed the abbot to be the Upachaya at my ordination and Ajahn Amara Thera as one of my two *Acariyas* – teachers and questioners. That considerably eased my nervousness about the coming ceremony because two of the three senior monks who would take part in the ordination already knew me well from London and would, I hoped, make some allowance for any mistakes I made. Phra Sumethadhibodi decided I should be ordained on 15th February at 9am, immediately after the morning service.

Ordination can be quite an expensive ceremony, especially in an important city monastery and when the senior monks taking part are very high-ranking. Although there is no fee involved, it is customary in Thailand for the ordainee to offer gifts to the monks who form the Sangha which accepts him into its midst during the ordination. There are a very limited number of things that can be offered and the gift usually comprises toiletries – toothpaste, tissue, soap and so on – or similar small items. It is also customary that each monk should be given a gift of money (in an envelope, so that the monk doesn't actually touch the money), with a larger amount for the two Acariyas and the Upachaya. The amount offered depends entirely on the ordainee's circumstances. In my experience, it may vary from a few baht in small rural monasteries, to several hundred baht in bigger city monasteries. If the ordainee or his family was very poor and unable to offer even a small gift, that wouldn't prevent the ordainee from becoming a monk. The ordainee or his family must also provide a set of robes, an alms bowl and other necessities for the new monk, but if they are too poor to do even that, it is the Upachaya's responsibility to supply them.

There were to be twenty-two monks at my ordination and on my behalf Phra Maha Laow had offered lunch to about sixty others afterwards, so the expenses were going to be quite high. I had already given most of my money away before leaving England, so the total costs were going to make quite a hole in what little I had taken to Thailand with me. To my surprise and amazement, a Thai lady named Khun Nit, who owned a restaurant in London and whom I had met only very briefly a few times, kindly offered to help towards the expenses and even flew to Bangkok to attend the ceremony. She wanted to 'make merit' by contributing to the cost of my ordination. Her generosity was to be the first of many examples of the Thai *jai dee* – good heart – that I have since encountered.

The night before a Thai man ordains is always the occasion for a big family party. Having no family in Thailand, my last evening as a layman was spent very quietly with Phra Maha Laow in his room in Section 24 of Wat Mahadhatu, going over the ceremony for the umpteenth time. In the final practice sessions I was word perfect. That night, he shaved my head and eyebrows, which was an extraordinary experience. I had been cutting my hair very short for a few months so that I would feel more accustomed to having none at all but, even so, the feeling of cold water on my head when I showered afterwards was very strange. Stranger still was the image which presented itself when I looked in a mirror. The sight of my very white bald skull on top of my naturally ruddy complexion, with two white gaps where my eyebrows had been, was quite bizarre!

The practice of shaving the head is a symbolic rejection of ego and vanity. The Buddha himself, as Prince Siddhattha, cut off his own long hair soon after he left his palace and renounced his princely lifestyle. In fact, although all monks shave their heads on the same day each month, the rule says only that a monk's hair should not be more than two inches long. Since this probably led to some minor controversies amongst individual monks, it simply became more convenient all round if everybody cut their hair at the same time. The shaving of the eyebrows is not a rule of the monks but is an old Thai tradition. I have read that it stems from a time when Thailand was at war with neighbouring Burma. The Burmese sent spies to the Thai court disguised as monks. When this ruse was discovered, the Thai Patriarch ordered that, in future, all Thai monks would shave their eyebrows off so that the Burmese spies could be immediately recognised. Of course, all that happened was that as soon as the Burmese got to hear of this, their spying monks shaved their eyebrows off too. But the tradition has remained in both countries.

I know of a few monks who dislike shaving their heads each month, but this practice is not only an important tradition in Buddhism but is also part of the monks' training. Most people, men as well as women, take good care of their hair, ensuring it is always clean, healthy and presentable. Besides simply taking care of their hair, people frequently also use it as a support for their own self-image, their ego, just as they do with their style of dress. Our hairstyle and clothes may sometimes be practical for our job but just as often they are a statement of how we perceive ourselves and how we would like others to perceive us.

I wish I had photographs of the many different hairstyles I have worn over the past thirty years. They would be an historical record not only of the changing times and fashions but also of my own changing mental outlooks and conditioning. They would also be quite embarrassing. In my early teens, my hair sported the Elvis-look, thick with Brylcreem. Then I became a 'mop top', copying the Beatles not only in hairstyle but also in dress, speech and outlook. In my late teens, as a flower-wielding hippy, my hair was past my shoulders and tied back from my forehead with a silk bandanna, complementing my flared tie-dyed loons and Fruit of the Loom t-shirt nicely. Later, very much into David Bowie and glam rock, my hair was still shoulder length but then sported green and red streaks. That nonsense past, it became much shorter and deliberately greasy.

By then I was riding a big motorbike, wearing filthy jeans and studded leather, and humming along to Meatloaf. Later still, by which time I had my own business and was Armani-clad, my hair became very neat and tidy, reflecting my perceived image as a serious businessman.

I suppose it could be said that shaving the head is also part of my image as a monk, just as the orange robes are part of that image. That's not the case, though. Since monks have no choice in the matter, shaving the head is a small training that helps to overcome our delusory self-image and ego. Wearing the shapeless (and, really, very impractical) robes is a rejection of fashion and our sensuous desire to wear clothes that make us look and feel good. I know I don't look good without hair and eyebrows, nor in the day-glo orange robes I currently wear, but it doesn't bother me at all. I don't need robes designed by Armani, or hair styled by Sassoon.

With my head shaved and about to enter the Sangha, I was known as a *naga*, or snake. In Buddhist legend, a snake took human form and tried to become a monk. It was discovered and the snake was refused ordination but it asked the Buddha if it could give its name to others seeking ordination. The request was granted and now all candidates for ordination are *naga*, which perhaps explains one of the traditional questions asked by the Acariya of the ordainee during the ceremony: '*Are you a human being?*'

On the morning of my ordination, I was dressed in a white sarong held up by a golden metal belt, and with a long, white lacy over-robe with fancy gold edging, which looked much like a net curtain. Usually, the ordainee walks barefooted to the main monastery building, the *Uposatha* Hall (or *Bote*), followed by his family and friends who carry his robes, alms bowl and other necessities, as well as the gifts for the monks. In the absence of family of my own, Phra Maha Laow rustled up about twenty shaven-headed and white-robed nuns from the women's section of Wat Mahadhatu to join our procession. Members of Phra Maha Laow's own family also joined in, together with Khun Nit and members of her family. I was very grateful for their moral support.

On our way to the Bote, we were all very surprised to meet my appointed Upachaya staggering towards us clutching his stomach. He had suddenly been struck by a malevolent bug and was obviously in no fit state to officiate at the ceremony. He informed us that Phra Sumethadhibodi would officiate instead as my Upachaya. In a way this was a great honour because the abbot of Wat Mahadhatu is usually too busy to officiate at ordinations himself and, as far as I know, had never ordained a Westerner before. But all my nervousness instantly returned and I found I couldn't remember a word of the ceremony, nor even my own religious surname, or *chaiya*. As it turned out that didn't matter because at the very last moment the abbot decided to change my Pali name from the one I had been given at Wat Buddhapadipa to another which gave me a greater association with the London monastery. I was to be Phra Peter Pannapadipo – Light, or Lamp, of Wisdom. My irrational nervousness made it a real effort to continue walking towards the Bote and I think I only managed it thanks to Phra Maha Laow's constant *Don't worry* liturgy.

Our little procession reached the Bote and we walked around the outside three times in a clockwise direction, a symbolic way of paying respect to the 'Triple Gem'- the Buddha, the Dhamma and the Sangha. Often the ordainee is carried on the shoulders of his friends during this circumambulation, symbolising, I believe, Prince Siddhattha's last ride on horseback when he left his palace and rejected his princely lifestyle. At most ordinations I have attended as a monk the followers do a lot of very loud wailing at this point, though I'm not entirely sure why. I'm glad to say that my nuns were blissfully quiet and well-behaved. I think twenty wailing nuns would just about have tipped my nerves over the edge!

Before entering the Uposatha Hall, it is a tradition in Thailand for the ordainee to turn to his followers and scatter coins, symbolising his rejection of worldly goods and materialism. I couldn't very well scatter money at the nuns since they had also rejected such things, so we skipped that tradition as well and proceeded directly into the Bote.

Inside, on a raised platform in front of a gigantic Buddha image, sat the abbot with twenty-one other monks ranged around him, leaving a small space for me in the middle. Phra Maha Laow was to be part of the Sangha which accepted me into its midst and he

33

was able to sit conveniently close to me so that he could whisper a prompt if I stumbled over a request or response. I approached the abbot on my knees, my package of robes resting on my forearms and my hands in a prayer-like attitude called *anjali*. The abbot took the package from me and checked that all the necessary robes were there. I made a triple bow, sat back on my heels, took a deep breath, and the ceremony started.

'*Esaham Bhante, sucira-parinibbbutampi . . .*''Venerable Sir, I go for Refuge to the Lord . . .'

The ordination ceremony is a series of requests from the applicant to the Upachaya, asking that he be allowed to ordain as a monk. The requests are repeated three times, so there can be no doubt as to the applicant's seriousness and the lack of any coercion. The two Acariyas, after questioning the applicant, also announce three times to the assembled monks that the applicant wishes to ordain. They ask the monks if they have any objections or know of any reason why the applicant should not become a monk.

Most Thai men I have seen ordained have taken the trouble to learn their lines and the correct pronunciation of the Pali, but I have seen others who haven't bothered at all and who have had to repeat their lines word for word after an Acariya. As far as I recall, I don't think I did too badly. Whether that was because I actually remembered the lines or because the abbot was making allowances for me I don't know, but there is a limit to how much allowance any Upachaya can make. Every Pali word is important and must be pronounced correctly, otherwise the tense or meaning may be altered. It is the Upachaya's responsibility to ensure that the ordination proceeds exactly in accordance with Sangha law and centuries-old custom. Any mistake or omission could invalidate the ordination.

People frequently say of personally important events that the time passed 'in a blur', or something like that. That's how my ordination ceremony was for me. I remember entering the Bote. I remember at some point being taken aside by two monks who helped me out of my white clothes and into my saffron robes. I remember being ordered by the Upachaya to go to another part of the hall, where I was asked traditional questions by the two Acariyas about my health and social standing: Did I have ulcers, ringworm, consumption or epilepsy? 'No, Venerable Sirs, I do not,' I replied. Was I a human being? Was I a man? Was I a free man? Was I without debt? Exempt from government service? Did I have my parents' permission? Was I fully twenty years old? 'Yes, Venerable Sirs.' I remember the beautiful chanting of the monks as I poured water from a small silver jug into a bowl during a ritual blessing. Lastly, I remember when my final response was made, all my lines said, and I looked at Phra Maha Laow with a great smile of relief on my face, as though to say, 'I did it! I actually did it!' And he had been right, of course. The whole ceremony only lasted about fifty minutes and there had been nothing to worry about at all.

Thai people love to take photographs and I was pleased to learn that someone had taken some during the ceremony. Hoping to send pictures of my big day to friends in London, I ordered a set of prints. I was absolutely horrified when I collected them from the photo shop. In one, I am bowing low before my Upachaya, wearing my white net curtain. My whole body is shiny wet with nervous perspiration, my face is glowing bright red from bending and my bald, white head is gleaming and reflecting the light of the altar candles. I looked like some hideous alien baby! Vanity prevented me from ordering prints for my friends.

At the end of my first day as a monk, when I was alone in my tiny room in Section 5 and was able to think clearly, I realised what an impressive ceremony I had been through. Even now, when I have been present at so many ordinations, I am still moved by the beautiful Pali requests and responses, the chanting of the monks and the traditions involved, by the feeling that this is how it has always been done and this is how it *will* always be done. And I am very glad about that.

I was now officially a monk and had my little yellow monk's identification book. With my shaven head and saffron robes, I certainly looked like a monk, but now I had to learn how to *be* a monk. More importantly, I had to begin ditching many of the concepts, delusions, opinions and ways of behaviour that I had accumulated over the previous forty years or so on my way to this new starting point.

4

One of the first problems I had to face was in adjusting to monk-style accommodation. I had been told I would live in Section 5, partly because the section had some experience of Westerners but also because it had some of the best meditation teachers of any monastery in Thailand.

Section 5 is listed in many guidebooks as an international meditation centre, though I think few Westerners actually attend residential courses there. That's partly because the section may sometimes have no English-speaking meditation teacher in residence, but also because some of the Westerners who visit and claim they want to learn about meditation really have little or no genuine interest and are simply looking for free accommodation for a while. There have been some problems in the past and the resident monks who act as the section's receptionists are now more wary about accepting foreigners for residential courses, though anybody is welcome to attend the three meditation sessions each day.

Many Thai monks come from all over the country to be taught sitting and walking meditation by the section's excellent teachers. I have also met Burmese, Sri Lankan and Korean monks there who have travelled from their own countries to learn Vipassana meditation in Thailand. Although Ajahn Amara Thera usually lived at Wat Buddhapadipa in London, he had a permanent room in the section and both he and Phra Maha Laow thought it would be the best place for me. I had some misgivings, even though I had met the section head, Phra Ajahn Maha Suparp, many times and knew him to be a kind and compassionate man.

The twenty-six sections of Wat Mahadhatu are built in terraces with alleys and paved areas separating the blocks. Each section has a senior monk as its head and most sections are home to at least five or six monks – sometimes many more – as well as a few novices, temple boys and an assortment of cats and dogs. In the *Pansa*, or Rains Retreat, when many Thai men traditionally ordain for a few months, the sections can be considerably more crowded.

Most of the single-storey, terraced buildings were originally built exactly alike but over the years many have been altered and added to by generations of section heads. Each reflects the style and resources of its past and present residents, exactly as a row of Victorian terraced houses does in England. Inside, some are rather like run-down but pretty Spanish villas, with terracotta floors and stucco walls. Some are filled with orchids and other tropical plants. Some are well maintained and clean but others can be gloomy, rat-infested hovels. At the time I ordained, Section 5 fell into the last category, though it has since been refurbished from top to bottom and is now a cleaner and more pleasant environment.

Section 5 had originally been the same type of building as most of the others, and like many others had been adapted and added to in a seemingly haphazard manner. When I lived there some monk rooms on the original ground floor of the building were large and airy; others in two additional floors that had been added to the roof were not. The rooms at the very top were tiny; about seven feet square. Although some had windows that opened onto fresh air, others were in dark and stuffy corridors. Section 5 was unusual in that it had a separate section within itself on the ground floor for white-robed and shaven-headed nuns. They seemed to me to be crammed into even worse conditions than the monks, though of course I never saw inside their rooms. The monks weren't allowed into the nuns' quarters and the nuns weren't allowed upstairs, where most of the monks lived. Taking into account resident monks, visiting monks, novices, nuns and temple boys, Section 5's residents probably numbered forty or fifty, and it was by far the most crowded and busiest section in the monastery. Despite the overcrowding, many monks had lived there for years and seemed perfectly happy to call it home.

At first I was allocated one of the tiny inner rooms on the top floor. My single window opened onto a partially enclosed space through which no air, let alone breeze, ever seemed to flow. The room had an electric fan, but in such a small area it just seemed to move the stifling air around without actually cooling it at all. It was rather like sitting in front of a hair dryer.

I had always had space in my life, lots of it. I am not claustrophobic but I needed space. All my flats or houses had been large and my last in London was a three-storey, three-bedroom house in which I lived alone. I liked space; clean, white, empty space, and had only ever owned the minimum of furniture that I actually needed. Even my furniture had to be one hundred per cent functional – 'minimalist', I believe it is called. My friends used to say that visiting my home was like visiting a clinic, it was so stark and antiseptic, but I had never been able to relax fully in a cluttered environment. I would quickly become agitated by the clutter, by ornaments, knick-knacks and by unnecessary visual distractions. I wasn't some sort of neatness freak who wanted to tidy up other people's homes when I visited – other people could have as much clutter as they liked – but I wanted none of it.

Well, my tiny room in Section 5 was about as minimalist as it is possible to be. It certainly had no clutter. Apart from the fan, it had a plastic sleeping mat on the floor, a bare fluorescent tube on the ceiling and a large number of ants. But it also had precious little space. I couldn't see any way I could adjust to living there; it was smaller than the toilet in my last house. 'Too small, too stuffy, too . . .' I whined to Phra Maha

Laow, but I had no choice. This was the room I had been allocated; this was where I had to live. I was just going to have to start the difficult process of adjusting my rigid ideas about what I believed I needed, or had to have. Not just about my living space but about many other things too.

I had thought for more than four years about becoming a monk but, sitting in that tiny room, some of the realities of my new life quickly started to hit me. I began to wonder whether I had given too much thought to the potential spiritual benefits and not enough to the practicalities, the hardships and discipline I would have to face. But I knew they were directly related and each helped support the other. My thoughts were confused and I started my first night as a monk in a miserable and depressed mood.

I had been lucky enough in the past to have travelled extensively, not just on holiday but sometimes staying for fairly long periods in exotic lands. I had never once felt homesick. But then I had always known that whatever adventures, difficulties or hardships I encountered on my travels, home was always there, just a few hours' flying time away. I could always return, full of tales and experiences to relate to my friends, and I could always resume my old lifestyle again.

My old lifestyle . . . a night out at the theatre or cinema, a wild party, long drives through the English countryside in an open-topped sports car, racing down to the coast on a big motorcycle late at night just for the hell of it, eating good food in expensive restaurants with a bottle or two of fine wine or curling up on my settee in front of the telly with a hot and spicy pizza in a warm cardboard box on my lap, shopping in London's West End, knowing I could buy anything with a flash of gold plastic, or happily deluding myself for a few hours that *this* time, with *this* person, it was the Real Thing.

It was all gone now and could never be regained. I had made sure of that. The smoke from my burning social and financial bridges could be smelt from London to Bangkok. Almost from the first moment, years before, when I had decided that one day I would ordain, I had deliberately started to cut myself off from it all. But now, today, was *the* day; the day I finally had to face the fact: there was no going back. That period of my life had ended utterly.

I had never experienced such feelings of great loss or uncertainty before and a part of me still clung to that past. Not, I think, because I had actually enjoyed any of it so much, but because it was what I had always known; it was *all* I had known. It was my life and I could cope with it. Now I was facing a new and totally different lifestyle, much of it completely strange to me. On that first evening I was, I think, a little scared. Lonely too.

But although my new lifestyle was largely unknown, one thing that was already known was that which had brought me to this strange new starting point: the teaching of the Buddha. In the Dhamma I could find all the strength, support and inspiration I needed to face whatever lay ahead of me.

I sat on the vinyl floor of my tiny room for a long time feeling quite dejected. Then I looked at my small pile of possessions: a couple of extra robes, my alms bowl, a few books and very little else. I realised that this was everything in the world that I owned, needed or wanted. Well, they didn't take up much space and what was this room for anyway? It was a place to sleep in, eat in, to study and to meditate in. None of those activities required vast expanses of floor, interesting angles or exciting lighting. There was, in fact, ample space for what I needed to do.

Luckily for me, after a few weeks a corner room on the top floor became empty and I was able to move from the inner corridor. Although my new room was just as tiny, it had the advantage of an extra window and both windows opened into fresh air. I also had a pleasant view across the monastery's colourfully-tiled rooftops. There was also a balcony just outside the room, where it was pleasant to sit in the cool early morning or evening. By the time I had scrubbed the floor and walls of my room, cadged a small set of bookshelves and a chair, I was sufficiently comfortable.

I rather surprised myself by adjusting fairly quickly and painlessly to my restricted living area, though then it was adjustment caused by necessity. It was some considerable time later, after I had stayed in different monasteries and lived in a variety of rooms or *kutis*, that I believe I really adjusted and started to become detached from such concerns. I realised that space or the lack of it – in fact my whole personal environment

43

– had ceased to bother me. The longer I remained a monk, the more uncluttered my mind became. It took quite a time, but my mind slowly started to develop its own space and a freedom that was confined neither by walls nor by preconceived or conditioned ideas.

As I write these words I am sitting in the bedroom of my present kuti, though it doesn't actually have a bed. It is a large, old and typically Thai-style wooden house perched on stilts, with polished wooden floors and many shuttered windows. It has three rooms and was originally intended as a residence for several monks, though I live alone. The area beneath the kuti has been turned into rooms for my three *looksit*, or temple boys, and the kuti is in a pleasant, walled garden with a small fishpond. Pots of colourful plants sit on the large balcony and there are cats everywhere, basking in the sun. It is quite charming and I am content to be here, but I know I could move tomorrow to a box room without a second thought. Any small possessions I have gathered or been given by lay-people will stay on here, a gift for the next occupant.

When I occasionally need to go to Bangkok, I stay at Wat Mahadhatu in Section 5. It's okay. Sometimes I am allocated a large room, sometimes a small one, but it's all the same really. Where I am is home and I carry my space with me wherever I go.

5

If there was one thing that really brought home to me that I'd started a completely new life, it was the fact that, at forty-five, I didn't know how to dress myself any more. I had exchanged clothes kept up and held together by belts, zips, buttons and press-studs for a large rectangle of cotton. Unless it was actually tied in a knot somewhere, I couldn't see how it could stay on. Often mine didn't. It not only fell off, it actually seemed to leap off me.

I was familiar with monks' robes from my years at the London monastery and had often seen monks wrap themselves in their outer robes but it always seemed to be done so quickly and effortlessly that I still didn't have a clue how to do it myself. Of course, I had never had the opportunity to wear one before and I think any monk would be genuinely horrified if a layman put on the robes, even for practice, before being properly ordained.

In modern times, the monk's wardrobe consists of

his outer robe (*civara* or *jivorn*) and an under-robe (*sabong*), which is worn around the waist, covering the navel and falling to just below the knees. The sabong is held up by a fold, a tuck, a cord belt and, in my case in those early days, a prayer. Worn on the upper part of the body, under the jivorn, is a sort of sleeveless, one-shouldered waistcoat (*ungsa*) which has a couple of handy pockets and is joined on the left side by tying tags. For religious services inside the monastery, the monk also wears an additional robe (*sanghati*) which is folded in a very particular way into a long rectangle and hung over the left shoulder. Novice monks do not wear the sanghati but in all other respects wear exactly the same robes as the monks.

A monk's seniority or status cannot be gauged by his robes. There are no badges or symbols on the robes to indicate the monk's rank and the Supreme Patriarch of the Thai Sangha wears exactly the same robes as even the most junior monk. Apart from sheer *presence*, which many senior monks most definitely have, the only way to gauge a monk's rank would be from his ceremonial fan. All monks have a fan but those of high-ranking monks may be very ornate and beautifully embroidered, though they are not usually used except at special occasions.

The monk may or may not wear sandals, depending on the tradition of his particular monastery, though most do. He may carry a soft bag, called a *yarm*, which is like a shoulder bag. The yarm is carried in the crook of the arm and should never be worn on the shoulder or slung over the back. Yarms are sometimes embroidered in coloured silk with the name and symbol of the monk's monastery, or may be commemorative of some special event, such as the opening of a new Bote.

Jivorns come in different sizes – all of them too short for me – and nowadays are usually made of cotton, silk, nylon or some other man-made fabric. They are always cut to the same pattern and design. They are made from many pieces of cloth sewn together in, according to Buddhist legend, the pattern of the paddy fields of Magadha in Northern India. They are made in many pieces to recall the days when monks made their own robes from scraps of cloth taken from corpses in charnel grounds.

The size and way of wearing the outer robe has changed since the Buddha's time and may vary a little from country to country but however it is worn the monk should always look neat and his body should be well covered.

In Thailand, the jivorn is large and is wrapped around the body with the two ends rolled together. This roll is taken over the left shoulder and under the left arm so that the end can be held in the left hand or pressed firmly between the arm and body. That prevents the robe from slipping off the shoulders, though even very senior monks may frequently have to adjust their jivorns. Inside the monastery the robe is worn so that the right shoulder is exposed, but outside the monastery both shoulders and arms are always covered. The colour of the robes varies from monastery to monastery. At

Wat Mahadhatu they are a reddish-brown but at others may be anything from very dark brown to brilliant yellow, or even day-glo orange, the colour I am now wearing.

On the morning after my ordination, I got up at 5am and tried to dress myself in my outer robe in preparation for breakfast in the section. Then I tried again. And again. The breakfast bell rang and still I seemed to have either too much robe left over, or not enough. Chanting from the dining hall signalled the end of breakfast and by then I was in an absolute sweat and still looked like a sack of potatoes, with lumps and bumps and bunches of cloth exactly where they shouldn't have been. One moment the bottom of the robe was at knee height, the next flapping around my ankles. Wrapping the outer robe is not a difficult task – once you know how – but I didn't know and I found myself getting intensely irritated. Each time I tried to wrap the robe it looked worse than the previous time. Even in the early morning, my tiny room was stiflingly warm and both my robe and I were damp with sweat. I was quite close to tears of anger and frustration. 'Calm down, calm down,' I told myself repeatedly.

One of the problems was that I am six feet tall and the ceiling of my room was only inches more. To get a neat roll of cloth to pass over my shoulder I needed to raise my left arm quite high while rolling the ends of the robe together, which was impossible inside the room. As my room was on the top floor I eventually clambered out onto the roof, where I had sufficient space to get the robe wrapped around me in something vaguely approaching the correct way, but only very vaguely. I looked a mess and the pigeons were not impressed. Phra Maha Laow's room was in Section 24 at the other end of the monastery, but I managed the distance without anything falling off and he was able to dress me neatly in seconds, as well as offering me what was left over from his own breakfast.

I think my biggest fear as a new monk was of my under-robe falling down in the street. I have seen it happen to other new monks. The sabong is held up by a narrow woven belt, which has two very long cords. The belt and cords are passed around the waist twice and the cords are tied in a bow at the front. The cords are a bit like over-sized versions of those round, nylon shoe laces, which I never found stayed tied together as well as the old, flat, cotton type. Many monks, including me, wear a key ring at the end of one of the cords and if the ring has several keys on it, they make that end quite a bit heavier than the other – enough to gradually pull a poorly-tied bow undone.

That happened to me in my first month as a monk as I was descending a very rickety staircase, when, for safety, I needed to support myself with both arms outstretched. As I came down the stairs I felt an unusual movement under my jivorn and was horrified when my belt slipped down past my knees and around my feet. I knew the sabong wouldn't be long after and it wasn't. I couldn't make a grab for it because I would quite likely have fallen down the stairs, which would have been even less impressive to the group of Thai people waiting at the bottom to come up. I sort of hopped out of my sabong, calmly gathered it and the belt up, put them in my yarm and walked away with as much dignity as I could salvage. But at least I didn't expose myself to total ridicule, as I did on a later occasion.

At that time, I was living in a remote rural monastery and had to shift some large rocks. Being in an isolated part of the monastery grounds, and as I was working alone, I'd taken off my robe and ungsa, just leaving my sabong wrapped around me. Staggering under the weight of a huge boulder, with my body arched backwards, I didn't notice that my belt had come adrift – until my sabong started to slide down my legs. There's not a lot one can do when both hands are full of boulder and, before I could drop the rock, my sabong was around my ankles, leaving me totally naked (except, perversely, for the belt, which was still hanging loosely around my waist). I had *thought* I was alone but loud screams of delighted laughter from behind a bush told me that, as usual, some of the village children had come to see what the strange foreign monk was up to. After that, I started to tie my belt so tightly that I often gave myself stomach ache!

I'm not sure at what point dressing myself neatly and securely became second nature, but of course it did and now I can't see why it was such a problem. Oddly, I have since taught other new Western monks and novices how to dress themselves and they usually get the hang of it within a few days, so perhaps I'm just a very slow learner. I now find that if I'm in a hurry to get dressed and sling my robe around myself very quickly, it usually looks quite neat, whereas if I take time and care trying to get all my little pleats and folds absolutely right, I look a bit of a mess. (Some of my friends have been amazed when they have seen my official studio photographs taken a couple of weeks after I ordained. They are head and shoulder portraits and show my robe wrapped absolutely perfectly, with impossibly precise pleats. What I don't tell them is that the robe is a fake one supplied by the studio. It covers only the neck, shoulders and part of the chest and the pleats and folds are sewn in. The only thing that might give it away is that the fake robe has a foam backing which makes it ridiculously wide at the shoulders, giving me something of the *Dynasty* look.)

I had to get used to dressing myself and learn many other practical daily matters as soon as I could because Phra Maha Laow was due to return to London a few weeks after my ordination. He had great patience and devoted endless hours in trying to teach me not only how to dress, but also how to walk in the robes, how to sit on the floor, change position, get up, how to make a perfect bow to a senior monk and so on, all without exposing myself. I had already picked up a lot of tips simply from watching the monks at Wat Buddhapadipa but there was a great deal more I hadn't noticed or even thought about. Many Thai men, especially in rural areas, wear little other than a sarong for much of the time and many of their daily activities are done at floor level.

They know instinctively how to make their movements neatly, politely and modestly. But I have also seen city-bred new monks who don't and they are frequently as immodest as I sometimes was.

Just about every aspect of the monks' behaviour is governed by the *Vinaya* – the 227 rules of the monks – many of which were laid down by the Buddha himself. They include almost every daily action and it is very necessary for a new monk to know all the rules and to understand the reasons for them. At the time of my ordination I knew the most important rules, but there were many other minor ones and even more Thai tradi-tional rules and customs that I didn't know.

If a Vinaya rule is broken, various penalties may be imposed, ranging from ejection from the Sangha for the most serious offences, or probation, or some sort of confessional ceremony. Although the rules are ancient and have remained unchanged since the Buddha's time, with understanding, commitment and a sensible atti-tude towards time and place, they are not difficult to live by and they really do work.

Every two weeks, all monks must assemble in a Bote to listen to a recitation of the rules by a monk who has been especially trained to chant them from memory. Such monks are usually very highly respected. As each Pali word is chanted, it is checked against a written version, so that no mistakes, changes or omissions can ever be made.

Some critics and reformists suggest that it's about time the rules were overhauled and updated, but it's not really necessary. Some rules have anyway fallen into disuse, or been temporarily laid aside, simply because of the changing times, but they remain rules. Times may change again to make them relevant once more. The point is that monks should understand the spirit of the Vinaya rules, not just the rules themselves, and live their lives accordingly. The monk's life and behaviour should be blameless and beyond reproach, regardless of the age or country in which he lives.

It's especially important for a Western monk to be aware of the training rules and he must be constantly mindful of his public behaviour and deportment. A Thai monk walking too quickly in the street, or swinging his arms as he walks, would probably go unnoticed by most Thai people simply because there are so many Thai monks. But a Western monk is such an unusual sight anywhere in Thailand that his every movement is watched with great interest, so his behaviour is more likely to be remarked upon.

I remember Phra Maha Laow telling me that if there were two monks sitting on a bench, one Thai and one Western, and both were smoking cigarettes, a Thai observer would be quite shocked by the Westerner but probably wouldn't even notice that the Thai monk was also smoking. I think that's probably true since, according to a report in the *Bangkok Post* newspaper a few years ago, eighty-five per cent of Thai monks smoke (though there is no specific rule preventing smoking).

So, my education and training were to be fairly intensive for the first few weeks and Phra Maha Laow would not allow me to go outside Wat Mahadhatu until he felt that I was able to conduct myself in public reasonably well. Even though I am usually a very shy person, I was desperate to walk in the streets and show myself off. That was pure vanity of course, and I knew it even then, but I had to start learning to be patient.

Happily, after a few days, Phra Maha Laow decided that I was probably able to behave myself in public and he suggested we should visit Wat Phra Kaew, the Temple of the Emerald Buddha. The temple is only a few minutes' walk from Wat Mahadhatu and another Section 24 monk decided to accompany us.

With my robe properly arranged for walking outside, my totally empty yarm placed on my left arm and my new and somewhat less-than-stylish plastic sandals with their irritating squeak doused with water to quieten them down a bit, we walked to the gates of Wat Mahadhatu. I was tremendously and unreasonably excited about my first public appearance, though of course I could not let my excitement show. Phra Maha Laow had instructed me that I must walk slowly and calmly with eyes downcast, being careful not to brush up against anybody. 'But Phra Maha Laow, how can I avoid brushing up against people if I'm looking at the pavement?' I asked. 'Don't worry,' he said. 'They'll see you.'

And see me they did. We must, I suppose, have presented a curious spectacle. Phra Maha Laow is very short, even for a Thai, and I tower over him. It is quite impolite in Thai society, and especially in Thai monk society, for a junior to have his head higher than that of his senior, but there was little I could do about that except to walk a few paces behind him.

Unfortunately, being tall, I also have a problem with walking slowly. It's not that I walk fast, but my legs are so long that I take huge strides. I tried to walk more slowly by shortening my strides, but I found that quite awkward and ungainly. Phra Maha Laow was constantly whispering to me to slow down, as I was frequently close to overtaking both him and the other monk.

Almost the instant we stepped over the threshold of Wat Mahadhatu, I heard someone say, *Phra Farang* – foreign monk. The first of dozens of times that day and the first of many hundreds of thousands of times since. *Phra Farang . . . Phra Farang . . . Phra Farang*. Even many Thai people who know me quite well, and even some of the monks at my present monastery, frequently address me as Phra Farang rather than as Phra Peter. I have never understood why, though I don't really care. I know that some Westerners who visit Thailand feel quite insulted when they are referred to as 'farang', though the Thai people rarely use the word in an insulting way. I have been told by a linguist that Westerners may find the word insulting because it has two syllables, like some of the racially insulting words or taunts used in the West. But I wasn't insulted; I was proud to be a Phra Farang. As we walked, people smiled at me. I smiled back. In fact, I positively beamed, until a warning glance from my teacher made me lower my eyes and fix a more neutral expression on my face. But I couldn't keep my eyes downcast for long, not with so many lovely Thai smiles being offered to me.

We certainly didn't have to worry about brushing up against anybody. At that time the area around Wat Mahadhatu was a very busy market and the footpath was crowded, but the crowds simply parted to let us through. '*Phra Farang* . . . *Phra Farang* . . . *Phra Farang*' . . .

Besides smiling, many people also offered me a very graceful *wai* as we passed; that lovely Thai gesture of both greeting and respect in which the palms are held together as if in prayer, and the fingertips are brought up level with the nose.

Of course, my vanity and ego were so inflated by all this that I didn't realise I might just as well have been carrying a big placard saying 'brand new monk'. My head was newly-shaved and shining brightly, whereas Phra Maha Laow's black hair had already grown noticeably since the last general head shaving day two weeks before. My robe still had its brand new sheen and creases, like an unironed new shirt, and although I tried to walk like a monk, it must have been obvious from the way I kept having to hitch my robe onto my shoulder, and my whole general demeanour, that I was new at all this. That didn't stop people smiling or wai-ing of course. In my experience, Thai people are usually genuinely delighted that a Westerner has chosen to follow Buddhism and has become a monk in their country, even though they often don't understand why.

But a monk like Phra Maha Laow, then with more than fifteen years spent in the robes, has developed an air of serenity that can't be falsified. It can't really even be learned. It is a reflection of true inner peace and comes from a genuine and deep understanding of what the Buddha taught and from long practice of Buddhist meditation techniques. Thai people seem to instinctively recognise this natural serenity, and I didn't have it.

None of that occurred to me at the time. There I was, in my lovely new robe and my lovely new haircut, walking on the streets of Bangkok while total strangers smiled and paid their respects to me. Oh, I was the bee's knees!

But not for long . . .

6

For me, Wat Phra Kaew is one of the most beautiful and fantastic religious monuments on Earth. Compared with some other such man-made monuments, Wat Phra Kaew is new, most of it dating back only about 200 years. But as an example of inspired architecture, of man's desire to revere his gods or spiritual teachers, the Temple of the Emerald Buddha is truly remarkable.

Golden pagodas gleam in the sun, soaring pillars and columns are covered with millions of tiny pieces of coloured glass and porcelain which glitter and sparkle, dazzling the eyes. Mythological giants and heavenly creatures stand guard at the gates and every surface is carved, coloured or embellished. The visitors who throng its courtyards are always quiet, perhaps stunned by the vibrant beauty and brilliant colour that surrounds them.

The origins of the image known as the Emerald Buddha are shrouded in mystery and legend. In 1434 it was found hidden in an old chedi in Chiang Rai in the north of Thailand, disguised with plaster and gold leaf. It was enshrined in various temples in the north, and later in Laos. In 1778, Chao Phraya Chakri, later to become Rama I and founder of the present royal dynasty, brought the image back to Thonburi, which was then the capital city of Thailand. The image made its final move in 1785, when Bangkok was established as the new capital and the Chapel Royal was built.

The image is really quite small, about sixty centimetres high, and is not made of emerald but of jade or jasper. Some historians believe the image is of Thai workmanship, possibly from the Chiang Sen period (about AD 1050) and that the material used probably came from Southern China. Other historians believe the image came from India.

What it is made of, or where it originated from, are unimportant compared to its meaning to the Thai people. It has become a talisman of the people, the religion, the nation and its sovereign. It is said that if the image should ever leave Bangkok, the 200-year-old Chakri dynasty will fall. The Chakri kings traditionally anoint the image and change its robes at the beginning of the three Thai seasons. The robes themselves are very beautiful. The rainy season robe is of gold decorated with rubies, with a gold and sapphire headdress. The cool season robe is covered in gold beads and the robe for the hot season includes a crown of gold and jewelled ornaments that almost cover the image. Great power is attributed to the Emerald Buddha. During a cholera outbreak in Bangkok in 1820, the image was carried through the streets of the city to end the spread of the disease. People travel from all over the country to pay respect to the image and to pray for some favour or relief from illness. Except for the King nobody may even approach the image, and it sits very high up on a pedestal, protected by a glass case, barriers and vigilant guards. It is also one of the very few Buddha images in Thailand that may not be photographed. I have frequently seen the guards exposing film of clandestine photography, usually very much to the tourists' annoyance, despite the fact that there are signs banning photography in the chapel.

I don't worship Buddha images. I respect them all, large or small, new or old, because they are symbolic representations of the founder of Buddhism and, for me, that symbolism includes everything that I believe, try to follow and practise. I sometimes use a small Buddha image to help focus my mind before meditation and I happily and humbly bow before the main image in any monastery I visit. That is a personal re-affirmation of my beliefs, but I cannot accept that any image is holy nor even ultimately important, nor do I accept that any image or holy relic can have magical powers. But I could be quite wrong and I am sure most Thais would say I am, and most certainly where the Emerald Buddha is concerned.

From the moment I first saw the Emerald Buddha, many years ago on my first visit to Thailand, I had been enthralled by this lovely object. On every opportunity, I always spent a half-hour or so sitting in the Chapel Royal staring up at the image and its surrounding altar decorations. Like any other visitor, I could not get very close. The only people who are allowed to pass the barriers are monks who come to pay their respects at the very base of the altar. Now I was to be allowed that privilege.

When I had visited Wat Phra Kaew and the adjoining Grand Palace before, I'd had to queue with other tourists to buy a ticket. Like many other historical attractions in Thailand, Wat Phra Kaew has a two-tier pricing system: tourists pay, Thais don't. In the case of the Emerald Buddha I think that's quite reasonable but on this occasion, my first visit as a monk, I wondered what my position would be. Would I have to queue and pay, or would I be allowed through the 'Thais only' gate? I was waved through with a wai and a smile and, for the first time, heard the phrase *Nimmon Luang Por* 'Invite Respected Father'. My vanity meter quivered, not sure whether to move up or down a point.

Inside, Phra Maha Laow and I wandered around for a while, studying the recently restored mural paintings depicting scenes from the *Ramakien*, the Thai version of India's *Ramayana*. I was aware that we seemed to have gathered quite a crowd of people behind us – a few Thais but mostly tourists – who followed us quietly from panel to panel. We decided to sit for a while in a small open-sided pavilion but, as soon as we sat down, we were surrounded by people, all pointing cameras and camcorders at us. Dozens of them. A Japanese man sat next to me while his companion took photographs. Then a couple of Germans, then an American. I expected that, at any moment, somebody would sit on my lap to pose with me, or plonk a 'kiss me quick' hat on my head, just for a laugh. I found myself intensely irritated and embarrassed, though I tried hard not to let it show. People were pointing their cameras at us as though we were just another tourist attraction, something to be photographed to show the folks back home. We were Buddhist monks, wearing the robes of that ancient order, but we might just as well have been wearing Mickey Mouse costumes for the benefit of visitors to Disneyland.

I personally felt insulted because I thought people showed not the slightest degree of good manners, but I was also irritated at a deeper level. Somehow, the robe and everything it represented and symbolised seemed diminished by this intrusion. I was appalled and deeply embarrassed. Phra Maha Laow seemed oblivious to it all and sat, smiling calmly.

I asked him if we could move on. We started walking towards the Chapel Royal, followed by our gaggle of tourists and preceded by others a few feet in front, walking backwards and keeping their camcorders fixed on our faces. Mine, I think, was bright red. A few yards from the hall, two young Englishmen, probably in their mid-twenties, sidled up to me and asked, 'Why are you a monk?' I replied that I had become a monk because I wanted to devote my life to following what the Buddha taught. 'You look like a bloody idiot,' said one, and they walked off, laughing.

I was trembling as we entered the Chapel and a guard led us through the assembly of about a hundred people, Thais and tourists, who were sitting on the floor. Now, there is a screen between the main floor of the hall and the area reserved for monks, but at that time there was only a low barrier and the monks could be seen at their devotions. We sat at the base of the altar in silent thought for a few minutes – mine quite different from Phra Maha Laow's, I'm sure – and then began to make the triple obeisance. My robe fell off.

I actually felt quite faint and nauseous and it was only with great effort that I got up and walked with any dignity at all through the crowds and into the sunshine outside. There, we once again found ourselves the focus of every camera and camcorder. Though outwardly I smiled, inwardly I was cringing with humiliation.

'Phra Farang . . . Phra Farang . . . Bloody idiot' . . .

When we got back to Wat Mahadhatu, I tried to explain my feelings to Phra Maha Laow, though I was confused and didn't really understand them myself. I felt I had been personally insulted by the two young men and I thought the robes and what they symbolised had been degraded by the tourists.

'You shouldn't worry,' said Phra Maha Laow. I don't know how many times I have heard my friend and teacher say, 'don't worry' during our long relationship.

It's his answer to most problems. In the West, we say it but I don't think we really know what it means, or how to do it. We know it's good advice, often the only advice, but we do worry; some of us all the time and about every little thing. That worry can lead to the most awful inner turmoil and suffering. Worrying *at* a problem may help unravel it and maybe a solution will present itself, but worrying *about* it will only ever make it worse. But when Phra Maha Laow used the term 'don't worry', or that most famous of Thai phrases, *mai bpen rai* – it doesn't matter – he really meant it. He doesn't worry. It doesn't matter. He seems to manage to keep both an inner and outer equanimity at all times. That was something I hadn't learned to do. I had no natural sense of *mai bpen rai* or, if I had ever had it, it had long ago been buried under layers of personal opinion, fixed views and habitual, conditioned response: '*I* think it matters' . . . 'it matters to *me*' . . . 'in *my* opinion . . .'. All just ego and all a source of potential mental conflict when things don't go exactly as we would ideally wish them to.

Phra Maha Laow said that if someone had shown impoliteness to me, either verbally or through his or her actions, it could only affect me and disturb my equanimity if I allowed it to. Maybe Westerners are more aggressive than Thai people in some situations. If someone insults us, our ego and pride are easily offended and perhaps we feel the need to respond in kind. That's not usually the Thai way and it certainly shouldn't be the monks' way. It cannot lead to inner equanimity or the overcoming of self-inflicted mental suffering.

I remember being told by the monk-teacher at one of my very first Sunday morning lessons in basic Buddhism at Wat Buddhapadipa: 'If you are playing tennis and someone hits the ball at you, there are two choices: you can either catch it, or hit it back.' Although he may have been a little confused about the rules of tennis, there was obvious wisdom in what he was trying to say. If you don't mentally respond to an insult in any way – if the mind doesn't move – the insult cannot cause hurt or harm. An insult is only the opinion of somebody else, who quite likely doesn't have any facts upon which to base that opinion; he's simply sounding off for some unrelated reason of his own and the words really have no validity. So why should the mind move? And if there is no ego, no vanity, there is nothing that can be hurt or offended anyway.

'You look like a bloody idiot' really means, '*I* think you look like a bloody idiot'. 'In *my* opinion you look . . .' Why should my equanimity suffer because of his opinion? Why should I be hurt, or humiliated? Why should my mind move?

I think on that day, only a few days after my ordination, I had my first real lesson about the false nature of ego and pride; something which I may have absorbed intellectually from studying at Wat Buddhapadipa, but which I didn't know experientially.

When walking to Wat Phra Kaew, I had been proud to be a monk, to show myself off to the people and to accept their traditional greetings and respect. But they knew nothing about *me*. The tourists offered no greetings or respect, because they also didn't know who I was or what I represented. One group of people thought I looked like somebody deserving of respect and another thought I looked like a 'bloody idiot'. Both opinions and reactions were based solely on what I was wearing and on my physical appearance. Ultimately, neither opinion had any validity but I had allowed pride and ego to respond to both, in different ways.

Inner equanimity is a state of mind that is unaffected by outside stimuli. The mind remains undisturbed by words, no matter whether they are flattering or insulting. All stimuli, whether they come by means of eye, ear, nose, taste or touch, are regarded with absolute tranquillity, with neither craving nor aversion. Equanimity comes from a true understanding of what the Buddha taught, not at an intellectual level but from really *knowing* for oneself at the Insight-Wisdom level. But it doesn't come easily. I was to have far more humiliating experiences in the future before I even began to know equanimity sufficiently enough to wrap it around myself as naturally as my robe.

Eventually, I began to see my robe in quite a different way as well. I saw it for what it was intended to be; a cloth to keep my body covered and to protect it from insects and the elements. It had symbolic significance as well, but that was something that had incidentally developed around it. The robe could neither be insulted nor flattered. It was just a piece of cloth, just a support for my particular way of life. Only I and my preconceptions and misconceptions could be insulted, but only if I allowed my mind to move.

Since that first visit as a monk to Wat Phra Kaew, I have returned many times. The tourists and visitors are still there, with their cameras and camcorders. Some are very polite and ask if they may take my photograph, which I never refuse. Some want to spend a few minutes discussing Buddhism, or why an Englishman should want to become a monk. Some don't ask before sticking their lenses in my face and just occasionally someone will surprise me by making an insulting taunt or disparaging remark about my physical appearance, but the insults are often witty and clever and only amuse me. My robe no longer falls off when I make the triple obeisance before the Emerald Buddha. If it did, I wouldn't worry. I'd straighten it up and put it back on. But that's now.

7

During my first visit to Thailand, I sent post-cards to friends in England showing monks on their early morning alms round, or *binderbaht*. The image of a line of shaven-headed, saffron-robed monks walking barefooted in the dawn streets was so exotic and so evocative of the country that I wanted my friends to see it too. Not that I actually saw monks on alms round myself; I was never out of my hotel bed early enough for that. But even the postcard photographs seemed to hint that, far from being what I then vaguely thought of as beggars, the monks had a nobility about them and that the custom was of great religious significance. Now I was a member of their community, I was excited by the prospect of taking part in the daily ceremony myself.

Alms round is an important part of every monk's daily routine. Besides being his way of getting food to eat, it also gives him the opportunity to reflect on his lifestyle and his relationship with the people. The monks rely on the people for all their needs, traditionally called the Four Supports: robes, food, shelter and medicines. When walking on alms round, the monk should reflect particularly on the food he is offered by lay-people, accepting gladly whatever is given and without concern for his own preferences or aversions for certain foods. Besides being necessary for his sustenance, walking on alms round is a training that the monk should use to help him overcome all his other preferences and aversions too, since in Buddhist philosophy it is these which are the cause of all mental suffering.

In return for the support of the people, the monks help to sustain the people's faith in the Buddha's teaching by good example and by practising well. The people then listen when the monks try to guide them by passing on the teaching. If the monks are seen to be lax in their behaviour or in their discipline in following the 227 Precepts, the people will no longer support them and their faith will decline.

Alms round is also important to the people because it gives them the opportunity to start the day with an act of generosity and compassion. In Buddhist teachings, these are qualities that should be practised and developed.

The monks' daily alms round is sometimes described as 'begging' and the alms bowl as a 'begging bowl', but neither term is correct. Monks do not beg nor, unless sick, should they ask for specific food or even hint at some need. On alms round, they simply walk in the streets with their bowls. If people offer food, they accept it. If people don't offer food, the monks go hungry. Monks who live in cities and towns usually get offered a lot of food, frequently more than they need, but in the countryside it can be quite different. If a rural area is suffering drought and consequent crop failure, the people may have very little to offer. The monk may have to make do with a few spoonfuls of rice and be content with that, and the way things are.

The Buddha walked on alms round and although the robes and alms bowl have changed over the centuries, it is still done in essentially the same way and for exactly the same reasons. The Vinaya includes many training rules about the conduct of the monk when he is walking on alms round. In modern times, it is not always possible to follow some of the rules to the letter but monks must try to follow the spirit of the Vinaya as closely as they can.

The original training rules, for example, say that the monk may accept food (i.e., curries etc.) in the proportion of one to four of rice. He can accept food only up to the top edge of his alms bowl and he must not hide curries under the rice in order to get more. But the nature of food itself has changed since these and other rules were laid down in India so many centuries ago. Now, at least in the towns and cities of Thailand, food offered to the monks is often in packets, bottles and cans, and even the rice may be in a bag or polystyrene box.

Thai people love to offer food to the monks since they believe they 'make merit' by doing so. Frequently, it is impossible to accept only a level bowl full and many monks carry a yarm or plastic bag in which to put the excess food they are offered. To refuse food, thus refusing to allow the people to make merit, would be considered extremely rude. So monks must compromise as necessary but still try to walk on alms round according to the ancient traditions.

Unfortunately, when lay-people offer excess food it can make alms round quite difficult for the monk. On some occasions, especially in Bangkok, I have not only needed both hands to carry a very full and heavy alms bowl, with its lid balanced precariously on top of a pile of packets and tins, but have also had several one-litre bottles of water dangling awkwardly in plastic bags from my fingers, as well as a bulging yarm hanging on my arm. Trying to cope with so much not only looks very ugly but is also completely distracting for the monk who is supposed to be trying to concentrate on the meaning of alms round. Once back in the monastery, all that excess food wasn't a problem for me and was never wasted, because I shared it with the nuns in Section 5, who did not walk on alms round.

Probably the worst alms round I've ever experienced was when I was living at Wat Mahadhatu and Bangkok was flooded. On that early morning, the rain was pouring down and I seemed to be the only monk on the streets. I had to wade knee-deep through filthy floodwater and was soaked to the skin. There were still plenty of people about, perhaps on their way to work, and I received so much food that it was piled at least a foot above the top of my alms bowl. I had to keep the lid on with my chin. It should have been obvious to anybody that I had quite enough food and was having difficulty even walking, but that didn't stop people trying to offer me even more. One lady even put a rolled umbrella on top of my alms bowl. I'm sure she meant well, but really it wasn't a lot of use, unless I held it up in my teeth.

At most city monasteries, the monks walk on alms round alone or in small groups. It is usually only in rural areas that the monks from the local village monastery walk together. Not all monks walk on alms round every day, though I think most do. In Section 5 of Wat Mahadhatu, the temple boys cook a simple breakfast every morning for the monks who, for whatever reason, are not able to go out on their rounds. In other sections, some monks go on alms round and then share the collected food with others in the section, perhaps on some sort of rota basis. In European and American monasteries, the monks do not walk on alms round at all because they live within cultures which are unfamiliar with Buddhism or its traditions.

Before being allowed out on alms round for the first time, I had to be trained. Phra Maha Laow was certainly not going to let me loose on the good people of Bangkok until he was confident that I knew how to walk on alms round properly.

For my first few days as a monk, I ate breakfast in Section 5, together with a monk with a broken leg, a couple of visiting Korean monks, and others who had various early morning duties. On about the fourth day, Phra Maha Laow decided that we would go out on alms round together.

That was to be only the second time I had stepped out of the monastery gates as a monk and I was not only looking forward to the experience of alms round, but also to the walk on Bangkok's pre-dawn streets. We were back within ten minutes, our bowls full. 'I want to go again,' I told Phra Maha Laow.

He was shocked. 'You can only walk on binderbaht once.'

'It wasn't long enough.'

'You can only walk on binderbaht once.'

'I didn't learn anything.'

Phra Maha Laow and I were well known at Wat Buddhapadipa for the frequency and futility of our arguments. He usually knew what was right and I always knew what I wanted. Usually he won, but on this occasion he gave in. We dropped off our first load of food at his section. 'We're like naughty novices,' he said, as we stepped through the gates for the second time.

In fact, the practicalities of alms round are simple and I quickly learned how to walk, stand, hold my bowl and accept food. There hadn't been much time to dwell on the spiritual significance of any of it. It was not until the next day, when I went out alone, that I really understood what I was doing. My teacher had been unable to prepare me for the spiritual and cultural shock I was to receive.

Spiritual experience was the last thing on my mind

that morning as I prepared to leave the monastery and take to the streets. My main concern was keeping a firm grip on my alms bowl and holding it level. Modern bowls are large, much larger than in the Buddha's time. They can be awkward to handle, especially when someone puts a bag or spoonful of very hot rice in them. The heat of the rice is transmitted immediately through the bowl to the hands and I have sometimes been scorched by the hot metal. Modern bowls, like mine, are often made of stainless steel with a very thin and lightweight tin lid. The lid fits only loosely on top of the bowl and is quite likely to fall off with a loud and embarrassing clatter if the bowl is tipped at the wrong angle. I was also still having a problem keeping my robe on, too. It was fine if I stood still with the roll of cloth that holds it together tucked tightly under my arm but as soon as I made any sort of movement the robe would shift on my shoulders and threaten to fall in a heap around me.

As I stood bare-footed at the gates of Wat Mahadhatu, my main thoughts were with these practical matters, as well as the state of the pavements outside. The vicinity of any monastery in Bangkok is home to countless stray dogs, since even the mangiest mutt is sure of a meal in the monastery. They leave evidence of their presence every few yards. Bangkok's pavements are themselves notoriously dangerous, with holes big enough and deep enough to break a leg in. Stepping off the pavement to walk in the road brings its own dangers. Slimy vegetables from yesterday's market fill the gutters, just waiting to be trodden on – banana skins in the most literal sense. I had all these potential hazards in mind as I prepared to step through the gate. And of course, I was nervous.

There is a form of meditation that focuses concentration on very precise movements of the feet. I decided to calm my nerves by treating alms round as a meditation exercise. After adjusting my robe one last time and clutching my bowl to my stomach tightly with two hands, I took a deep breath and stepped over the monastery threshold.

I had decided to go on a less populated route for my first solo alms round so that I could be out longer. My route was to take me around the perimeter of Wat Mahadhatu, past Wat Phra Kaew, and to a small market about a kilometre away.

I had never experienced anything in my life like that forty-five-minute walk. I had intended practising only the simplest walking meditation, concentrating on each foot as it was moved forward – *right goes thus, left goes thus* – but my concentration level quickly became so high that it soon encompassed my whole body. I'd been practising walking meditation for several years but for the first time I really understood walking. Each step seemed to be a unique experience. I was totally aware of the movement of each muscle in my legs and feet, aware of my own body weight as each foot touched the ground, the texture and dampness of the surface I was walking on, the cool air on my shaven head, the feel and weight of the bowl in my hands – everything seemed to take on a higher clarity. In fact, I was so absorbed in my meditation that I failed to see the first person waiting to offer food. I walked straight past her and she had to run after me!

Walking past Wat Phra Kaew was also an odd experience. As I walked past, eyes downcast, the pavement beneath my feet started to vibrate slightly. I could hear rhythmic stamping behind me, but I didn't turn around. Suddenly, a squad of about twenty Thai soldiers, marching at a trot in two lines, came level with me and, as they did so, the lines opened up to flow past on either side of me. It totally broke my concentration for a few seconds, but I thought what an amazingly surreal black-and-white photograph that moment would have made – a Buddhist monk walking on alms round, totally surrounded by armed soldiers!

The ceremony of offering food is simple but full of symbolism. The layperson waits at the side of the road with a basket or tray of food, usually rice and curries packed in little plastic bags, a piece of fruit, perhaps a cake or other sweet, and occasionally a ten or twenty baht note in an envelope. The monk approaches with eyes downcast, looking only at the pavement, mindful of every step. As the monk draws near, the layperson invites him to accept food by saying '*nimmon*'. Without looking up, the monk stops walking and stands perfectly still. These few moments of complete stillness enable the donor to consider the merit of his or her action and the monk to contemplate the meaning of the food as a support and necessity for his body. Then, bending forward very slightly from the waist, the monk raises the lid of his bowl and the donor gently places the food inside. The monk should not look at the donor, but keep his full attention on the bowl. The donor pays respect to the monk with a graceful wai, the lid of the bowl is lowered, and the monk walks on his way. The monk should never say 'thank you', but occasionally may murmur a very short blessing in Pali. Usually, no words are spoken and none are necessary. Both monk and layperson are aware that they have followed a tradition that has barely changed for thousands of years.

To me, this was not only beautiful and spiritually moving, but also quite surreal. I was a forty-five-year-old former businessman from London, who now found himself walking bald and barefooted in an exotic city at dawn, wearing a robe and accepting food from complete strangers in total silence. And the oddest thing was, it felt *right*.

The first time I returned from alms round alone it took me some time to recover from the extraordinary experience. I was humbled by the kindness of the people and, at the same time, spiritually uplifted by this simple little ceremony that takes place hundreds of thousands of times every morning throughout Thailand. It took me a while to sort out my thoughts and emotions but I realised that the people gave not just to the monk as an individual, but also to the order of monks – the Sangha – and that when they pay their respects it is to the robe and all it symbolises for them. And the respect seemed totally genuine.

The same people do not necessarily offer food every day. They may do it once a year to make merit on the anniversary of the death of a parent or loved one, on their own birthday, or for some other reason known only to themselves. The alms round I followed each morning when I lived at Wat Mahadhatu took me through a small market, so I was frequently offered food by the same stall-holders each day. One lady always placed a piece of Swiss roll and a carton of milk in my bowl, another an apple. Once I was given a cheese sandwich. I was quite touched that people were taking the trouble to offer food that they thought the Phra Farang might like, though the type of food offered is of little importance.

Each day I returned from alms round and sat cross-legged on the floor of my tiny room in Section 5, to eat breakfast in solitude and contentment. Even after a few weeks, I found I was beginning to forget the businessman that I once had been and it became increasingly difficult, and unnecessary, to relate to his hedonistic pleasures and desires. He was someone who lived a very different lifestyle in a distant land and a seemingly distant past. I was beginning to find a new and hitherto unknown satisfaction in my life; a spiritual satisfaction that I had never experienced before. Slowly, I was becoming a monk, on the *inside* as well as the outside.

8

I haven't lived at Wat Mahadhatu for more than five years. On the rare occasions when I need to go to Bangkok, I stay in Section 5 and I am happy to do so. There are always many monks there as temporary residents that I do not know but there are also some who live in the section permanently, as well as others who live there for several years whilst studying at the university. With these monks I seem to have a perfectly good relationship, within the limits of our communication skills, and we are polite and helpful to each other. With the few who can speak English well, and those I have known for a few years, I seem to have a particularly good relationship and some go out of their way to look after me. But we didn't start off that way.

A month or so after my ordination, Phra Maha Laow and Ajahn Amara Thera had both returned to London and I began to feel alone and isolated in Section 5. Although I was sure some of the monks must have been able to speak English, they seemed to be a most unfriendly bunch. The spirit of comradeship and brotherhood that I had expected to find in the Sangha didn't appear to extend to me. Some of the monks had been friendly to me before I ordained, at least to the point of smiling, but the smiles had disappeared and had been replaced by total blankness.

I was taking a shower when another Section 5 monk actually spoke to me. I had only been in the shower a few minutes when the monk tapped on the door and said impatiently, in English: 'Do you know the meaning of hurry up?'

'Yes,' I replied.

'Well, hurry up,' he said.

I hurried and when I emerged from the shower the monk was waiting outside, looking quite surly. He was only a young man, though as a monk obviously my senior. At a time not so long before, I might have reacted, or over-reacted, aggressively to him, but I was determined to be less confrontational. I quietly apologised in Thai and gave him a respectful wai.

At that time I could hardly speak any Thai but I wanted to be friendly and tried speaking in both Thai and English to some of the other monks and novices in the section. Often they would not even acknowledge what I had said or, if I had tried to speak in Thai, would simply laugh. On one occasion, I approached a monk that I knew spoke English well; the monk who had been impatient with me at the shower. 'I understand you have been studying English for many years. You must be fluent,' I said.

'Yes, I am,' he replied, and walked away without another word.

I started to think they were rather a snooty lot and either disliked me personally, which I could accept, or that there was some resentment against foreign monks in general. Some of the Section 5 temple boys were particularly impolite and would quite openly snigger at me or behave in ways that I was sure would be unacceptable to a Thai monk, even a very new one. I didn't know the reason for any of this, so I could see no way to improve the situation.

I am naturally shy, but even more so with Thai people. I am constantly aware that Western and Thai cultures are very different and sometimes totally opposed. It is very easy in Thailand to be unintentionally impolite or offensive, either through actions or words. Thai society is fairly rigidly structured, the Sangha even more so, and I had to be very careful about my speech and behaviour. Short-time visitors to Thailand probably don't notice this so much because they usually only meet Thai people who frequently have more understanding of Western ways than the visitor has of Thai ways. To hotel staff, tour operators, restaurateurs and so on, the tourist is the customer and is therefore likely to be forgiven for any social or cultural blunder. The Thais are usually a very forgiving and easy-going people anyway.

Some aspects of behaviour that may be quite acceptable in Western societies are most certainly not acceptable in Thai society. For example, in the West there is no particular taboo about touching another person on the head. In Thailand, that's about as impolite as one can be.

How you use your feet is also very important. In the West, we tend to use our feet for much more than helping us stand upright or walk. We open and close doors with them, move things at floor level with them and even have household gadgets like vacuum cleaners that are designed to be operated with them. We frequently use our feet as an extra pair of hands, to the point where in Thailand Westerners' feet are sometimes referred to as 'farang hands'. In Thailand, to use the feet for almost any purpose other than walking is generally unacceptable. To point a foot at another person, especially at a monk or Buddha image, and most especially at the head, can cause very great offence.

I was aware of these and other potential cultural hazards because I had taken the trouble to learn from my Thai friends in London, but I knew there must be many others of which I had no knowledge. Was I unconsciously and unintentionally breaking some cultural or religious taboo? I couldn't think of anything, but I became so unhappy and concerned about the other monks' apparent unfriendliness to me that I started to stay in my room, not talking to anybody, in case I made the situation worse. In retrospect, *that* behaviour added to the problem because I'm sure the other monks thought *I* was being snooty.

It was only by chance that I discovered my cultural understanding, or lack of it, was not really the problem at all. I passed two temple boys in the section one day and heard one sneeringly whisper to the other: 'Star monk.' Star monk? *Star* monk? What on earth did it mean? Over many lonely hours in my tiny room, or sitting on the roof with the pigeons, I thought about it, reviewing everything that I had done or that had happened to me since my ordination.

Slowly I began to see the problem and its various inter-linked aspects. I realised that it could be a problem that would follow me wherever I went as a monk. In that I was right, for I have since been known not only as 'star monk', but also as 'one-man show' and 'Phra Farang Superstar', though in quite different and friendlier circumstances.

The problem was that I am, quite simply, unusual. I don't mean in my physical appearance or personal habits – I don't think there's anything especially weird about me. Physically, I am tall and thin and sometimes because of shyness I tend to stare into some middle distance without seeing anybody, without catching their eye, unless I am actually talking with them, of course. All this can lead people to believe I am haughty, though I don't think I am at all. But my apparent haughtiness wasn't the crux of the problem.

Once, when I was at the Immigration Bureau in Bangkok arranging for a visa extension, I asked an official how many Western monks lived in Thailand. He told me that there were probably no more than about a hundred at any one time and that most lived in fairly isolated international forest monasteries in the north-east of the country. There were only four or five Western monks living in Bangkok monasteries, he said. There are usually around 300,000 monks in Thailand and that figure can rise to nearer 500,000 in the rainy season, when many Thai men ordain for a few months. Those numbers make the Phra Farang, the foreign monk, a rare sight indeed. Additionally, I had been ordained by the abbot of Wat Mahadhatu, a famous, important and very high-ranking monk. He is an extremely busy administrator and does not usually have the time to ordain people himself. As far as I was aware, I was the first Westerner to have had that honour, even though it was only because of my appointed Upachaya's sudden indisposition.

So, I was a rare Western monk who had been uniquely ordained by a high-ranking Upachaya. But even that wasn't the total issue.

Lay-people frequently invite a section head and a group of monks, always totalling nine, to take breakfast or lunch at a house. It may be the occasion of a wedding ceremony, house blessing or because the layperson wants to 'make merit' for a deceased loved one. At these ceremonies, the monks chant relevant Pali blessings and are offered food. After the meal, the monks are invariably given a small gift of flowers or toiletries, together with an envelope containing money. In my experience, in rural areas that may be twenty or fifty baht, but in Bangkok is likely to be several hundred baht. On one occasion in Bangkok, I received 1,000 baht.

I hadn't then even begun to learn any of the Pali chanting, some of which is long and difficult. Yet I was being invited daily, and sometimes twice a day, to attend these house ceremonies. I would sit in silence at the end of the line of monks while they chanted – usually feeling an absolute idiot, since the assembled lay-people rarely took their eyes off me. Monks sit in order of seniority so I should always have been at the far end, but often the senior monk would move me up the line so that I could sit next to him. That would *never* happen to a new Thai monk. Usually, a new Thai monk would have to wait many months before receiving an invitation to have breakfast or lunch at a house and would probably only then be invited if he knew the necessary chanting. Being moved up the line always caused me great embarrassment because I knew it could be considered impolite by the other monks, but I could hardly refuse. I would eat the fine food that was always offered and then be given gifts and money. Because I was a novelty.

Many of the Section 5 monks rarely had the opportunity to attend these ceremonies. They attended university every day and spent most of their free time in study. Most of them, I think, worked very hard indeed, not just at their university studies but also in trying to learn the Pali chanting.

I was sure my unresponsive colleagues in Section 5 were not concerned about the money I was receiving almost every day. Whenever I returned from a house breakfast or lunch, I made a point of dropping the envelope containing the money into the section's donation box in the reception area. In all my time at Wat Mahadhatu I never kept a single baht that was given to me. However, the other monks were understandably beginning to resent all the special treatment and attention I was getting. There were many examples of that, even within the section. One particularly embarrassing incident was when a very important Thai lady visited me at the section's reception area. I didn't know her, but she presented me with a beautiful folding lecture chair, which I kept, and 4,000 baht, which I didn't. Unfortunately, she was rather rude to the monks at reception and gushingly over-polite and respectful to me. That didn't endear me to the more senior monks on reception at all, though why I should be held responsible for other people's good or bad manners is beyond me.

I was a brand new monk who knew nothing but I was being treated like a celebrity. I was being photographed and videoed every time I stepped out of the monastery and was generally getting the star treatment. Perhaps my apparent haughtiness added to the impression that that's how I saw myself. I totally understood the resentment that seemed to be building against me because of it all, and I rather resented it myself. I didn't want to be a celebrity or star monk and be shown off because I had novelty value. Like my colleagues in Section 5, I wanted to study the Dhamma, Vinaya and meditation and I wanted to become a good monk, an ordinary monk.

I couldn't do anything about being a Phra Farang,

nor about the circumstances of my ordination. I found myself in a difficult and delicate position. I didn't want to offend the various section heads by refusing their invitations and I didn't even know whether I was allowed to refuse. At the same time, I very much wanted to live in harmony with my fellow monks in Section 5. I certainly didn't want to be the unwitting cause of any discontent.

I really had nobody to turn to for advice. I could have approached the head of Section 5, especially as he was one senior monk who did not constantly invite me to have meals at houses. His English was good and he was a kind man, but I felt the problem in part crossed cultural barriers and that he wouldn't fully understand my position. If he didn't *fully* understand, I feared there might be further repercussions in the section. So I said nothing to him or anybody else and the situation got slowly worse. It got to the point where, if I saw one of the monks who passed on invitations to me from a section head, I would hide so that I wouldn't have to accept the invitation. I didn't know what to do at all and became miserably distracted from my studies and meditation and quite desperate for somebody to talk to.

Whenever Phra Maha Laow is in Thailand, he stays at Section 24 of Wat Mahadhatu and I had spent many hours in that section. There was a resident monk there, Phra Maha Weera, who I guessed must have been able to speak some English because that was part of the course he was studying at the university. Although he had frequently listened with apparent interest and understanding when I talked with Phra Maha Laow, I don't recall that he had ever spoken. At that time he had been a monk for six or seven years and he seemed a very gentle and friendly person. He was quite big and sort of soft – not fat – and he had a pleasant open face and a rarely seen but lovely smile. Someone had given him the nickname of 'Giant', which he seemed to quite like.

At the height of my problems in Section 5, in desperation I went to see Giant to see if he could offer me any advice. It turned out that, like me, his verbal reticence was due only to shyness and he could actually speak English very well. In fact, he was totally fluent and had just completed translating George Bernard Shaw's *St Joan* into Thai! I hadn't even read it in English.

We quickly became friends. He used to call us comrades in arms, no doubt influenced by St Joan, and I sometimes spent hours each day talking with him in Section 24. Often we would go out together to visit other monasteries in Bangkok where he had friends, and he became my adviser about many things a new monk should know.

I explained the problem in Section 5. Giant was sympathetic but I don't think he fully understood it from my Western point of view. He accepted that it was a problem for me, but could see no way out of it that would not cause more problems. My idea of transferring from Section 5 to Section 24 was immediately ruled out; the section head would lose face, he said. I started to spend more and more time in Section 24 with Giant, avoiding my own section as much as possible.

Giant was just about at the end of his formal studies at the university but as part of his course he had to teach Dhamma and undertake social work in a rural monastery. He had chosen a little monastery called Wat Nahoob, which was close to his own village in the northern province of Nakhon Sawan, about 240 kilometres from Bangkok. He was to leave Wat Mahadhatu permanently in a few months but, before that, planned to make a visit of a few days to Wat Nahoob.

Two important things happened then which were to lead to an ending of my unhappiness in Section 5. Giant invited me to join him on his short visit to Wat Nahoob, and I fell down the stairs.

9

I was riding my motorcycle through London one night when a Ford Cortina appeared where no Cortina should ever be: broadside on to a 1200cc, 7-hundredweight Harley-Davidson travelling at speed. The car driver had tried to jump the lights and had stalled in the middle of the junction. There was nothing to be done but hit the wretched thing dead centre. The bike came to a sudden halt, embedded in the side of the car, but I didn't. I sailed through the air, trailing a screamed obscenity behind me.

When I came to in hospital I naturally enquired first about the state of my Harley and then asked how I was. The bike was wrecked but I was luckier. Nothing broken, no internal injuries. Amazingly, I was only slightly bruised and battered. Years later, it became apparent that I had weakened both my knees when I hit the road on the other side of the car, my left knee more badly than the right. That never really caused me any problems until I started to practise sitting meditation at Wat

Buddhapadipa. Even then, I had no great difficulty or discomfort. My meditation was not excessive and I alternated between sitting and walking meditation, but that started to exacerbate the slight damage caused by the accident years before.

One of the reasons I ordained was to devote myself to the study and practice of meditation. Foolishly, instead of building up my meditation time slowly at Wat Mahadhatu, I went straight into long periods of sitting. Several hours at a time was not unusual for me. Additionally, all monks spend a lot of their time on their knees; during morning and evening chanting, in paying respects to other monks or Buddha images, or sitting cross-legged for eating. Gradually my left knee started to ache. Then it started to swell. Then it simply started giving out on me entirely and I would fall over. I never actually fell down the stairs but I would have done if someone hadn't been quick enough to support me.

Something had to be done and a visit to a hospital close to Wat Mahadhatu was the first limping step.

The doctor could speak English and he said that the cartilage in my left knee was cracking, crumbling, or whatever cartilage isn't supposed to do. He said that it wasn't a great problem and he could operate. He showed me some photographs of what the operation entailed. I'm not especially squeamish, but I wasn't really into brightly-coloured – mostly red – pictures of a leg without its rightful kneecap, particularly if it was potentially my leg.

More off-putting than the operation was the recovery time. The doctor said I would probably have to stay on crutches for a couple of months. I couldn't believe that was necessary, and said so. Couldn't something be done with lasers, masers or phasers, whatever they were called? Regrettably, no. Although the excellent and very expensive private hospitals in Bangkok had the latest medical technology, public hospitals did not. They do the best they can, of course, but they just don't have the funds. But the doctor assured me he had some very sharp knives. He told me that even if I didn't have the operation, the knee would not be a great problem provided I avoided putting any strain on it, which meant not doing anything that a monk has to do every day. He even warned me against using Asian squat-style toilets!

The last thing I felt I needed at that time was to be cooped up in Section 5 on crutches for a couple of months. I didn't think I would be able to cope with the bad atmosphere my presence seemed to be causing. But if I didn't have something done about the knee, I wasn't going to be a very effective monk, at least not in my terms.

I made a phone call to a friend in London, a nurse. She told me it wasn't always necessary to have surgery for a simple cartilage problem. In some cases, she said, it could be an in-and-out of hospital in a one-day job. I decided to go to England and another phone call to Wat Buddhapadipa assured me that the London monastery would be able to accommodate me.

Phra Maha Laow once accused me of running away from my problems. At the time that struck me as very odd. I had always considered that I faced my problems head-on. But his comment always stayed with me and I still examine any intended action to see if it is such a case. Yes, I wanted to be away from Section 5 for a while in the hope that my novelty value would wear off and that the situation would settle down. I couldn't see any other constructive action that I could take without potentially creating more disharmony. The only course seemed to be to remove the apparent problem – me – even though I believed it was the attitude of other people towards me that was the real problem, and not me at all. Anyway, the fact was that something had to be done about the knee and I had every intention of returning to Thailand after it was fixed.

I had a small sum of money in a Thai bank for just such an emergency, though I hadn't expected to need it so quickly. I booked a seat on a flight to London, but not for an immediate departure. I felt that if I followed the doctor's advice and didn't put any strain on the knee, there was no reason to cancel the planned visit to Wat Nahoob. I invested a few baht in a heavy-weight knee support bandage and Giant and I made our plans.

The bus from Bangkok's Morchit terminal takes about three and a half hours to make the 240-kilometre journey to Nakhon Sawan. About an hour of that is spent just getting out of the capital's infamous traffic. Giant and I set off at about 9.30am, later than we intended, which meant we had to buy sandwiches and fruit to eat on the bus during the monks' lunch period.

Before I ordained, I had never been particularly conscious of 'breakfast time', 'lunch time' or 'dinner time'. I ate when I was hungry regardless of the time and had never liked any aspect of my life determined or regulated by the clock. Within the obvious requirements of my business life, I ate, slept and did most other things when I felt the need and, if I didn't feel the need, I didn't do them at all.

A monk cannot be so casual. Most monks eat twice a day, a minority only once, but all monks must finish eating by noon and should not eat again until the following dawn. Monks who eat twice usually have their first meal immediately after returning from alms round, and their lunch between 11am and noon. Others may have a single meal at around 10am. Because monks know they can't eat after midday, they become very conscious that they must eat before, so they will not be hungry in the evening.

I've always been skinny and have never seemed to require much food intake, so I'm not too bothered if I miss lunch sometimes. If I'm planning to undertake a long evening meditation, I'll deliberately skip lunch or might even fast for the day, depending on the circumstances. But I'd rather not. Physical hunger can be ignored but it can also become a discomfort and distraction to the body's sense of wellbeing. In my experience, a comfortable, healthy body, not stuffed full of food but with just sufficient for its needs, leads to a comfortable mind and good physical and mental conditions for meditation. Though I still eat very little, over the years of my life as a monk I also have come to rely on the clock, rather than the rumbling of my stomach.

Giant and I ate our sandwiches and fruit on the bus whilst being driven northwards on a good motorway. The countryside we passed through was fairly uninspiring, though it became more picturesque the further we got from Bangkok. One thing that was worth seeing on the route was just outside the town of Ang Thong. There are a number of factories alongside the motorway that make traditional Thai wooden houses, in the beautiful Central Plains style. Some of them, known as 'cluster houses', are very grand, being made of a number of single-family houses joined together by balconies and open areas, making then suitable for the Thai extended family. Look out for them if you ever travel on that motorway.

Before setting off on our journey, I'd looked up the details of Nakhon Sawan Province and city in a couple of international guidebooks. What little information the books gave was very dismissive of the city, almost seeming to say, 'don't bother'. One even called Nakhon Sawan 'the least friendly city in Thailand'. At first sight, the city does seem rather drab and lacking in interest, certainly compared to more well known cities in Thailand. But, as I was to eventually discover, Nakhon Sawan is much more representative of the real Thailand than some of the other places which visitors usually include on their itineraries.

All main provincial cities in Thailand share their name with the province in which they are situated. Nakhon Sawan is theoretically in the northern region of Thailand, though on a map it appears to be fairly central. The city is an important crossroads but neither it nor the province have any obvious attraction to entice the average tourist to stop off whilst en route to Chiang Mai in the far north. Just about the only attraction is Bung Boraphet, which is a vast lake and bird sanctuary just outside the city. During the rainy season the lake covers an area of about 120 square kilometres.

It is this very lack of tourist attractions that gives Nakhon Sawan City its own special character. Neither the city, the province nor the people have had to compromise in any way to cater to the whims or demands of the international tourist.

Some cities in Thailand that rely heavily on tourist income have had to make many compromises, as have the inhabitants of those cities, but Nakhon Sawan has managed to remain an ordinary little provincial city. Its skyline is dominated by the roofs of monasteries, rather than high-rise hotels or apartment blocks. I don't think there is any building in the city higher than seven storeys, and very few of them, even. The streets are crammed with little Chinese noodle shops, rather than hamburger or pizza restaurants. There are no souvenir or postcard shops, no traffic jams nor, as far as I am aware, strip joints or sleazy nightclubs.

Through the centre of the city flows the Ping river, quite literally, in the rainy season. It is in Nakhon Sawan

that the Ping joins the Nan, Wang and Yom rivers from
the north to form the mighty Chao Phraya, the River
of Kings, that runs from the province, through Bangkok
and to the sea. Unlike in Bangkok, the beauty and calm
of the river is not disturbed by the irritating buzz of
long-tail speedboats or river buses. Almost the only river
traffic is a little ferry that runs from one side of the
river to the other.

Nakhon Sawan is an ordinary, peaceful little city –
until February, when it goes slightly crazy.

Just as Chiang Mai is the place to be for the Thai
New Year *Songkran* festival in April, so Nakhon Sawan
is the place to be for the Chinese New Year celebrations in February. The population of the city is about
200,000 and, although if asked their nationality most
would respond 'Thai', the majority of the people are in
fact Chinese. Not the Chinese-Thai combination found
throughout Thailand, but one hundred per cent
Chinese. Nakhon Sawan is *the* China Town of Thailand.
Many shop signs are written only in Chinese, some of
the older inhabitants cannot speak Thai and many
young people speak Chinese when at home with their
families.

In February, the normally drab rows of 'shop houses'
are spruced up and decorated with fairy lights and
bunting and many thousands of Thai and Chinese visitors pour into the city from all over the country for the
traditional, colourful and noisy celebrations. For nearly
a week, the atmosphere is more like that of Singapore
than of a provincial Thai city. Forty-foot long dragons

and troupes of 'lion dancers' perform in all the main streets. Some years, dragons are invited from many neighbouring countries, adding even more variety to the amazing spectacle. Many streets are closed to traffic and the major road junctions are spanned with red-lacquered, dragon-decorated arches which, apart from the 'sponsored by Pepsi' signs, give the city something of the look of imperial China. Hundreds of red Chinese lanterns supplement the normal street lighting and many streets are hung with red and yellow banners, covered in Chinese characters. At night spectacular fireworks displays, street theatre and traditional dance performances keep the carnival atmosphere going.

I didn't know any of that when Giant and I first arrived in the city. At first sight, it seemed as ordinary and uninteresting as the guidebook had led me to believe. Giant wasted no time in showing me around and instead we found a beaten-up thirty-year-old Toyota taxi for the forty-kilometre journey to Nahoob village.

I was delighted to be out of Section 5, out of Bangkok and in the green countryside. The province isn't known for spectacular scenery but, away from the motorway, it does have a sort of soft beauty about it that I found attractive and quite reminiscent of the English countryside. There were vistas that could almost have been Sussex or Norfolk, except that those English counties don't have banana trees and Nakhon Sawan doesn't have windmills. Although the countryside was mostly flat, it was occasionally broken up in the most dramatic way by granite mountains. I'm not sure if they really qualify as mountains but that's what the Thai people call them. They were really just huge piles of rock, many hundreds of metres high sometimes, which seemed to have been dropped about the countryside quite haphazardly, bearing little apparent relationship to the flatness all around them. Some were rounded tree-covered humps, while others were treeless, broken and craggy. Some of them were very beautiful indeed and the most stunning, a sort of mini-Alpine range with multiple peaks, seemed to lie at the end of the road on which we were travelling.

Nahoob village lies in the district of Banpotphisai and we were through Banpot town in a few minutes, it is so small. I renamed it 'Pisspot', much to Giant's amusement, though it is a very nice little town sitting on both sides of the Ping river. A few more kilometres down the road and the taxi turned onto a rough dirt track, lined on one side with fields of tall sugar cane and on the other by traditional Thai farmhouses. At the end of the two-kilometre-long track lay our destination, the village of Nahoob. A few kilometres beyond that were the beautiful mountains of Khao Nor.

The monastery lies to one side of Nahoob so we didn't need to drive through the village to reach it. Even at that time, I had seen many different types of monasteries and temple buildings. Some were huge and spectacular, others were neat and pretty and some were . . . well, they were like Wat Nahoob. It was a typical, ordinary, rural monastery. In such monasteries, there will usually be a small Uposatha Hall, an open-sided sala or meeting hall, a small crematorium, a bell tower and a collection of other buildings and kutis. Some will be ramshackle and made of wood (with a great deal of charm to my Western eye) with others made of cinder blocks, functional and ugly. There is usually a big, grassy area for fairs and football matches, a pond, the inevitable plot of waste ground where all the rubbish is dumped, and a few trees, some of which may be very old. There is always at least one *Bo* or *Bodhi* tree, the type of tree under which Prince Siddhattha meditated and became the Buddha. That was Wat Nahoob.

It's pretty much the same picture that can be seen in thousands of villages all over rural Thailand. These monasteries are not built to house priceless images or relics, or to impress tourists, or even to glorify the Buddha. They are working monasteries, built with funds raised by the local villagers themselves to serve the needs of the village and the monks who live within the community.

Each year during the Pansa, or rainy season retreat, the monasteries will be home to at least a few of the village men, who will ordain for three or four months. Some who have left the village to work in the big cities will return home at that time to devote a few months to studying the teaching of the Buddha, or simply to fulfil their social obligations and 'make merit' for their parents. During the Pansa, monks are not allowed to travel so much or be away from their monastery overnight. Each night must be spent in the same monastery, so monks who usually wander from place to place frequently return to their own village monastery for the retreat.

The abbot of Wat Nahoob and the one other resident monk were both away from the monastery when we arrived, so I took the opportunity to wander around on my own. The monastery covered four or five acres and in one corner was a group of old trees, shrubs and twenty-feet-tall stands of bamboo, perhaps a remnant of a forest that may well have covered the area years before. Inside the mini-forest was a shady clearing. I sat there on a fallen tree, enjoying the smells and sounds of the forest and the clean air, so wonderfully pure after having breathed Bangkok's fumes for a couple of months.

Through a break in the trees, I could see a vast expanse of paddy fields, stretching away into the distance to the base of the mountains, hazy in the afternoon sun. A bright green metre-long snake slithered across the clearing. Huge butterflies of the type usually seen pinned in glass boxes fluttered silently on black-and-yellow wings through the trees. A chameleon clung to a branch a few feet away from me, its head cocked and regarding me without apparent fear. The silence was broken only by small sounds in the undergrowth and the occasional bird call.

I sat for more than an hour in the cool shade. My unhappiness in Section 5 came into my mind but I let the thoughts drift away. This really didn't seem like the time or place for such worries. I felt my body and mind relaxing and just enjoyed each moment, with no particular identifiable thoughts to disturb me. My mind became quite calm and I slipped easily into meditation.

Giant eventually came looking for me and said that the abbot, Ajahn Waow, had returned. We walked back to the main kuti block to meet him. Giant must have already told him that I had a problem with my knee because as I started to kneel to offer my respects with a triple bow, the abbot indicated that it wasn't necessary and that I should sit in whatever position I found most comfortable.

Ajahn Waow couldn't speak any English, but with Giant to translate we had a long and very friendly conversation. The abbot was in his mid-fifties and had been a monk for more than thirty years. Nahoob was his home village and his mother and other family members still lived there. He seemed to be related to just about everybody in the village, though Thai people frequently refer to 'my brother' or 'my cousin' even when there is no blood relationship. It can sometimes be very confusing but usually doesn't matter.

The abbot was tall for a Thai, at more than six feet the tallest I had ever met, and he was very thin. His height and build gave him a sort of stateliness that wasn't in the least diminished by the eighteen-inch-long, pink plastic back scratcher he carried. This piece of 1950s Americana had a little curled hand on the end. I never saw Ajahn Waow actually scratch himself with it and I'm not even sure if he knew what it was for, but he seemed to find plenty of other uses for it. Senior monks are allowed a little eccentricity.

I liked Ajahn Waow almost immediately. Many senior monks I have met seemed to have developed a deep calmness, or 'coolness', but sometimes at the expense of any trace of compassion. Or perhaps they have reached some higher level of compassion that I do not yet comprehend. Ajahn Waow seemed to be 'cool' but he also seemed to be a very caring and compassionate man, in an ordinary sense, with a deep concern for the wellbeing of the villagers who were under his spiritual care. To me, he became Ajahn Wow and, for good measure, with an exclamation mark: Ajahn *Wow!*

The abbot told me I was very welcome at Wat Nahoob and that I was to relax and enjoy my visit to the countryside. One of the temple boys had prepared rooms for Giant and me in the main kuti block where Ajahn Waow and another monk, Phra Maha Pern, also lived. The room had been cleaned and drinking water, bedding, an electric fan, towel, soap and toothpaste had all been laid out for me. I was sure this consideration was not at all because I was a Phra Farang, or especially honoured in any way. It was a simple and friendly welcoming gesture that I knew would have been extended to any visiting monk.

Wat Nahoob owned a car, another thirty-year-old Toyota donated by a villager, and Ajahn Waow had arranged for one of the village men to drive us to Khao Nor the following day so that I could see the mountain's monkeys. By the time we had finished chatting it was late afternoon and I very much wanted to take a walk through the village. Giant accompanied me in case

I gave the villagers too much of a shock. Most of them had never seen a farang before, let alone a Phra Farang!

Nahoob village is a collection of about 150 houses spread over a wide area and surrounded on all sides by paddy fields and sugar-cane plantations. Most of the houses are built in traditional Thai style; not the Thai style seen on picture postcards, but ordinary houses for ordinary country people. All the houses are made of wood, though rarely of teak, with many gaps in the walls to allow breezes to flow through, and with corrugated tin or asbestos roofs. Most stand on stilts to protect them from floods and from at least some of the local wildlife. There are frequently concrete additions to the houses and lots of ramshackle wooden barns and rice stores, and huge stone water barrels for storing rainwater in case the village wells dried up.

As I strolled around the village, I saw beautiful old buffalo carts stored in barns, rarely used since rural mechanisation has been so strongly promoted by successive Thai governments. The old businessman in me immediately surfaced to wonder what one would be worth to an English country pub, parked outside in the beer garden and full of flowers. There were ducks and chickens everywhere, apparently under no sort of control and I wondered how anybody could know which belonged to whom. Presumably the ducks and chickens know to whom they belong. Some chickens were kept for eggs and others for the much-loved Thai 'sport' of cock fighting. These fighting chickens are highly prized, as well as quite aggressive, so they are often kept under large, woven baskets to prevent them from wandering.

On the whole, Nahoob seemed to be a neat and tidy village though inevitably, as in every Thai village I have ever visited, there were many unsightly piles of plastic bottles, broken glass and other household refuse. These were eyesores, of course – no doubt to the villagers as well – but there is no weekly rubbish collection in rural areas, nor municipal tips where rubbish can be dumped, nor the recycling bins that have become a common feature in European towns. Although Thai people are natural recyclers, especially in rural areas, some household rubbish is left to pile up, to be dispersed eventually by wind, dogs and children.

There was nothing in the village that a Westerner would call a shop, though a few houses had open fronts and sold a small selection of everyday essential items. One had seasonal fruit, vegetables and cheap whisky, another had toiletries and cheap whisky, and another had petrol and cheap whisky. Nahoobians obviously liked a drop of whisky now and again.

The one exception to the traditional and slightly decrepit houses was a very large, concrete Western-style house, its new paint gleaming brilliantly white and contrasting starkly with the surrounding drab, wooden structures. All over Thailand, in villages and 'new towns', Thai architects have taken the general shape and style of the 1930s detached English suburban villa, then added to it. They've added Roman pillars, Georgian windows, Victorian balustrades, Art Deco doors, Art Nouveau balconies with Grecian statuary of flowing ladies holding flaming electric torches, and lots of other decorative touches that would probably give a European architect a nervous breakdown. There's usually nothing about them that is even vaguely traditionally Thai, but that doesn't matter. The Thai people who live in such houses obviously like them. The Nahoob house wasn't entirely unattractive, even though it did look out of place in its village setting. I wondered whether in twenty or thirty years' time all the old wooden houses would be gone, replaced by this type of house, with concrete roads and pavements instead of dirt tracks and buffalo paths.

We met many villagers on our walk. They were mostly very old and infirm people, for all the younger men and women were working in the paddy fields. I saw very few young children and when I mentioned that to Giant, he said they were there, but they were hiding because they were frightened of me! A lot of the old people knew Giant because he had been born in a village nearby and was a frequent visitor to Wat Nahoob. They all greeted him very courteously and there was obviously a great deal of respect for him in the village. I don't think they knew what to make of me at first, because they had never seen anything quite like me before. But at least nobody whipped out a camera or camcorder.

A few people asked me polite questions. Did I like Thai food, Thai weather, Thai people and so on, but I was amazed and delighted that even after a few minutes they just seemed to consider me as an ordinary new monk and had little interest beyond the normal politeness they would extend to any visitor. They seemed to be a pragmatic people and easy to like, especially some of the old ladies. After a lifetime spent working in the paddy fields, bending to plant seedlings, some of them couldn't straighten up any more and were permanently bent at right-angles from the hips. But without exception, they had beautiful (and usually toothless) smiles on their lined and lovely old faces, and they smiled frequently.

I was delighted to meet these people and was greatly touched by what seemed to be their genuine and straightforward friendliness towards me. Before I became a monk, I had travelled extensively in Thailand and like most visitors I had mostly stayed in cities or large towns that were on convenient routes, good roads, or close to airports or railway stations. Large cities and towns, anywhere in the world, often attract local people on the make and looking to take advantage of the innocent or stupid visitor in one way or another. It's happened to me frequently in Thailand and, to an extent at least, had tarnished my original impression of Thai people, making me a little cynical about the famous Thai smile. But, as I have discovered, rural Thai people in their own environment genuinely deserve the Thais' reputation for openness and friendliness, no strings attached. They are simply not sophisticated enough, or perhaps not Westernised enough, to consider every stranger an easy mark. They happily open their hearts and homes to strangers and their smiles are always genuine.

That night, I sat alone on the balcony of the kuti block, listening to the night sounds and sipping at a cup of cocoa. I felt totally at peace and perhaps for the first time understood the much-used Thai word, *sabbai*. It can mean healthy, well or comfortable, depending on the context, but it can also mean much more. It can be a deep, inner feeling of wellbeing and contentment; of being at peace with oneself and with the environment. Sabbai. That's how I felt as I drifted off to sleep.

10

I t's amazing how many people you can fit into an old Toyota if you really try. The Thais are wonderful at that and genuinely seem to enjoy going on a journey with someone else's elbow in their ear. And there's always room for another brother, sister or cousin. I'm not sure how many people were crammed into the car for the outing to Khao Nor but it was considerably more than the manufacturer's recommended number. On a later occasion in the same car, we managed to squeeze in the driver and nine monks.

The drive to the mountain was quite splendid. We followed a meandering dirt road that ran alongside rice paddies and sugar plantations, through shady bamboo groves, remnants of forest and past delightful little streams, their surfaces covered with lotus flowers. Dotted about in the fields were enormously tall and straight teak trees, once a source of great wealth for Thailand but now, with stocks greatly diminished, it is illegal to cut them.

At the foot of the mountain lies a monastery, Wat

Khao Nor. The monastery extends a little way up the mountain itself to several cave kutis, intended for monks who want to meditate in isolation. The monastery has an interesting collection of very realistic concrete sculptures, which illustrate basic Buddhist teachings. Such sculptures are fairly common in the grounds of rural monasteries, though their quality may sometimes be quite crude. One showed the 'Four Sights' – the four people Prince Siddhattha saw on secret journeys from his palace: a sick man, an old man, a corpse and an ascetic. The first three caused him to realise the suffering that all people must endure and the fourth showed him possible release from it. Another sculpture was a very realistic pile of skulls and there was one of Prince Siddhattha as an ascetic, before he became the Buddha, sitting in meditation, every vein standing out from his skeletal body, but his face serene. I have seen this particular sculpture in several monasteries and it never fails to move me. After his Enlightenment the Buddha declared that ascetic practices were too extreme and did not lead to Awakening, but the agony and determination that the sculpture manages to portray is inspirational.

Apart from a striking new Uposatha Hall, the monastery was a rather scruffy, dusty place, but it's probably difficult to keep anywhere clean and tidy when it's home to several hundred monkeys. Almost every hill and mountain in Thailand seems to have its share of these mischievous animals. The monkeys at Khao Nor were clever and quite capable of opening a car boot or bonnet in their endless search for edible titbits. They would even make a grab at a monk's bag and run off with it. The babies were cute but some of the adult males were aggressive and dangerous. Visitors to the monastery were occasionally bitten.

Giant and some of the villagers decided to climb to the top of one of the mountain's lower peaks, but that actually meant *climbing*. There was a marked trail but in places it was a case of hauling oneself up fairly sheer rock faces and clinging to exposed tree roots for support. Although the doctor in Bangkok hadn't specifically mentioned avoiding mountain climbing, I'm sure he would have done if he had thought of it. I decided to go only a little way up to a flat ledge that extended over the rock face and the forest below.

I sat on the ledge with a bottle of water, looking out over miles of paddy fields. Some had been flooded after planting and others were already brilliant green with growing rice. The sun sparkled on the water and on the intermittent squares of bright colour. Distant clumps of trees marked the location of villages and I could see the multi-tiered, multi-coloured roofs of several monasteries glistening in the afternoon sun. It was a view straight from a guidebook to Thailand; the real Thailand, rural Thailand, a land of small villages where the vast majority of people spend their lives in backbreaking rice farming.

A few monkeys came to pester me for a while but they soon lost interest and I was left alone. The only sounds were the distant and diminishing voices of Giant and the villagers as they ascended to the top of the mountain. In the treetops beneath my ledge, monkeys dashed madly from branch to branch, seemingly never still. I thought for a long time about the famous Buddhist simile of the 'monkey mind'; the mind that must be trained to stop its constant movement before it can know real peace. I tried to put even those thoughts aside and settled into meditation. Once, when I opened my eyes, I found a young monkey had joined me on the ledge and was sitting only a few feet away, watching me intently. I wanted it to come closer but it ran off as soon as I moved. I was reminded of an occasion years before in London when I was walking in the heavily wooded part of Wat Buddhapadipa's grounds. I saw a young Thai monk sitting on a log, deep in meditation and with a serene expression on his face. Sitting on the palm of his hand was a squirrel, busily washing its face. Each seemed oblivious to the other. It was a beautiful scene but I crept quietly away, not wanting to disturb either of them. How much I wanted to achieve that same absolute stillness of body and mind!

After about an hour, the voices of Giant and the villagers became louder as they descended the mountain, dirty and sweaty but obviously having very much enjoyed their exercise. They hadn't got to the peak because monks' robes are really not very suitable for clambering about on rocks or hanging from tree roots. It was a happy and peaceful afternoon and as we drove back to Nahoob, I looked frequently through the car's rear window at Khao Nor. It was silhouetted against the setting sun and looked magical and mysterious. In fact, I think I preferred it more from a distance than close to. I don't like monkeys much anyway.

That evening I had another long chat with Ajahn Waow and we were joined by the village headman and other people that I hadn't met on my tour of the village the previous day. Everybody was very friendly and polite to me but in a perfectly straightforward and honest-seeming way, which I much appreciated.

The following morning Giant and I were due to return to Bangkok and Ajahn Waow had arranged for a driver to take us to Nakhon Sawan bus station in the car. As we were saying goodbye to the abbot, he spoke at length with Giant. That was mostly about Giant's future duties at the monastery and I let my attention wander around the abbot's room. Photographs of famous monks covered the walls, including one of my own Upachaya. Calendars, some years out of date, were pinned one on top of the other and a board showed a list of names of villagers who had donated towards building the Uposatha Hall years before. Suddenly, my attention was brought back to the conversation as I heard Ajahn Waow mention my name. I didn't understand everything he said, but I picked up the key words: 'Peter . . . Pansa . . . *nii*?' Giant never had a chance to translate. 'Yes,' I said immediately. And I bowed in respect and gratitude to my new abbot.

It's not really that simple, of course. A new monk has responsibilities to his Upachaya, just as the Upachaya has responsibilities to those he ordains. The new monk is supposed to stay at his home monastery for five years, serving his Upachaya and being taught by him. I wasn't at all sure if the abbot of Wat Mahadhatu would allow me to leave that monastery and go gallivanting off to the wilds of Nakhon Sawan after only a few months. Certainly it would be unusual, but I very much wanted to live at Wat Nahoob. I wondered if in this instance my unwelcome special status could be made to work for me.

It would have been totally impractical for me to go to live at Wat Nahoob on my own. I couldn't speak Thai and Ajahn Waow couldn't speak English, so we could not communicate effectively. There was nobody in the village who could translate for us. I supposed I would eventually learn Thai but to be able to talk in Dhamma or Vinaya terms requires considerably more effort than the sort of tourist Thai which can be picked up relatively easily.

I also needed a lot of help to learn some of the Pali chanting. Chanting has never been particularly important to me but it is of great importance to many Thai people. There are some chants which are used frequently and which every monk should know. Besides spending time in his meditation and Dhamma study, almost every monk has contact with the lay-people at some time, especially at 'cycle of life' ceremonies. At funerals, for example, monks chant Pali passages concerned with the impermanence of all things and these passages are a great comfort to those who have been bereaved. It would have been immensely difficult for me to learn the chanting on my own and without guidance.

But I wasn't going to be on my own. Giant would be there and he was both willing and able to be my teacher. Apart from his fluency in English, he was also a *Maha*, a title earned by a monk following an examination to test his proficiency in Pali. He was very capable of teaching me to chant correctly. He would also, we thought then, be able to teach me Thai, though as it turned out that was a rather optimistic idea.

We were back in Bangkok, and for the following week Giant and I sat in Section 24 discussing – plotting – how we could convince the abbot to allow me to go to live in Nakhon Sawan. At the same time we would have to tell him that I needed to return to England, though I didn't think that would be such a problem because it was a medical necessity and I would be back before the Pansa started. We made an appointment to see the abbot and, as usual, I was very nervous when we went to his section with our request.

Phra Sumethadhibodi is a very busy man with far-reaching responsibilities. Every time I have seen him in his kuti he has been surrounded by monks and lay-people, with a queue waiting for advice or to have a form or letter signed, or on some other religious business. He always sits on the floor, surrounded by two-feet-high untidy piles of paperwork, files, photographs and books. But despite the apparent lack of organisation, he is known to be a very organised man indeed.

115

The abbot has a wonderful air of controlled calmness about him. After someone has spoken to him, he frequently remains quite still for a moment before replying. I get the impression that he never says anything until he has very carefully considered his words. If a question has been asked, there is no expression on his face, no body language, to give a hint as to what his answer is going to be.

Our turn in the queue came and Giant and I made our most respectful bows to him. My robe fell off. Giant did all the talking and he talked for a long time. I constantly searched the abbot's face for some indication as to how he felt about what was being said but apart from the occasional glance at me, when I quickly lowered my eyes, there was no reaction at all. No hint of approval or disapproval.

Giant stopped talking. There was a silence. '*Dai*,' said the abbot. It was settled. I could go. We bowed again and, much to everybody's surprise, my robe stayed on.

I was going to England. I was going to get my knee sorted out. And then I was going to live at Wat Nahoob.

11

Anybody unfamiliar with Wimbledon could probably drive down Calonne Road and be completely oblivious to the fact that hidden behind one of its grander houses is one of the most extraordinary buildings in Europe. It can hardly be seen from the road at all, except in winter when the screening trees have lost their leaves. Then, the sun glinting off the orange-glazed roof tiles might attract the eye. Drivers sometimes come to a screeching halt and reverse their cars back down the road for confirmation that what they thought they saw was not an exotic illusion.

On a man-made rise, behind a large, late-nineteenth-century mansion, set in four acres of gardens and woodland, stands a Thai temple. A real Thai temple. This is not a building that compromises in any way to Western architectural taste. It is straight from Thailand and, from the outside at least, is replicated all over that country.

The temple is small but it rises from its marble base with proportions that make it appear larger and grander than it really is. It positively glows as the sun reflects off the gold leaf and mosaics of coloured glass that decorate its pillars, roof and doors. Little bronze bells with Bodhi leaf shaped pendants tinkle in the eaves. On the roof, massive, golden hook-like finials, called *jo-fa*, rear into the sky. These jo-fa hook the building onto heaven or, I have also heard, prevent flying demons landing on the roof. This is the Uposatha Hall of Wat Buddhapadipa.

Inside, the building is even more extraordinary and there is nothing like it even in Thailand, or anywhere else for that matter. Its walls, every square inch of them, are covered with mural paintings. These are not the traditional murals of Thai temples. Here within the story of the Buddha's life are characters well-known to Westerners: Charlie Chaplin, Superman, Presidents Nixon, Reagan and Bush, Colonel Qaddafi, Saddam Hussein, Ninja Turtles and many more. Elephants stand side by side with nuclear missiles. Aeroplanes and spacecraft fly across painted skies with heavenly beings, a Henry Moore sculpture and Stonehenge occupy the same wall panel – and isn't that Margaret Thatcher over in one corner directing things? Like it or not, it is a most incredible artistic achievement which took fourteen artists seven years to complete, sometimes working with the tiniest of brushes and magnifying glasses for the most detailed work.

When I was studying at Wat Buddhapadipa, I sat in this building for many hours, examining every panel. Even then I did not see it all for there are hidden things too, disguised details known only to the artists. They have long since returned to Thailand, their great effort rewarded without a single coin. This great endeavour was their way of making merit and contributing to the spread of Buddhism in the West.

The Uposatha Hall houses the monastery's main Buddha image; a massive 700-year-old bronze work from the Sukhothai period of Thai history, presented to the monastery by His Majesty the King of Thailand. Originally, the image may have been covered in gold but now it gleams dully black, reflecting the gold of a second large image from a later period. On each side of the main image stands an almost life-size image of the leading disciples of the Buddha – Sariputta and Moggallana. There is also a reproduction of the Emerald Buddha, though it conveys little of the beauty of the original in Bangkok's Wat Phra Kaew.

Wat Buddhapadipa was the first official Thai monastery to be established in Europe. It was originally located in a small house in East Sheen in 1965 at the invitation of British Buddhists. The present much larger site was acquired in 1976 so that the Uposatha Hall could be built and because of the increasing interest in Buddhism throughout Europe, with a consequent increase of visitors and students to the monastery.

The acquisition of the site by the Thai Sangha caused something of a shock for the residents of Calonne Road. The road is full of very upmarket and expensive houses and some residents didn't fancy the idea of a Buddhist monastery in the area. They made their objections to the local council. The retired colonel who owned the property was keen to sell it to the monks and he had rather cleverly also gained planning permission to build about sixteen town houses on the extensive site. Given a choice between a monastery and an estate, objections from the neighbours were quickly withdrawn. Although the monks get on well with most of the other residents, there are still a few who disapprove of having a Buddhist monastery on their road. When I lived at the monastery, I had to deal with a very irate neighbour who complained that the monastery's bees were causing her a nuisance by flying about in her garden. She called them 'your Buddhist bees'. I had to gently explain that it wasn't Buddhist monks who made mead and that we had no bees.

Wat Buddhapadipa is very much a working monastery. The monks are missionaries and they have a job to do which they undertake with great enthusiasm and energy. Although missionaries, it is never the job of Buddhist monks to try to convert people to Buddhism. They simply present the philosophy to those who wish to listen. Besides teaching meditation for beginners and advanced students at weekly classes, there are also several one-week-long residential retreats each year. During those retreats, weather permitting, the retreatants live in the monastery's forested area, meditating and sleeping in special tents imported from Thailand for the purpose. There are weekly classes in basic Buddhism and in the *Abhidhamma*, or Buddhist metaphysics, and the monks are frequently invited to lecture at schools and colleges all over London. They produce several monthly magazines and additionally officiate at cycle of life ceremonies, mostly for the Thai community in England, at which they chant relevant suttas and blessings. It is a very busy monastery but is well-supported by a large number of Thais and Europeans who visit not just for the religious environment, but also to meet with others for social and cultural activities.

There are usually nine Thai monks at Wat Buddhapadipa and they live in the main house. Some younger monks come and go, perhaps staying only for a year or two, but most of the more senior monks have been resident at the monastery for many years. Without exception, those who lived at the monastery when I stayed there before my ordination were quite extraordinary characters. Most of them had a terrific sense of fun and laughed a lot, but they were also very wise men and were always willing to give their time to listen to the problems of other people. Most communicated in English very well and those who had been in England for many years were totally fluent, though occasionally even they had verbal blind spots.

My good friend and teacher, Phra Maha Laow, communicated particularly well, especially when talking about meditation or the Buddha's teaching. He had a more limited vocabulary about other matters. He quite often amazed visitors by telling them about the monastery's ancient daffodils and the squirrels that nested in them. Some of these daffodils, according to him, were more than a hundred feet tall, and the squirrels apparently much enjoyed their diet of daffodil nuts. My friend was referring to the oak trees that grew in the monastery grounds. His knowledge of European flora was so poor that he referred to anything green and growing as a 'daffodil', though perversely I once heard him call a real daffodil an oak tree.

Although most of the monks spoke English well and even had a certain understanding of the British character, they hadn't always totally grasped the occasionally offbeat English sense of humour.

A friend of mine, Lawrence, studied at Wat Buddhapadipa and he had a great Spike Milligan-ish sense of fun. At the time, we were both students of a particular monk who was quite old and had been a monk for a very long time – nearly fifty years, I think. We liked and respected him very much but, as sometimes happens with senior Thai monks, he had become quite pompous, believing that anything he said or did was beyond reproach. That's understandable because senior Thai monks are usually surrounded by Thai lay-people who wouldn't dream of disagreeing with a monk, or criticising him, or telling him he had said or done something daft. That would seem to be showing disrespect.

Despite his fluency in English, our dear old teacher really didn't have much understanding of the English sense of humour and he was easily perplexed by some of Lawrence's Milligan-ish comments.

On one occasion, the monk and the two of us were passing through a room when the monk saw the monastery cat lying underneath a radiator. 'That cat is dead,' the monk said to Lawrence, 'take it out and bury it.'

Lawrence looked at the cat. 'It's not dead, it's asleep,' he said.

'That cat is dead,' insisted the monk loudly, 'and don't argue with me.'

Just then the cat sleepily stretched its legs. Lawrence immediately fell to his knees, hands clasped in prayer, eyes heavenwards and proclaimed, 'It's a miracle, a blessed miracle!'

The monk stomped off in a huff.

Soon after I started studying at Wat Buddhapadipa, I suggested to the abbot that the monastery should have a resident European monk. There are some Pali concepts used in teaching Buddhism and meditation that are taken almost for granted in traditionally Buddhist countries but which may not always be clear to a Westerner, regardless of the teacher's fluency in English.

I first realised the need and usefulness of a resident European monk when the abbot of Wat Buddhapadipa received a request from a local Catholic convent. The Mother Superior thought it would be a good idea for a Buddhist monk to give an inter-faith talk at the convent – something she may later have regretted. The abbot happily agreed. Although I was still a layman, I was asked to accompany the delegated monk to the convent as that was to be one of his first public talks in English and he needed moral support.

The monk who was to give the talk usually had quite a good command of English, though it sometimes let him down. Lawrence and I had tried to help him improve his communication skills and, at his own request, had also taught him a few earthy phrases. Our justification for agreeing to this was that it is important that non-native speakers should understand what might be said to them, even if they shouldn't necessarily use the words or phrases themselves.

When we arrived at the convent, the monk took his place next to Mother Superior at the head table, though with a respectable distance between them. I sat on the floor by the monk's feet. The monk looked almost outrageously colourful in his orange robes, amidst the roomful of nuns in their sombre black gowns. Some of the older nuns looked rather stern and seemed not at all approving of having to listen to this heathen Buddhist rubbish but the younger ladies were a very happy, smiling group and seemed quite ready to be enlightened by whatever the monk had to say.

On that occasion the monk started his talk in a routine and sensible manner by explaining one of the basics of the Buddha's teaching, concerning the suffering that all living creatures endure. He gave the usual examples:

'The Buddha taught that birth is suffering. Sickness is suffering.'

The older nuns seemed to relax a little and a few nodded their heads at this profound wisdom.

'Old age is suffering. Dying is suffering.'

Murmurs of agreement: yes, we can relate to that all right.

Then, after a dramatic pause for inspiration and smiling beatifically, he added, 'Going for a shit is suffering.'

The older nuns exchanged horrified glances, some of the younger ones giggled and one actually fell off her chair in hysterics. Mother Superior buried her face in her hands. I reached out and shook the monk's foot and he bent down to see what I wanted.

'What are you *talking* about!' I hissed at him. 'You can't say that!'

'Why not? We all have to go to the toilet and sometimes it's really suffering. Sometimes if you've eaten too many chillies you have to . . .' he started to reply, forgetting that he was holding a microphone in his hand.

'Shutupshutupshutup!!!'

Unfortunately, after being interrupted so early in his talk, the poor monk lost his confidence entirely and became so careful about what he was saying that he often lapsed into Thai, so that occasion wasn't a great success and we weren't invited back. But it illustrated the difficulties that many Thai monks have in communicating the Buddha's teaching in English and how helpful it could be to the monastery to have a resident European monk.

Of course, I wasn't really a resident, merely a visitor, but nevertheless in some ways I felt I had come home. Not because I was in England but more because I was at Wat Buddhapadipa. It was in this same old house, set in these same tranquil grounds, that I had realised years before that I wanted more than anything else to become a monk and to follow the teaching of the Buddha. It was here, in the underground meditation chamber beneath the Uposatha Hall, that I had my first lesson in walking meditation, when my dear old teacher forgot to tell his naïve students to keep their eyes open, with the consequence that we ended up walking into pillars and falling over each other. Here, in these grounds on a warm summer evening, I had made my first attempt at an all-night meditation, sitting under the trees by the side of the lake, and fell asleep after about ten minutes.

It was at Wat Buddhapadipa that I first met the extraordinary men who, in some cases, had already spent more than thirty or forty years in the robes and who stimulated me into asking questions on subjects which I had never even thought of before. Often they taught without knowing it. Merely being with them, by observing them, I could see the results of those years in the robes. It could be seen in their controlled movements, their calm faces, their innocent smiles and in their precise and measured reaction to any situation. And it could also be felt, for being with the monks was to experience their tranquillity for myself, and to share a little of what they had learned.

It was delightful for me to be back in that environment. I was happy to be able to work for the monastery and to take part in some of the ceremonies in which the monks must be involved, despite my lack of chanting skills. I think many of the European visitors were also pleased to have an English monk at the monastery, even though he was a very new one and knew little or nothing. On Sundays, when the monastery received many visitors and students, I was kept busy simply talking, though I frequently felt awkward when it became clear that many of the students knew far more about Buddhism than me.

I think my meditation teacher, Phra Ajahn Amara Thera, also saw the value of having a European monk in residence at the monastery. He asked me if I would like to stay for the Pansa in London. I was tempted, but I said no. If I stayed at Wat Buddhapadipa, I would naturally have to do my share of teaching, either Dhamma or meditation, and at that time I didn't feel anywhere near ready. I could probably teach meditation, at least to beginners, though I would be teaching largely from others' theories and experiences. I wanted to teach from my own experience. I wanted to teach what I had personally realised from my own practice. I wanted to be able to say, 'This works. I *know* it works.' So far I had done very little practising. I explained to my Ajahn that I wanted to undertake the Pansa at a remote monastery where I would have little contact with people or the distractions they can cause. I needed to be where I would be able to meditate undisturbed and in isolation.

The first thing anyway, the reason that had brought me back to England, was to get my knee fixed. If I didn't get that done I wouldn't be meditating much anywhere. A visit to a doctor was the priority on my London agenda.

All the monks at Wat Buddhapadipa are registered with a medical practice in Wimbledon. I went to see a doctor there. After examining my knee, he said he would arrange for an appointment with a National Health Service – NHS – hospital, which might take two or three months, and then if I required an operation the hospital would make a further appointment, which could well be another three or four months. Five months or more! But the start of the Pansa was only three months away. If I couldn't make it back to Thailand by the day the Pansa opened, I would have to stay in London until it ended in October. There had to be another option. There was, but could I afford it?

Wimbledon Parkside Hospital is, as its name implies, alongside Wimbledon Common and only a short distance from the monastery. It looks like an elegant, discreet, exclusive and very expensive hotel. As soon as I walked into the reception area I added another zero to my mental estimate of what the private treatment there might cost. I would have walked straight out again if I hadn't already made an appointment.

I was shown immediately into the consulting room of the doctor who specialised in joint problems. I very much regret that I can't remember his name for he was, without doubt, the kindest doctor who has ever laid hands on me. He wasn't actually titled 'Doctor' any more for he was a consultant at a government hospital and, for some reason I have never been able to fathom had, in the way of consultants, reverted to 'Mister'.

Mr Doctor didn't seem in the least bit surprised to

have a bald and orange-robed patient and didn't even make the mistake of asking me to take my trousers off. After an X-ray, he prodded and probed at my knee and confirmed that there was a small piece of cartilage that had broken away and should be removed. I told him I had to return to Thailand quite soon and needed the operation done quickly. 'How about tomorrow?' he asked. 'How much will it cost?' I countered, feeling as though I was haggling in a Thai market. '£1,600, plus £75 for this consultation,' he replied, with a perfectly straight face.

I'm sure his patients don't usually turn a hair at such breath-taking figures and simply reach for their gold cards. I'd cut mine in half a couple of years before. I sat calmly, trying to think of some polite way of extricating myself from the situation. The doctor and I looked at each other for a few moments, our faces equally expressionless, then both of us burst out laughing.

'You're a Buddhist monk,' he said. He was quick all right. 'Why did you become a monk?'

He seemed genuinely interested and we chatted for about another fifty pounds' worth of consulting time. I had to tell him that I couldn't afford the operation although I was, of course, quite prepared to pay for the consultation. He told me not to worry about the consultation fee, he wasn't going to charge me. He added that if I telephoned his secretary at the NHS hospital she would book me in for an operation on the National Health Service as soon as possible. He wouldn't let me jump the queue, he said, but he would slip me in between other scheduled patients and would just work a bit faster that day.

I was already well used to sometimes extraordinary acts of kindness and generosity from Thai people but I was especially delighted to find it extended to me as a Buddhist monk in England. Of course, kindness and generosity should not be restricted within denominational limits and they remain the same virtuous acts whether they come from a Buddhist heart, Christian heart or Muslim heart, and to whomever they are extended. But I was still greatly touched by the doctor's *jai dee*.

A week later I checked into hospital early in the morning and was back at Wat Buddhapadipa in the afternoon. I stayed on crutches for only about a week. My knee was fixed. I could go to Nahoob.

12

As my problem knee was sorted out so quickly, I had ample time to return to Thailand and take up residence at Wat Nahoob before the Pansa started in the middle of July. I decided I would stay another month or so in London to help at Wat Buddhapadipa and also take the opportunity to see some of my old friends.

During my travels to visit various people, I had to make use of public transport. That sometimes led to potentially confrontational and humiliating situations, especially when waiting at bus stops or walking to the railway station. The Thai monks are a familiar sight in Wimbledon Village and I think they are mostly greeted politely by residents and shopkeepers. At worst, they are simply ignored. Apart from the annual Wimbledon tennis tournament, the Thai monastery is probably the most well known attraction in Wimbledon and certainly draws more people annually to the suburb than the tennis. On special Thai cultural celebrations, thousands of people may visit the monastery in one day. That's good for local traders but apparently objectionable to some of the other residents of Calonne Road. The monastery is so well known in Wimbledon that many local stationery and gift shops sell picture postcards of Wat Buddhapadipa's Uposatha Hall. When the Thai monks need to go into Wimbledon Village there is occasionally some minor unpleasantness – mostly verbal insults – though on one occasion a monk had a tomato thrown at him. The monks don't respond to any of that and I am sure that as well as remaining both outwardly and inwardly calm, they are also genuinely understanding and forgiving.

It was much worse for me. Because they look exotic anyway, the Thai monks can get away with their unconventional dress and appearance and people are mostly quite tolerant towards them. I, however, am pale, tall, skinny and very English looking and I frequently became the target of all sorts of abuse. That was at least partly because members of the Hare Krishna group are sometimes a nuisance to local residents and cause some minor problems on the streets of Wimbledon with their dancing, singing and begging for donations. (One time, a group of them walked down Wimbledon High Street with a buffalo, which caused some residents to complain to Wat Buddhapadipa.) Many people mistook me for a member of the Hare Krishna group since we dress in a vaguely similar style. Other people seemed to take it as a personal affront that I wasn't Christian.

When walking on the street, I was frequently

followed by jeering groups of youths and children chanting 'Hare Krishna, Hare Krishna' and so on. That didn't really bother me too much. On one occasion, someone threw a stone at me. On another occasion, a group of youths flicked ink down the back of my robe; the same robe in which I was ordained. The stains are still there, even after many hundreds of washes. Frequently, people would quite openly giggle and point at me. Although that was totally harmless, it sometimes made me feel like some sort of freak.

All that was the complete opposite to my reception when walking on any Thai street. Although Thai people openly stare at me in amazement, nobody has ever been abusive to me and I always bear in mind my experience at Wat Phra Kaew a few days after I ordained. Whether people are being respectful or jeering, it's really much the same thing. No ego-response, no movement of the mind, is necessary. That's the theory, but the practice can be considerably more difficult and I never really felt comfortable outside of the monastery. Incidentally, a monk living in a Thai monastery in America told me that the resident monks *never* leave the safety of the monastery unless in a car; they feel it is simply too dangerous.

The closest I came to physical abuse was on the underground. I foolishly got into a carriage that was occupied only by a group of teenagers. I should have known I was asking for trouble and the abuse started the moment the doors closed behind me. The boys obviously saw me as an easy target and were constantly egged-on by the girls, though at first it was just the usual bad language and idiotic insults. I kept my face as calm and expressionless as possible, my eyes fixed on the floor in front of me. I knew that if I responded in any way I would probably worsen the situation – this was definitely not a receptive audience for a Dhamma talk about tolerance and compassion. My apparent calm seemed to make the boys quite angry and I realised I was in for a bashing, especially when the boys started to leave their seats and approach me.

Though calm on the outside, my heart was pounding and I was quite scared. I thought I would get off the train at the next station but then I decided against it. I would stand my ground – in a way I had to – and refuse to be intimidated just because I had no hair and was wearing a robe instead of jeans. I would remain as calm and collected as possible, which wasn't much, and I mentally prepared myself for whatever was to come.

The train pulled into a station and by some miracle two railway policemen got into the carriage and sat on the same bench seat as me. I don't know if they were aware of the situation when they got on the train but they smiled at me and I smiled back, though I felt like giving them both a hug. The youths shut up and I continued my journey in peace.

I remembered a funny story another English monk told me. He had been visiting his home in the north of England. He was walking down a street and was suddenly attacked by a newspaper seller. The man grabbed hold of the monk's alms bowl and started to beat him about the head with it, whilst screaming that he should 'Come to Jesus!'

I've always believed that everything that happens to us, positive or negative, can be taken as a lesson. I certainly learned something from my experiences of walking and travelling around London. I don't think I've ever been racist or bigoted against any minority group on the grounds of skin colour, religious beliefs or sexual orientation but I began to understand and experience for myself how members of such groups probably feel when they are subjected to mindless abuse – often a lot worse than the mostly harmless stuff I had to put up with. I began to understand a little of their humiliation, their anger, frustration and fear. Suddenly, in the city of my birth, *I* was a minority. *I* was the 'Paki', the 'nigger', the 'queer' and a target for anybody with a grudge against the world in general. It is an unhappy feeling. I never told any of the other monks or my friends about these and other incidents. They were something I had to face and come to terms with on my own.

I have always considered myself lucky to have made a few, just a few, very good friends in my life. I don't mean acquaintances. I mean people for whom I would do virtually anything and who I believe would do anything for me. Friends who have been friends in some cases for ten, twenty, thirty years or more. I have always been a bit of a loner and have never made friends easily but those I have made I have kept for a long time because I have worked at it, just as they have. We have sometimes drifted a little apart while following different interests but we have always come back together again at some point on the road. But then our roads were all going in roughly the same direction.

My friends had seen me at my lowest moments and had been supportive. They had seen me during my highs and had rejoiced in my happiness or good fortune. We had stuck together in relationships that seemed indestructible by time, distance or circumstance.

The last time I had seen any of my friends in England, I was a layman and staying at Wat Buddhapadipa full-time. I was then living under the Eight Precepts of an Upasaka and had some restrictions on my behaviour but nothing that really affected our relationships very much. Now I was a fully-fledged monk, living under the 227 rules of the Vinaya, I wondered what my friends' reactions would be and whether our relationships would change drastically.

Naturally, I didn't expect them to greet me in the same way that a Thai person greets a monk, with a graceful wai or a triple bow and always deferentially referring to the monk as *Luang Pi* or *Luang Por* – 'Respected Brother' or 'Respected Father'. Some of my friends had known me for a very long time and had seen me in situations and circumstances that were not at all respectable! They would not be treating me as though I had suddenly turned into a holy man, that was for sure.

In the event, reactions to my changed physical appearance ranged from screams of delighted mock horror to embarrassed laughter. Some of my friends tried to cover their real reaction by not reacting at all, but instead behaved as though I'd just popped out for a minute: 'Oh, hello Pete, come in . . .' that sort of thing, and put the kettle on for a cup of tea, just like old times. My only aunt, a lovely seventy-five-year-old, completely ignored my appearance and flung her arms around me and gave me a big kiss; totally against the monks' rules but I wasn't going to spoil an old lady's pleasure by telling her she couldn't hug me any more. (I'm very glad about that because that was to be the last time I ever saw her.) One friend of more than thirty years' standing met me at his local railway station with a paper bag over his head so that he would be spared the embarrassment of being seen with me! That was very amusing of course, as it was meant to be, but there was a more serious side to some of these reunions.

The rules that monks live by are to be practised in every waking moment, not just when the monk is on duty at a religious ceremony, or in the public eye. Even when he is entirely alone the monk should not relax his vigilance or mindfulness of his behaviour. He should develop and refine his behaviour until he is relaxed according to the rules of the Vinaya; until following the rules becomes natural and comfortable for him. He can't live his life by one set of rules in public and another in private.

I remember reading something that a monk wrote which has always stayed with me: 'When you are with a lot of people, behave as though you are alone. When you are alone, behave as though you are with a lot of people.' In other words, keep to one standard; the standard set by the Vinaya.

Although I've left Thailand only three times as a monk, I do change some aspects of my behaviour when I travel, but that's really just exchanging one set of social norms for another. As long as I don't have to compromise my position as a Buddhist monk, nor go against the spirit of the Vinaya, my mind is untroubled.

With one exception, my friends are not Buddhist and know nothing about Buddhist meditation, the Dhamma or the Vinaya. There's no reason why they should. When I arrived on various doorsteps, they saw an old friend who was now dressed in robes instead of jeans and a t-shirt, or the business suit that they were more accustomed to seeing. The outward superficialities were probably not too hard for them to accept but I don't think any of them could fully understand or accept that, through my practice, I was actively encouraging change and development to occur within myself; to develop the very thing they had loved just as it was before: me, Peter Robinson. They could see the robe wrapped around my body but they couldn't see that it was also wrapped around my heart.

All my friends were interested in my new life and tried hard to understand why I couldn't do this, or had to do that, as a monk. But without an understanding of what the Buddha taught, why he taught it, and a background knowledge of the Vinaya rules, their understanding had to be superficial. There was sometimes an awkwardness between us that we were all aware of and which had never existed in our relationships before. I felt especially embarrassed about that because I knew it was the changes in me, rather than any changes in them, which were the cause.

One friend of more than twenty years wrote to me, 'Understand if some of us might be human enough to be embarrassed, after so many years, by having to call you by your chosen name, or to go out with you in your robes. You have changed, we have not.'

I cannot quantify the changes that are happening within me. I know that my meditation practice and my lifestyle are helping to develop certain qualities and to rid me of others, but any change is such a gradual process that I cannot see it, nor do I have any way of measuring it. Each day I am what I am. If I am even a tiny bit better today than I was yesterday, I have made progress. Just putting on the robes does not itself bring about any great change or improvement. It is the practice of meditation and of living the Dhamma and Vinaya that achieves the goal.

What some of my friends called my 'monkish behaviour' was already mostly quite natural to me, but it will never be natural to them. I know most of my friends have great respect for what I am doing, even if they don't fully understand the 'why' or 'what for'. They try hard to adjust to my new circumstances but it is extremely difficult for them. Understandably, they want me to be the same old Peter that they have known for so long. But it cannot be.

It is fundamental to the Buddha's teaching that all things, situations and phenomena are impermanent, subject to change and eventual decay. Perhaps some of my old friends and I will eventually drift irrevocably apart and our relationships will decay, because our lives are now so different. I can identify with their lives because I've done it all and shared the same aspirations and dreams. But they will never again be able to identify with mine, no matter how much they try. That was a very sad realisation for me.

The warm weather was approaching in England and rain clouds were gathering in Thailand. It was time to leave. On my last evening at Wat Buddhapadipa, I sat in my favourite spot in the monastery's meditation garden; a little clearing on the edge of the lake. The lights of the Uposatha Hall were on and the building was brilliantly reflected in the still, dark water. I sat there for a long time, as I had done on so many occasions in the past, relishing the beauty and silence of the evening. Phra Maha Laow came out to join me for a short time but he could see I was lost in my own thoughts and he left me alone. I let those thoughts wander where they liked. They frequently wandered to another clearing, another monastery, 10,000 kilometres away; to the place that was not only to be my new home but also my meditation workshop.

I felt ready. Most of the practicalities of the monks' daily life were already familiar to me. Now it was time to start the real work. I knew it wasn't going to be easy. I didn't know it would be quite so hard.

13

I was very happily surprised when I arrived early in the morning at Bangkok's Don Muang airport to find not only Giant waiting to meet me, but Ajahn Waow as well. Both had been convinced that I wouldn't be on the plane at all, suspecting that I might succumb to the temptation to stay in London. They had come in the old Toyota, which fairly amazed me considering the distance, but I was very happy to see both my old friend and my new abbot again. I was flattered that they had made the effort to meet me and to make the journey to my new home as easy as possible.

Giant had moved to Wat Nahoob while I was still in London, taking my few belongings from Section 5 with him. When I arrived at the monastery, I found my new room in the small kuti block already cleaned, arranged and prepared for me. During my first few days there, I had a constant stream of callers from the village, all coming to welcome me and to offer small gifts. After my unhappiness at Wat Mahadhatu, that seemed like a very positive new beginning.

Although I had accepted Ajahn Waow's invitation to spend the three months of the Pansa at Wat Nahoob, I was to live there for more than a year. My days usually passed pleasantly, peacefully and productively. Most days were much the same, as I knew they would be, as I wanted them to be, as I needed them to be. Within a month at Wat Nahoob, I started to develop a very strong feeling of being at peace with both my environment and myself. Sabbai.

An observer, especially a Western observer used to the hustle and bustle of daily life with all its sensory diversions, would probably have considered my life to be boring. That depends on one's point of view. My life certainly wasn't boring to me. Although each day followed much the same routine and I had few duties, I became more and more conscious of small changes within myself that I would possibly not have been able to recognise, acknowledge or even experience at Wat Mahadhatu, Wat Buddhapadipa or anywhere else.

Those small changes were not obvious on a day-to-day basis, but I would occasionally find myself thinking something, doing something or reacting to something in quite a different way and with a new attitude, instead of with my usual conditioned and habitual response. I also found that sometimes I genuinely seemed to have no reactions or attitudes to some situations at all, neither negative nor positive. Things were as they were and didn't seem to require a reaction or attitude from me at all. As the months went on, my whole perspective on life seemed to gradually change. Slowly, I felt I was becoming more of an observer; an observer not only of what was happening around me but also of what was happening to me and within me.

Through the Buddha's teaching and through following the Vinaya, I believe I started to develop a deep and genuine interest in life, and a greater understanding of it, yet with an objectivity I doubt I could have gained in any other way. I started to see that my life had some meaning and depth. I clearly recognised that before I became a monk I was merely filling up an emptiness, gratifying the senses more as a way of passing the time than because of any great need. I am convinced that is what most people do, though I think few are prepared to examine their lives closely enough to realise it, much less admit it.

Some years after I left Wat Nahoob, I read Henry David Thoreau's words in *Walden*, which seemed so apt to what I had experienced at the little monastery: 'I went to the woods because I wished to live deliberately, to front only the essential facts of life, and see if I could not learn what it had to teach, and not, when I come to die, discover that I had not lived. I did not wish to live what was not life, living is so dear; nor did I wish to practise resignation, unless it was quite necessary. I wanted to live deep and suck out all the marrow of life, to live so sturdily and spartan-like as to put to rout all that was not life, to cut a broad swath and shave close, to drive life into a corner and reduce it to its lowest

143

terms and, if it proved to be mean, why then, to get the whole and genuine meanness of it, and publish its meanness to the world; or if it were sublime, to know it by experience and be able to give a true account of it in my next excursion.'

As I could see and experience for myself that the Buddha's teaching worked, even in the smallest of ways, each day brought a strengthening of purpose and a new commitment, not only to my life as a monk but to my life as a *person*. There was to be a black, confused period when I was full of despair, feeling lost and alone and believing that I lacked not only the strength to continue, but also any sense of where I was going. With the Dhamma as my support, I persevered.

Although the environment at Wat Nahoob was the right one and helpful for me at that time, I was always conscious of the danger of becoming too attached to it or of allowing myself to think that any results from my practice were due to the environment. They weren't. The peaceful, untroubled environment and the simple routine of my life were merely aids to help me, just as the robes were an aid, just as the cushion I used for sitting meditation was an aid. Any progress or lack of it in my meditation was not due to the cushion; its job was to make me less aware of the hard floor and allow me to settle into my meditation quickly, easily and comfortably. The results of my meditation and every other aspect of my life were concerned only with my mental state.

I believe my sense of wellbeing and any progress I

thought I was making in my meditation was due as much to what I didn't have as to what I had. At Wat Nahoob I had everything I needed for my physical and spiritual or mental nourishment, and nothing more. I had a conducive environment, sufficient food, a pleasant companion in Giant if I needed company, clothes on my back and a roof over my head. I had my books and my purpose. What I didn't have was pressure; pressure to be, to do, or to achieve anything. I wasn't even under any self-imposed pressure to achieve results in my meditation. I had a meditation programme but it didn't have a timetable. I was just doing it and was content to see what, if anything, I would learn.

I also didn't have much in a material sense to cling to or become attached to, which I was beginning to realise quite clearly had been the cause of much of my background discontent before I ordained. That is the most basic teaching of the Buddha; that clinging, attachment and craving of various kinds leads only to mental suffering. Through my meditation I began to see just how much clinging I had done in the past; clinging to things, to people, to situations and to my personal concepts and ideals. I saw how all this clinging and attachment had led to what had been a largely unsatisfactory and disappointing life. It had been fun on the surface, but trivial and not satisfying in any deep sense. It had lacked real purpose. It was only as I slowly began to investigate my mental states that I realised how much clinging I had been doing and how much I had suffered mentally as a result. I began to recognise for myself that all my previous ambitions and desires, my seeking after material success, comfort and sensual diversions, my conditioned fixed views and my blind acceptance of society's values had been largely pointless. I had been sidetracked and deluded.

Some months after I moved to Wat Nahoob, I wrote to a friend in England: 'It is difficult for me to explain what a joy my life has become. Every "now" in my life is just right, just as it should be, just as it is. Even the occasional not-so-good moment is fleeting and affects me only if I let it. "Now" quickly becomes "then" and is forgotten. But there are few not-so-good moments any more. Wat Nahoob, here, now, is the place I am and the place I am content to be. There is nothing I miss, nothing I want. There is no "I wish . . ." or "If only . . ."'

I worked hard at my meditation and for a time I was profoundly content. I don't think there had ever been a period in my life when I had felt so genuinely and deeply content, though I think few of my friends in England really understood why. In my letters to them, I usually wrote only about the interesting or amusing practicalities of my life in Thailand, rather than about any deeper significance of it. I didn't want to seem to be lecturing about the spiritual satisfaction I was discovering in Buddhism in case it might have seemed that I was making comparisons with their lives. I would never do that. I genuinely believe that everybody must find his or her own path through life. Someone else's path could be quite different from mine but no less satisfying to them. Being a monk was just my way of life; it suited me but it didn't suit my friends and that was fine.

Lawrence, my friend at Wat Buddhapadipa, seemed to sense my deep spiritual satisfaction from my letters. He wrote to me saying that he would like to join me for a time at Wat Nahoob, as a layman, but that he would 'have to *be* something'.

I tried to explain in my reply that, in fact, it was this very grasping at 'wanting to be something' that was causing much of the discontent from which I knew he suffered. At Wat Nahoob, we were attached neither in trying 'to be' nor in trying 'not to be'; we simply *were*, but it didn't seem to make much sense when written down; it's something which can only be understood experientially.

Once when I wrote to a friend describing my daily routine, he wrote back simply: 'You must be mad.' A few years before, I might well have agreed with him, but then 3.45am was often the time I staggered into bed. Now it was the time I got up. Adjusting my waking and sleeping times proved quite difficult at first. I don't have any particular problem about getting up and seem to require very little sleep, but I have never found it easy to get to sleep early. For many years I had rarely gone to bed before 1am or 2am, but now to get sufficient sleep – I reckoned five or six hours – I was having to go to bed at 9.30pm. My body clock eventually adjusted – it had to – but it took rather longer than I expected and there were many mornings when I dragged myself up after only a couple of hours' sleep.

It was difficult in letters to friends to make my daily routine sound even interesting, let alone fun. I had only a few light duties and my routine was simple: up at 3.45am to ring the bell for morning chanting, walk on alms round through the village at about 6am, breakfast with the other monks at 7am, lunch at 11am and ring the bell for evening chanting at 5pm. Periods in between were spent in meditation and study or helping to keep the monastery grounds swept and tidy. I also gave myself the job of cleaning the Uposatha Hall and its many Buddha images each week. In addition to my daily routine, there were also occasional special services to be attended, such as funerals and ordinations, and some-times an invitation to take breakfast or lunch in a villager's house.

Because I had the job of ringing the bell in the morn-ing, I was always the first one up. The bell was also the villagers' alarm clock. Everybody in rural Thailand tries to get as much work done as possible in the early morn-ing, before it gets too hot.

When Ajahn Waow had given me the bell-ringing duty my heart had sunk and I was tempted to ask for another duty instead, but I didn't. The huge brass bell was hung at the top of a concrete tower, about forty feet high. It looked much like the training towers used by firemen in England, except that it had lots of red and yellow curly decoration. It wasn't the duty that bothered me, nor the getting up early or the height of the tower. It was climbing up there that filled me with trepidation.

The tower had narrow concrete steps up to the first level. They were no problem but to get to the bell on the top level, I then had to climb a twelve-feet-tall ladder. I've never liked ladders at the best of times, no matter how sturdy their construction or how securely they are fixed. Put me halfway up a ladder and I freeze, unable to go up or down.

The ladder at Wat Nahoob was neither well-constructed nor securely fixed. I don't really think it qualified as a ladder at all. It was just lots of bits of rough old wood, held loosely together with nails and lengths of string. The so-called rungs were especially disconcerting since they were not an equal distance apart. Some were twelve inches apart and some were sixteen, and the ten rungs were not rounded but square, with rough splintery edges that were really painful on bare feet. This terrifying contraption went up almost vertically and disappeared through a hole in the ceiling. The greatest hazard was that it extended only about two inches above the hole in the second floor and there was nothing to stop it slipping at the bottom. For the morning bell-ringing, all this had to be negotiated in the dark.

On the first morning of my duty I climbed about three-quarters of the way up and froze. I found myself clinging on for dear life, quite unable to move. I tried to calm myself with some deep breathing but all the time I was seeing a middle-aged Englishman, a former businessman, wearing only a sabong up a dangerous ladder in a remote Asian village at four in the morning. And I asked myself, '*Why*? What the . . . am I *doing*?' and other great philosophical questions to that effect. I had to give myself a good talking to before I could throw myself up the last few feet. But I made it, stood up – and cracked my bald head against the edge of the bell, almost causing me to fall back down the hole in the floor. A totally out-of-sequence 'bong' echoed across the countryside, followed by several unseemly oaths which happily were unlikely to have been understood by any citizens of Nahoob who were already awake. Nobody but a Thai would think of placing the bell directly above the access hole.

The mallet used to beat the bell had its own built-in hazards. It weighed several pounds but the head sometimes came off as it was swung and would go whizzing over the parapet, necessitating another scary journey on the ladder to retrieve it. There was a long sequence of about forty strikes in the morning and for some notes the bell had to be struck really hard on its rim. If I missed, the weight of the mallet plus the momentum of the swing could easily have sent me over the edge of the parapet, or headfirst down the hole in the floor. The vibrations when the mallet came into contact with the metal would jiggle my eyeballs and nobody warned me that it was necessary to steady the bell with one hand. After about a dozen strikes, the heavy bell would be swinging about all over the place, while

I ducked and dived to keep out of its way, leaping backwards and forwards over the hole, whilst still wildly swinging the mallet to keep the sequence going. I'm sure Quasimodo never had any of these problems.

For several days I dreaded my early morning duty, but I found my fear of the ladder slowly disappeared. After about a week, I was up and down it like a little Khao Nor monkey. I have never lost my dislike of ladders in general, but that particular one became part of my life and ceased to bother me. And I really enjoyed bell-ringing. There was great satisfaction in getting exactly the right note out of that great old bell. When I finished, I would look out over the village and watch the lights come on in the houses, as a new day began for Nahoob.

For the monks, the day began at 4.15am when we would all assemble in the monastery's tiny Uposatha Hall. Although 4.15 didn't really seem to me to be a civilised time to do anything, I always looked forward to morning chanting. It was an illogical feeling, but I felt that through the chanting I was able to reaffirm my personal belief in my teacher and all that he taught. The Bote's main Buddha image, made from bronze and slightly bigger than life-size, was one of the most beautiful I had seen. Even though I knew intellectually that it had no ultimate significance, I actually enjoyed bowing before it and the totality of what it represented.

At most monasteries in Thailand, all monks assemble twice each day in the Bote for morning and evening chanting. Although the chanting is preceded by a triple bow to the main Buddha image, that is not an act of worship. When bowing, the monks are paying respect to the Buddha as their teacher, to what he taught, and to the monks before them who have preserved the teaching for so many centuries. I know many Westerners don't understand the frequent bowing that monks have to do, either to images or to more senior monks. The point is that if done mindfully and in full awareness of what one is paying respect to, it can be a form of meditation, as can everything in the monks' life. It's also a good way of humbling oneself, something that many of us ego-orientated Westerners find difficult to do.

I have heard some English-speaking monks translate the Thai word *suat* – chanting – as 'prayer', but that's quite wrong. There is no prayer in Buddhism, since there is nobody to pray to or seek requests from. All chanting is in the ancient Pali language which, for me at least, is very difficult to learn. Most of the chants are the teachings of the Buddha and many are believed to be his own words. I've caused myself some problems when trying to learn various chants by substituting similar sounding English words or phrases for the difficult Pali. Hence, for a time, instead of chanting *upakappati*, I'd be chanting 'have a cuppa tea'. In other chants the words 'beef casserole' and 'cat gets up my nose' would always spring into my mind. But how do you pronounce a word like '*Siridhitimatitejoyasiddhimahiddhimahagunaparimitapunnadhikarassa*'? Despite my difficulties with the Pali, I found morning and evening chanting a very satisfying way to start and end the day. The acoustics in Wat Nahoob's little Bote were wonderful and although I don't think my voice added anything to the harmonies, I always chanted with great enthusiasm. Ajahn Waow never complained. (Unlike the monks at Wat Buddhapadipa, who asked Phra Maha Laow to have a quiet word with me because my hideous chanting was putting them off!)

After about thirty minutes of chanting, I would usually go into the forest for about an hour's meditation before going out on alms round. The early morning was one of my favourite meditation times. The temperature was usually still cool and the local insects seemed to get up late.

At Wat Nahoob, a huge ancient drum was sounded to warn the monks and villagers that it was time for alms round; the time traditionally being when there is sufficient natural light to see the lines on the palms of one's hands. The drum beat reverberated across the village and the surrounding countryside and was frequently faintly echoed by other drums, far away in other monasteries.

Walking on alms round in a rural village is quite different from in a city or town. At Nahoob we all walked together in single file, followed by a rickety old cart pushed by a couple of rickety old men. The villagers would be waiting outside their houses and would put only steaming rice into our alms bowls. That was frequently 'sticky rice' – great lumps of difficult-to-digest glutinous rice, the staple diet of north-eastern Thai people. The curries, fruits and sweets would be put into little pans on the cart. The round was quite a long one and took about an hour but it was always a good opportunity for reflection on the life I was leading.

I made a rather embarrassing mistake one morning on alms round. After my arrival, a few other monks had also come to spend the Pansa at the monastery. The newly arrived monk who walked directly in front of me seemed to have some sort of digestive problem and was unfortunately very flatulent in the early morning. His constant body explosions seemed to thoroughly amuse the other monks, but they weren't immediately behind him. I decided one morning to walk at the end of the line of monks instead. As we walked through the village, I became increasingly mystified by the number of knowing smiles and 'nudge nudge, wink wink' type of looks I was getting from the people. Giant hadn't walked on alms round that morning and when we arrived back at the monastery I asked him why the villagers had seemed so amused. He roared with laughter and explained. Apparently, being made to walk at the end of the alms round line is frequently the punishment for a monk who has confessed to masturbating! Next day I resumed my normal place. (But I've often wondered, what about the most junior monk who has to walk at the back of the line every day anyway?)

Some of the people who lived along the dirt track that led from the main road to the village came to see Ajahn Waow one day. They were between the alms round routes of two monasteries, Wat Nahoob and another on the main road. Monks from neither monastery walked on alms round past their homes. They wanted the opportunity to offer food to the monks and asked the abbot if some of our monks would walk on alms round along the track.

Next morning, Giant and I went that way instead of through the village. The track was about two kilometres long and was made from a reddish earth on which were scattered very sharp pieces of granite and other stones. It was absolute hell to walk on with bare feet and Giant and I were both limping by the time we got back to the monastery. But Ajahn Waow decided that one monk should walk on alms round down the track each day. I volunteered immediately.

I'm not a masochist and I certainly didn't enjoy having my feet lacerated by the granite chips, but the pain was worth enduring in return for the solitude that the track provided. Alms round in Nahoob village was a much more casual affair than I had become used to in Bangkok. In the village, the monks were well known to the people and most were related in some way. Alms round often turned into a sort of social outing and an opportunity to chat with family or friends. I suppose that was quite natural but to me it seemed that the spiritual significance of alms round had become secondary to the pleasant stroll and opportunity to socialise. I wanted to walk on alms round alone.

Ajahn Waow gave me a temple boy to carry the curries and other food offered by the people living along the track, though often I would walk without him and carry my own pans, as well as my bowl. Because the track was so rough and used by so many vehicles, including buffalo carts, the surface had become very rutted and full of pot holes. Often in the morning these shallow holes would be full of dirty but cool water and I took every opportunity to stop for a moment to bathe my aching feet. That seemed to amaze my temple boy, but for me it was a great relief, until the boy pantomimed in very graphic detail that the puddles were actually a great relief to the buffaloes and I had been pickling my feet in their urine. I carried on doing it anyway.

Despite the difficulties of walking along the track, it was well worth it for the beauty of the surroundings at that time of the morning; not that I could enjoy it too much because I had to be mindful of every step I took. Most of the farms were set back on one side of the track, screened by trees or stands of bamboo. On the other side were miles of sugar-cane plantations. Frequently in the early morning there would be a ground mist lying across the fields at a perfectly equal depth of several feet, all the way to distant Khao Nor. The mountains looked like black, primeval islands rising dramatically from a white sea. That early in the morning, the air was still cool and there was never a sound from anywhere. In that peaceful rural setting one morning, much to my astonishment, the silence was broken by the most bizarre music coming from a long way off, rolling towards me across the mist-covered fields. It was a twenty-year-old recording of Frank Ifield yodelling!

On the whole, Nahoob was not a poor community.

Most of the farmers owned their own land and some had fairly substantial holdings. They weren't materially wealthy – few Thai farmers get rich from their toil on the land – but they were able to offer very generous amounts of food to the monks. After returning from alms round, the monks would sit down together on the floor of the open-sided sala, often with more than thirty dishes of food for breakfast.

Eating was always preceded by a short chant to remind us that we relied on alms round and the generosity of others for all our food. The chant also reminded us that the food was merely a requisite, or fuel, for the physical body and was not to be eaten merely out of greed or a desire to gratify the sense of taste. After breakfast, there was another short chant to thank the donors. The chanting never became routine for me. It helped me not to take my food or its availability for granted, as I had done in the past. Food had always come from Sainsbury's, the fridge was always full and I could stuff myself with all the foods I found most delicious and most satisfying to the senses.

There were a few very poor landless families in the village and they would usually come to the sala to share the monks' food, though always politely waiting until the monks had finished eating. Very little food was wasted.

After breakfast, I would spend the rest of the morning in study or trying to learn Thai with Giant. If I could get out of that, I would disappear into the forest for meditation. My periods of sitting meditation were always preceded by a short time in *jongrom* – walking meditation – and I had cleared a path in the undergrowth about twenty feet long and two feet wide for the purpose. Before any meditation outdoors, I would first carefully sweep the leaves from around my meditation platform (built for me by the village carpenter from an old wooden bed) and from the walking path.

There were a few dangerous creepy crawlies lurking in the forest, scorpions being the most frequently seen. They liked to hide from the sun under fallen leaves so it was always important to keep all paths carefully swept. We had one type of scorpion that I was told was very dangerous. Locally, it was known as an 'elephant scorpion' on account of its huge size. I had seen them more than five inches long. They were extremely beautiful in a scary way; jet-black and shiny and with huge claws, like something Sigourney Weaver would pit herself against in the *Alien* movies. I found the scorpions fascinating and loved to watch them, but I always kept my distance. I once picked up a broken piece of asbestos in the forest and found at least twenty 'elephants' lurking underneath, so I left the asbestos undisturbed. We had lots of the smaller green and beige scorpions too, much less dangerous but still capable of giving a painful sting.

An old tractor cogwheel hanging in the *sala* was beaten each day to announce lunch at 11am. It made a lovely 'ding', which was perfectly audible even in the forest, though I would often ignore it and continue my meditation. Lunch was usually whatever was left over from breakfast, which was sometimes very little.

I was rarely disturbed in the forest. Ajahn Waow had told the villagers that my main purpose in coming to Wat Nahoob was to follow a strict programme of meditation and that I wanted to be as isolated as possible. The villagers understood but, because of the natural friendliness and curiosity that is so much a part of the Thai character, many couldn't resist coming either to just stand and silently watch me, or try to talk to me.

The villagers of Nahoob were all descended from Laotian people and spoke a weird mixture of Thai and Laotian, wrapped up in a very local dialect. I couldn't understand it at all and none of the villagers were ever able to understand my atrocious Thai. Communication was almost impossible and most of them eventually stopped coming to visit, but we were all on very friendly terms and did a great deal of smiling at each other. The villagers were usually extremely considerate towards me whenever I was in meditation. My platform was close to a dirt track that ran alongside the monastery boundary. The farmers would slow down their tractors as they drove past that point, so that the engine noise would be less disturbing to me.

I think some of the villagers, especially some of the old ladies, found me very strange and were perhaps a little frightened of me. Although rural Thai people usually have great respect for monks who practise meditation, they are often quite wary of them, believing that meditation helps develops supernatural powers and attracts ghosts or spirits to be near the monk. Although that is entirely untrue, at least as far as I know, it did help keep people away from the forest.

Although I tried to spend as much time as possible in the forest, frequently, like all the other monks, I had to help with various jobs around the monastery. I very much enjoyed sweeping leaves, using a broom made of slim slivers of bamboo. Some of our trees had leaves more than a foot long, which would drop off and quickly dry and curl in the sun. Sweeping them up became a form of mindfulness meditation for me, as I mentally watched the movements of my body and the actions and sounds involved in the activity.

Sometimes, all the monks were invited to have breakfast or lunch in a villager's house but that was much less frequent than at Wat Mahadhatu, which suited me. Occasionally, we also had to go to other nearby monasteries to take part in ceremonies that required a specific number of monks, such as ordinations or funerals. Although most of the local monasteries were large in area, they were generally home to only a few monks, so we all had to help each other out.

At 5pm each day I had to climb the tower again to ring the bell for evening chanting, and by about 6pm was ready to spend the rest of the short evening in study or meditation. Most days followed much the same pattern and many days were spent in silence. Quite frequently, I wouldn't say a word for several days, except in Pali during morning and evening chanting. There was no vow of silence, but even the Thai monks rarely spoke to each other unless there was some need to.

There was little idle chatter, no gossip between us; there just didn't seem to be much that needed to be said. I was glad about that. Like people everywhere, but possibly more so in the West, I had talked far too much in the past, often using conversation simply to get my own opinions and views across; just another way of massaging my own ego. At Wat Nahoob we each got on with our own practice in our various individual ways and felt little need to talk about it. It was the time for silence and contemplation.

14

Strangely enough, the one person I did regularly talk with was a farmer who couldn't speak a word of English and could hardly understand a word of my Thai. It was a decidedly odd relationship, but he seemed to enjoy it as much as I certainly did. The farmer's name was My, but in common with all laymen and laywomen, his name was prefixed with *Yom* if being spoken to or referred to by a monk.

Yom My was in his early forties, married, and the father of several children. He owned only a little land and his house reflected his small income. I think he earned only about 5,000 baht a year from his rice crop. The house was little more than a shack but he made me most welcome there on several occasions, though he would more usually visit me at my kuti. As a child he had been a temple boy at the monastery and then, for a short period, a monk. His life revolved around Wat Nahoob and he was very helpful to all the monks, especially Ajahn Waow to whom he was, of course, related in some obscure way.

We communicated initially with the aid of a couple of dictionaries; a Thai-English version for him and an English-Thai for me. Additionally, we would both enthusiastically draw little pictures on a pad that I kept for the purpose, to try and illustrate what each of us was trying to say. Yom My amazed me with his ability to remember English vocabulary and although he never wanted me to teach him English in a formal way, he was keen to try and communicate. He'd received little education as a boy but was very knowledgeable about the birds and animals, the seasons, and the plants and herbs that grew around the monastery. He had endless patience in trying to explain things to me. Over the months, our level of communication gradually improved as we each began to know which Thai or English words the other had so far learned.

Sometimes he would come to see me late at night, often after a whisky drinking session. He would apologise profusely for his near-drunken state and bow most respectfully, though I usually had to help him get upright again. I would lecture him about the dangers of alcohol, wag my finger at him and threaten to give him the Five Precepts, but all in a very good-natured way.

One day Yom My and his wife, Yom Noi, asked me if I would like to go on a picnic to Khao Nor. Yom My explained that there was something he wanted me to see, though he wouldn't say what. I said 'yes' to the picnic immediately. At every breakfast or lunch in the monastery, the monks were surrounded by villagers who seemed fascinated watching me eat. It initially irritated me a bit, especially when they would come and sit only a couple of feet away from me, staring with intense interest at every movement I made. I soon got used to it, but I still longed for a meal alone. That was partly due to my shyness at being constantly watched but also because there is a form of mindfulness meditation which uses eating as its subject and which I like to practise occasionally. It requires every movement involved in eating to be done slowly and thoughtfully, which is not at all suitable for a group meal, or with dozens of pairs of eyes watching.

Early in the morning on the day of the picnic, Yom My and Noi came to pick me up in their tractor. That was a delightful machine, really little more than a mechanical buffalo cart. At the front, where one would expect a buffalo, there was a two-stroke motorcycle engine and two small wheels, then seven-feet-long handlebars, which acted exactly like reins. They were joined to a two-wheeled cart with a high seat for the driver. Such tractors are common throughout Thailand and are extremely versatile machines. The front wheels can be changed to heavy corrugated metal grips for working in the mud of the paddy fields, or to road wheels. The cart and rear wheels can be unhitched and various strange bits of farming equipment can be attached to the front to make a hand-held motorised plough. On the road, they are neither particularly comfortable nor fast and the journey to the mountain took about three hours. It was great fun for me and I very much wanted to drive the tractor, but Yom My was rather shocked at the idea and wouldn't let me.

We skirted past Wat Khao Nor and continued driving along the base of the mountain, which is entirely encircled by a fairly good road. We eventually came to a halt under a huge, old Bodhi tree which was surrounded by massive, half-buried boulders that had crashed down from the mountain many years before. The whole of the base of that part of the mountain was covered in a thick bamboo grove and it was a delightfully cool, shady and silent place. The only sounds were bird calls and the cries of monkeys high up on the mountain.

Yom Noi laid out a tablecloth on the ground beneath the Bodhi tree and then *pracaned* the food to me. That is a respectful way of passing food to a monk and must be done with two hands, barefooted and followed by a graceful wai. They had gone to a great deal of trouble to cook food they were sure I would like; nothing too spicy (although I enjoy very spicy food), no fish and plenty of fruit and vegetables. After the food was presented they left me alone, for monks and lay-people do not eat together. They wandered off into the bamboo grove to pick shoots for their evening meal and I didn't see them again for several hours. In fact, I didn't see anybody at all for several hours. Not a single car, tractor or pedestrian passed by on the road.

I had my very slow meal in perfect peace and it stands out in my mind as one of the most successful mindfulness meditations I have ever practised. After the meal, I chanted quietly and then settled under the tree to practise sitting meditation. Unusually for me, I had eaten too much and fell asleep almost immediately. I didn't wake up for a couple of hours, when Yom My and Noi came back down the mountain. I told Yom My that we should be heading back to the monastery. The journey by tractor was a slow one and I had to ring the bell for evening chanting. '*Mai bpen rai,*' he said.

With a stick, he drew a clock in the earth to show that we had to stay on the mountain until 6pm.

'Why?' I asked.

He wouldn't say, but he did tell me that he'd already cleared my late return with Ajahn Waow.

We climbed back onto the tractor and drove for a couple of hours further round the mountain, frequently stopping at little streams or interesting old trees, so that I could explore a little. We eventually arrived at a very desolate spot where the mountain had a great piece missing from its side. A little track turned off from the road there, leading us into a wilderness of gigantic boulders and stunted trees. Yom My told me that the mountain had collapsed at that point many hundreds of years before. He finally stopped the tractor. It was about 5.45pm, the air had cooled and there was a slight breeze. We sat in absolute silence, with me not quite knowing what was going on.

What I was to see may be very common in Thailand, and all over the world for all I know, but I had never seen or experienced anything like it before. At a few minutes before 6pm, all the birds, insects and monkeys suddenly fell totally silent, as though a signal had been given. That instant ceasing of every sound was eerie and I really felt quite strange. If there had been any hair on my neck, I'm sure it would have stood up. There was a definite tension in the air, as though something extraordinary was about to happen, which indeed it was.

Very slowly, a sound started to roll down from high up on the mountain. Almost inaudible at first, it quickly built up until it was a very loud, hissing ululation; so loud that Yom My couldn't hear me when I asked him what it was. It rose and fell quite distinctly, but it wasn't just a sound, it was also a vibration that could be felt as a tingling in the air and on the skin. It was coming from *inside* the mountain, almost as though the mountain was breathing. Quite suddenly, the sound stopped. For perhaps a minute, there was absolute silence from the mountain, then the eerie sound started again, built up, and stopped again. It went on like that for about ten minutes. Each time, the sound was a little louder and the silences between a little shorter. If I'd been on my own, I'd have run a mile.

Yom My silently and, I thought, rather dramatically, pointed to a narrow fissure about 400 feet up on an almost sheer rock face. I strained my eyes but at first there was nothing to see. Then, without warning, what I thought could only be thick, black smoke started to pour from the fissure. But it didn't behave haphazardly like smoke. It was more like a great black snake, twisting, turning, coiling back on itself and writhing in the air, but in a consistently wide and dense 'tube' about fifteen feet across. It was bats, literally millions of them, maybe tens of millions of them, but so many that I thought the mountain must be entirely hollow. But they didn't come out in a great mass; they came out in an orderly line that never seemed to vary in its width.

Soon this twisting column of bats stretched for perhaps twenty miles or more across the countryside. Only then did the leaders start to fan out. The front of the column became a widening and indistinct haze in the distance as the bats separated in their nightly hunt for food. The black umbilical cord of bats was still attached to the mountain and they continued to pour out for about fifteen minutes. Then, quite suddenly, the column came to an abrupt end, with not a single straggler. Yom My told me that the same thing happened every day at exactly the same time. He said that as far as he knew, the cave or cave system inside the mountain had never been explored. The fissure was inaccessible except to the most professional of rock climbers.

I've since met several other Westerners who have visited Khao Nor to see the spectacle. All of them have been as enthralled as I was but none of them have been able to find the same fissure that I saw the bats leave from. I've been told there are many exits and that millions of bats leave at the same time by each one, so the total number of bats living inside the mountain must be quite staggering.

Our journey back to Nahoob was exhilarating because it started to rain very slightly, much to Yom My and Noi's discomfort, but to my great delight. I love the rain but Thai farmers only like it when it falls on their crops. Most Thai people seem to loathe getting wet, especially on their heads. I looked back. The sun was setting behind Khao Nor and, although I had long since ceased thinking of the mountain as fancifully magical, I was delighted to know that it did in fact hide a secret.

The rain got heavier. Yom My looked at the sky. 'The rainy season is coming,' he said.

15

Before the start of the rainy season, every monk must decide on the monastery he will stay in for the duration of the Pansa. On the day the Pansa starts, he must chant a determination in his kuti in Pali that he will not move to another kuti or monastery until the three-month period is over.

When I had made my first visit to Wat Nahoob and meditated in the clearing in the little forest, I had sat in the centre of a group of four trees. They weren't particularly old trees; each was only about twenty feet high but by some accident they formed almost a perfect square, each side being about fourteen feet in length. The two at the front faced Khao Nor, and each of these had a branch growing from about halfway up its trunk. The branches curved upwards and towards each other, making a beautiful Gothic arch shape. The topmost foliage of the four trees made a roof over the space beneath, keeping it shaded at all times of the day. I thought at the time that it was a delightful place, but

I never imagined that, one day, I would have a little house on that exact spot.

When I returned from England and moved to Wat Nahoob, I stayed in the main kuti block with Ajahn Waow, Giant, Phra Maha Pern and another monk who joined us but whose name I never knew. I was perfectly happy in the main block and thought I would live there for the Pansa, so I was quite surprised at breakfast one day when Ajahn Waow announced he was going to have a new kuti built for me in the monastery grounds. Its size, style and location would be entirely up to me, he said, though within the very precise limitations laid down by the Vinaya.

After breakfast we all walked around the grounds, together with the village carpenter and an assortment of other interested villagers. But of course, I knew exactly where I wanted the kuti to be: in the centre of the four trees. I imagined something about twelve feet square, which would not only be large enough for my needs but would also fit into the space neatly. No good, said the carpenter. He explained that whatever size the kuti was to be, we had to allow an additional three feet all round for the roof to overhang, as a protection during the rainy season. He indicated with his machete that it would be no problem to chop the trees down. No, I said hastily, as he started to swing his machete, that wouldn't be necessary. We would simply reduce the size of the kuti with the overhanging roof until it could fit into the space. I had to settle for a room about nine feet square, but that was perfectly adequate for me and my few belongings.

We all squatted in the clearing and with a stick I drew a design in the dirt of how I envisaged the kuti. There's not really a great deal one can do with a building only nine feet square and the final plan showed it to have a window in each side, each window with two wooden shutters, and with a door at the front facing the mountain. The kuti would stand on three-feet-high concrete legs, there would be four or five wooden steps up to the door, and the roof would slope from front to back. I particularly wanted the door to be more than six feet high, so that I could stop banging my head, and the ceiling had to be high enough for me to raise my arm to get my robe wrapped around me. The abbot approved all that but also suggested we should add mesh windows and a mesh inner door as a protection against mosquitoes and other insects.

The conversation then got into the practicalities of building the kuti and I wandered off a little to observe the scene. There were about a dozen people in the clearing, monks and villagers, all squatting on the ground and chatting animatedly. Each had his own idea of how the kuti should be built. I thought how marvellous that picture was; how very Thai. These people did not know me, we could hardly communicate, they knew nothing about my culture and they didn't know whether I would still be there the next day, but here they were, discussing how to build the Phra Farang a kuti in the forest. Someone was donating the wood, someone else the concrete, and the carpenter was giving his labour free. (Long after I left Wat Nahoob, the carpenter retired, ordained as a monk and ended up living in the kuti he had built for me.) A friend in England once told me that she couldn't understand what she called my 'curious affection' for the Thai people. Here at least was part of the answer: the Thai *jai dee* towards strangers.

At that part of the forest, the perimeter of the monastery was only about six metres from where my kuti was to be sited. I wandered outside the monastery boundary. Parallel to the perimeter trees was a dirt track and on the other side of that was an eight-feet-wide concrete irrigation ditch. Beyond the ditch there was nothing but unbroken miles of paddy fields, stretching in every direction. Dotted about in the paddies were little wooden platforms on stilts, with straw or palm leaf roofs. They were shady shelters in which the farmers could eat their lunch, or take an afternoon siesta. Exactly in the centre of the horizon was Khao Nor. The scene was a ground level view of what I had seen from my visit to the mountain. Bright green paddies and sparkling lakes in every direction. There were villagers working in the fields, each wearing a colourful sarong and a traditional lampshade-shaped straw hat. A lone buffalo tethered to a tree watched me mournfully and silently. The air was clean and fresh and there was no sound of cars or motorcycles. I sat beneath the shade of a palm tree thinking, I *live* here, and I could hardly believe how lucky I was.

Over a period of a few weeks, the kuti began to take shape. It looked like a cross between a little Swiss chalet and a rather grand garden shed. It was perfect. Inside, it was clean and dry and smelled sweetly of the mango wood which had been used for the floor boards. It was spacious enough for me to live simply but comfortably and to undertake my nightly meditation. I couldn't use my outdoors meditation platform very successfully at night because mosquitoes, moths, bats and other flying things were a big distraction – though I have never once been bitten by a mosquito in Thailand.

When the kuti was almost complete, the village electrician arrived with his bag of cables, plugs and switches. He wanted to know where I wanted the fluorescent light fitted. 'But I don't want electricity,' I told him. 'I'm going to have candles.' He looked at me as though I was quite mad and went off to report to the abbot his failure to connect me to the mains. Soon after, Ajahn Waow came to see me and asked why I didn't want electricity. Candles would be sufficient for the simple life I wanted to lead, I explained, and asked if he would allow me to have the stumps of last year's Pansa candles, which I had seen in the Bote. These special candles are often five or six feet tall and about nine inches thick and are made to burn throughout the Pansa. With a few of the leftover stumps I was sure I would have ample light to see by.

I realise, now, that this was a stupid piece of vanity, which I'm sure Ajahn Waow realised immediately. I was already seeing myself in the role of the old forest monk, meditating and studying by candlelight, and probably writing my notes with a quill pen as well. The abbot smiled and said that of course I could have the candle stumps.

On my first night in the finished kuti, I sat surrounded by five blazing candles. It was like sitting in the middle of a bonfire. The candle flames were fully seven inches high and the temperature inside the kuti was soon unbearable. It was also extremely hazardous. My robes were hung on a rope stretched across one wall and I was flapping around in my sabong in constant danger of setting both the kuti and myself on fire. And I still didn't have enough light to read or write by. On that first night, I got a headache from the flickering light and blew the candles out to go to sleep. The kuti was immediately filled with thick smoke and acrid fumes from the smouldering wicks. I had to sit outside in the forest for a while to let the air clear, feeling like an absolute idiot.

A few days later, Ajahn Waow asked me if I was sure that I didn't want electricity.

'Well, okay,' I said, 'if it pleases Ajahn.'

We both smiled.

Soon after that, I not only had a fluorescent tube on the ceiling, but also a spot lamp, an electric fan, a kettle and a small stereo on which to listen to my chanting tapes. So much for the ascetic forest monk. Never mind, I was now ready for my first Pansa.

Khao Pansa, or *Vassa*, the three-months-long rainy season retreat, was an established practice in India before the time of the Buddha. At the beginning of the rainy season, monks and ascetics of many religious philosophies would take up residence in a particular place and stay there until the monsoon season had passed. There were practical reasons for that. Much of the low-lying land was flooded and what tracks or roads existed were frequently washed away, making the traditional wandering life of the monks impossible.

When the Buddha established the Sangha, there was no prohibition against his monks continuing their wanderings during the monsoon period. According to Max Muller's *Sacred Books of the East*, that worried some of his disciples. They asked the Buddha if it was right that ascetics belonging to other religions stopped travelling during the wet season whilst: 'Sakyaputtiya Samanas (Buddhist monks) go on their travels alike during winter, summer and the rainy season, crushing the green herbs, hurting the vegetable life and destroying the life of many small things.'

The Buddha agreed that it was not right and told the monks: 'I prescribe, O bhikkus, that you enter upon the Vassa.'

The purpose of the Buddha's decree was not just so that his monks would cease damaging crops but also so that they would have a fixed period for study, meditation, and to teach newer monks. Although in modern times monks could travel regardless of the weather and without damaging crops, the tradition of the Pansa as a period of study and intensified practice remains.

At Wat Nahoob, we were to have five men ordain for the rains retreat. Three of them were about twenty years old, that being the minimum age at which a man can become a monk. They had all been born in the village but, like so many of its young people, they had left

Nahoob to find work in the cities. The other two ordainees were older men who lived in the village. They ordained a few weeks before the rains retreat started.

The three young men returned to Nahoob about a week before their ordinations to discuss the details with their families and Ajahn Waow. Ajahn Waow was an Upachaya, so he would be conducting the ceremony himself. He decided that the three men should all be ordained together on the same day – the day before the start of the Pansa. (Strangely, although Ajahn Waow had ordained many hundreds of monks, I was told that he refused to conduct the ceremony for his own monks who wanted to disrobe. He always sent them to another Upachaya. One of his little eccentricities, I suppose.)

Never having seen a rural ordination before, I thought the triple ceremony would be much the same as my own in Bangkok: a quiet, sober and sombre affair. I was quite wrong. Although the ceremony itself was exactly the same as mine, the build-up to it was anything but quiet and sombre – and it certainly wasn't sober.

The day before the ordinations, lorries started arriving in the village loaded with marquees, chairs, tables and sound systems with speakers so large I thought Iron Maiden or some other heavy rock band had included Nahoob on a world tour. Although Thai people usually conduct their daily lives in a quiet way, they have a natural exuberance. An ordination party is a good excuse for making a lot of noise and letting off a great deal of steam.

The night before the ordinations, the noise from

the village was deafening. Nobody got any sleep. Everybody in the village was celebrating and they were still at it when I dragged myself up the bell tower at 3.45am, supposedly to wake everybody up. From my vantage point at the top of the tower, the village looked wonderful; almost Christmassy. Every house and barn, and even many trees, were covered in flashing fairy lights! The ordinations were to be held directly after the monks' breakfast, and the village festivities continued up to the very moment that the three young men were carried over the threshold of the Uposatha Hall.

Just as I had walked from Section 5 of Wat Mahadhatu, so the three ordainees walked from their family homes in the village. The head of each man had been shaved the night before but their heads had been smeared with some sort of bright yellow lotion, giving them a very odd look. Each was wearing the white net robes, but they also had net veils over their faces and carried flowers, making them look somewhat like brides-to-be but without the expensive hairdos. Each walked to the Bote under a huge red, white or gold umbrella carried by a family member and, when they reached the hall, each was hoisted onto the shoulders of friends for the triple circumambulation.

The three processions entered the monastery grounds from different directions and every inhabitant of the village was in one procession or another. There were several hundred people altogether, for the ordainees were accompanied by friends and supporters who had travelled in hired coaches from Bangkok and the other cities where they worked.

Unlike my orderly procession with the silent nuns, these were each preceded by what might loosely be called a percussion band, each with a mobile loudspeaker system. The purpose of the bands seemed to be to make as much noise as possible and to compete with each other in the decibel stakes. It was not until I had attended many such ordinations that I realised the noise they were making actually had a tune. I came to think of it as the 'Ordination March'. At the time, it seemed to bear no resemblance to music as it is known anywhere else in the world. I think I would have preferred Iron Maiden.

The three processions were timed to reach the Bote at the same moment but the bandsmen had started banging away at their drums and bashing their cymbals at different times, with the result that there was the most hideous cacophony of noise. That was accompanied by women wailing away at the top of their voices and everybody 'ramwonging' like mad. The *ramwong* is a traditional Thai dance involving a graceful weaving of the body and arms, whilst walking or moving in circles. But it wasn't graceful on that occasion, when many of the dancers were not only hungover, but falling over too. The dance dropped any pretence of elegance.

From my vantage point high up on a balcony that circled the Bote, I watched as the three ordainees and their hundreds of supporters circled the hall three times. They were all going in the same direction, thank goodness, and carefully stepping over fallen fellows who were flat on their backs but still managing to ramwong. It was absolute bedlam but everybody was so happy. As they passed, many looked up at me and smiled or gave a wai to their Phra Farang. I smiled back, happy to be their Phra Farang; happy and proud to be part of that important day in Nahoob.

The next day, right on cue, the rain arrived.

16

In Europe we think we have rain but until I experienced a tropical rainstorm I really had no idea of what it could be like. When the rain hit Nahoob, it seemed to be almost solid water falling from the sky. On the occasions when I was caught out in it, I had to hold my hand over my nose, otherwise breathing was actually difficult.

Within a few minutes of the start of a rainstorm, rivers, streams and lakes would appear in every depression and hollow. The wells overflowed, the irrigation ditch overflowed and, unfortunately, the toilet cesstanks overflowed. If the rain was accompanied by high winds, which was usual, coconuts would be blown off the trees and would fly through the air like cannonballs. On one occasion, a flying coconut killed one of the monastery dogs.

During a storm one night, a fifty-feet-tall coconut palm fell over, missing my kuti by only a few feet and bringing several other young trees crashing down all around. A tree fell across the roof of the main kuti block, directly above the abbot's bedroom, causing extensive damage to the roof but none, happily, to Ajahn Waow.

If the downpours were accompanied by thunder and lightning they were especially dramatic, particularly at night. The inside of my kuti would be brilliantly lit by the almost continuous flashes, as though it was daylight, and the concrete foundations would shake with the reverberations of the thunder. I thoroughly enjoy storms, but when a storm was directly overhead I was sometimes both awed and a little scared of the incredible forces that were hurling themselves around me and sometimes, it seemed, directly at me.

My kuti was on a slight rise. As the rain increased in frequency and intensity through the three-months-long season, I slowly became surrounded by a lake that crept nearer to my steps each day. Through the lake swam black and green snakes, some six feet long, in search of the bullfrogs that had appeared in their thousands and which kept me awake at night with their throaty calls.

As the water in my lake rose, every creature that had been flooded out of its own home in the vicinity seemed to take refuge under, above, or in my little ark. A female wild cat moved into the gap between the roof and the ceiling, where she had a litter of kittens. She always ate the rice I left out for her but she would peer and hiss at me from her refuge in a most unfriendly and ungrateful way whenever I entered or left the kuti. I feared that, one day, she would pounce on me from the roof and rake her claws across my bald skull. My kuti started to smell very badly of dead things so I sent Yom My to climb one of the trees to see if there were the remains of dead animals in the cat's lair. He was most reluctant but anyway got nowhere near close enough to see. A great paw with what appeared to be titanium-plated claws appeared at the gap, ready to do battle in protection of the little ones.

A lovely little squirrel-like animal appeared one day in a downpour and made a dash into the roof gap; a bad choice of refuge considering the cat-from-hell was living there at the time. I never saw the squirrel again.

A twelve-feet-long boa constrictor hung around beneath the kuti for a few days. It was sick, having been captured by a villager in the paddy fields and brought to the monastery in a very large, stone, water jar. The villager had caught it with a looped cord and the loop was still tied tightly just behind the snake's head, which I think must have made it difficult for it to breathe or eat. I have no particular fear of snakes and when it first arrived at the monastery I put my hand into the jar, to the horror of the onlooking villagers, and tried to cut the cord away. It was too tight and I couldn't see how to do it in the confined space without hurting the snake.

The snake stayed in the jar for a few days and then, to my delight, escaped one night. It was seen a few times around the monastery and I kept track of its movements. It smelled very badly and I guessed it must have been suffering from the cord around it neck, but

I couldn't get close enough to cut the knot. I knew that boa constrictors killed their prey by crushing with their coils but I hadn't realised until my hand was in the jar that they also have teeth – big ones – so I was a little more wary of it. Finally, it arrived under my kuti and just lay there for a couple of days, apparently too sick to even move. I guessed it was safe to approach it. I gently lifted the snake's head, placed it on my lap and cut the cord without difficulty. I had never been so close to such an animal before and I was thrilled at the experience. I very much hoped the snake would stay around but after a few days, and presumably after a few bull-frogs, it slithered away into the paddies.

Although I'm not frightened of snakes, I did move pretty quickly when a cobra slithered up my kuti steps and poked its head around the partially open door. Some frantic swishing with a broom chased it out. Yom My told me that there were also king cobras in the monastery grounds. I never saw one, but just before I moved to live at Nahoob a local woman was bitten by a king cobra and died.

Sometimes I found twelve-inch-long, bright red millipedes on my steps, and even in the kuti itself. I was told they are quite dangerous. There were also huge centipedes and scorpions everywhere, looking for somewhere dry to spend the night. I discovered that although the plank walls of my kuti were snake-proof, they were definitely not scorpion or great-big-hairy-spider-proof and these creatures were frequent refugees from the rising water.

I am both fascinated and terrified of big spiders and I really don't want them anywhere near me. I acknowledge their right to live – somewhere else. They were extremely difficult to shoo out with a coconut-hair broom and I sometimes spent hours looking in every nook and cranny for any that had escaped my frantic swishing, but I could never relax if I knew there was one anywhere in the kuti. Every night before going to bed, I would take all my bedding outside the kuti and give it a good shake, just in case a spider or some other creepy-crawly had decided to spend the night with me. On one occasion, I woke up in the morning on my floor mat to find a saucer-sized spider sitting on the floor only inches from my face, sort of throbbing at me. Even though I knew that particular species was not dangerous, I leapt straight up into the air with a childish scream of terror. The spider was even more terrified and fled.

As the paddies flooded, so the monastery grounds became over-run with land crabs. They look much the same as the ordinary English seaside crab, rather dull and about four inches across, but they had an enormous claw which I'm sure could give quite a nip. There were thousands of them and we had to be very careful when walking about at night to avoid treading on them. Unfortunately I did once, though quite unintentionally. It was a most disgusting feeling, though I'm sure more so for the crab than me.

One day, I found a small bat hanging on the ceiling in a corner of the kuti. That was a surprise because there seemed no particular reason for it to be there, rain or no rain. Khao Nor was probably only a few minutes' flying time away. The bat was beautiful and I very much wanted to hold it, but I thought it might be sick. Believing that bats can carry rabies, I avoided that corner for a few days. The bat suddenly dropped off the ceiling one evening, stone dead. I burned its little carcass in the forest.

A sort of flying ant caused me the biggest problem during the rainy season. Every time it rained, literally thousands of them would find their way into the kuti. They would fly around for a while, then their wings would drop off and they would crawl about on the floor. Soon after, they would die and the floor could be almost covered with their bodies. Occasionally, I could sweep up a whole bucketful of them in one evening.

It wasn't only my kuti that became a refuge for every little creature and creepy-crawly. Going to the shower block, especially at night, was like going on a safari. I think the BBC could have made a whole series of wildlife programmes just about the creatures that took up residence in the showers and toilets. It could be quite a nerve-racking experience, standing there naked, not knowing whether something horrible was going to drop out of the roof or come crawling out of the waste hole in the floor – and things sometimes did.

Often it would be raining when we went on alms round. Monks don't use umbrellas during alms round and we would trudge through the village on dirt tracks six inches deep in slithery mud, our sodden robes clinging to our shivering bodies. It didn't really bother me too much, in fact I rather enjoyed it, much to the disbelief of the other monks, who absolutely hated it.

Like everybody else, I suffered with continuous colds and bronchial infections throughout the rainy season. My kuti was constantly damp, as was my bedding, books and all my robes. I shivered, shook and sneezed my way through the three months, until the day came when I thought I was *really* ill.

I began to experience an ache around the top right-hand side of my chest and under my right arm. It wasn't particularly bothersome at first, but it slowly got worse. After a few days, I discovered that all that area was covered in small red lumps. The lumps themselves were neither painful nor itchy, but they seemed to be hot.

My first thought was that some hideous insect had laid its eggs under my skin and that at any moment I could expect maggots or something to come crawling out of the lumps. I've heard of this happening in Thailand, though I don't know if it's true. Yom My came to visit me and I showed him the lumps. He recoiled in horror at the sight and said in his most dramatic English stage voice: 'It's the . . . it's the . . . *Leum!*'

Oh God, I had the Leum and I was going to die. From the look on Yom My's face, I would probably take the rest of the monks and the entire population of the village with me. But what is the Leum, I asked, and what does it do?

Our communication skills didn't extend to medical

terms, so Yom My drew a picture of a very thin torso – my torso – on a piece of paper. Then he added spots to one side. He looked at me enquiringly. Yes, yes, I understood so far, I said, get on with it. He added more spots until they travelled all the way across the chest. Then he turned the paper over and continued drawing spots until they had entirely encircled the paper. When all this spot drawing was finished he looked at me with a very sad expression. 'Dead,' he said.

All this rang a distant bell in my mind. When I was about six years old my mother had been quite ill and it was something to do with spots or lumps on her stomach. An unkind neighbour had told me that if the lumps circled my mother's body and joined up, my mother would die. I seemed to remember that my mother had been suffering from shingles, but wasn't it an old wives' tale about the sufferer dying if the lumps joined up? I had no idea. I looked up shingles in my dictionary. Well, I certainly didn't have small pebbles lying in masses along a seashore, but if one took pebbles for lumps and the seashore as my chest, it was actually a good definition of what I seemed to have.

What was I to do, I asked Yom My. He indicated rather belatedly that I wasn't to worry and that he would fetch a doctor. Off he went, while I lay on the floor quietly dying and trying to work out how many hours it would take for a doctor to come from the nearest hospital. Within minutes Yom My returned, accompanied by a very old man carrying a plastic shopping bag with a picture of Father Christmas on it.

I had seen this old man in the village a few times but I hadn't realised he was the local shaman. Many Thai villages have these 'doctors', usually very knowledgeable about Animism, fortune telling, folklore, massage and herbal medicines, but I had never seen one work before. They are frequently highly respected and consulted on all sorts of matters, not just medical problems.

I would really have preferred a paramedic team but since the old man had been kind enough to come out in the pouring rain, I smiled my most grateful and bravest smile and turned myself over to his ministrations.

The doctor looked at my chest. Then he looked at Yom My. Some sort of understanding seemed to pass between them, as though to say, 'It's hopeless, but we'll try.' Nobody spoke. The doctor rummaged in his plastic bag, probably for his stethoscope, I thought. Instead he pulled out a very straight, very prickly, twelve-inch-long cactus.

'*Yar*,' said Yom My solemnly. Medicine.

And what, I enquired nervously, was I supposed to do with it?

'Boil it,' said Yom My.

That was a relief. And then I was to drink the liquid, I supposed.

'No, no,' said Yom My, as though he had never heard anything so ridiculous in his life. I was to pound the boiled cactus into a poultice and smear it on the lumps. But first, the doctor would give me the main treatment.

The doctor made three rheumatic but very respectable bows to me and then held my right arm straight up. He started mumbling a chant. I couldn't recognise the language but it wasn't Thai, Lao, or Pali. Perhaps it was a combination of all three, but it had a definite rhythm and he certainly wasn't making it up as he went along. This was a deadly serious charm he was weaving and his old face was screwed up in concentration.

After a few minutes of chanting, the charm had been cast and then, much to my surprise, he suddenly blew into my armpit. I nearly burst out laughing but I thought that would be entirely inappropriate, so I kept my face as serious as possible. Yom My heaved a sigh of relief. I thanked the doctor who, apart from the chanting, hadn't said a word. He bowed again and Yom My helped him back to the village.

Word spread quickly that the Phra Farang had the Leum and over the next few hours a stream of villagers came to wish me well, wish me goodbye or blow in my armpit. I wasn't sure if a monk should let ladies do anything quite so intimate but they seemed to think it was respectable so I let them get on with it.

Later that night, as I lay miserably on the floor of my kuti stinking of boiled cactus, I heard someone coming along the forest path. That was unusual. At night especially, the villagers avoided my part of the forest like, well, like the plague really. They believed it was haunted even before I arrived. Yom My occasionally visited at night but I could recognise his footsteps because they were usually broken up by drunken falling-over noises. To my surprise, my night caller was one of the village lads, a boy of about sixteen named Rabbit.

I knew him because he and a bunch of his friends would sometimes visit me in the daytime to try and teach me rude Thai words on the pretext that they were very polite and should be used often. They once suggested that I should ask the abbot if he had enjoyed the traditional Thai sport of kite flying when he was a lad, without telling me that in Thai, 'kite flying' is the same word as masturbation. It turned out that the shaman was Rabbit's grandfather.

Rabbit had brought me a small pot of white cream that had obviously come from a hospital. There was a big scoop out of it but the pot was still half full. '*Yar*,' said Rabbit.

Yes, but what was it for? I asked. He said I was to apply the cream to the lumps and assured me that they would be gone in a few days. I asked where the ointment had come from and it then became clear why the boy had come to my kuti so furtively. The year before, he had suffered with the same symptoms so his grandfather had taken him secretly to the hospital. No cactus poultice for the shaman's grandson! Rabbit asked me not to tell anybody because his grandfather would lose 'face' in the village.

I showered the evil-smelling green gunk from my body and applied the white cream. Within a couple of days, the lumps and aching had entirely disappeared. Was that due to the cactus, the cream or the very sincere chanting and arm-blowing? Maybe a combination of all three? I really don't know.

I also don't know what the disease was called, but it

wasn't the Leum. Some time later, when my Thai vocabulary had improved a little, I discovered that 'leum' is Thai for 'forget'. 'It's the . . . it's the . . . I forget!' Well, it remained the Leum to me and I suffered no harm, and I'd had a fascinating glimpse into Thai rural life.

17

Although Ajahn Waow was consulted by the villagers on any matter of importance, the ordinary monks didn't usually have much contact with them except during cycle of life ceremonies. The most frequent of these during the rainy season were funerals. The wet season and the following cool season usually bring an increase in the number of deaths in rural areas, especially amongst old people. Fairly elaborate rites are usually involved in Thai funerals, though in the poor north-eastern region I have seen bodies carried into a field and burned on a pile of wood with the minimum of ceremony. I think that's probably less frequent now that most village monasteries have built crematoria.

At Wat Nahoob, we had a new crematorium that had never been used, but it was to see a very great deal of use during the rainy season when I lived at the monastery. It seemed that almost every week one of the village patriarchs or matriarchs passed away. When families are bereaved anywhere in Thailand, they try to do the best they can for the deceased by making merit on behalf of that person, believing that the merit can be transferred to the dead to help him or her achieve a better next life. Relatives and friends of the deceased will invariably offer food and gifts to the monks on behalf of the dead person and male relatives will sometimes ordain as novice monks for a few days, or even just for the day of the funeral. Ordaining, even for a very short time, is considered a very meritorious act and the best gift that anyone can make to the dead.

The dead are not usually cremated before the seventh day after death. Occasionally the body may be kept for much longer, to allow as many people as possible to pay their respects. When especially important or highly respected people die, the body may sometimes be kept for one hundred days, or even longer, before being cremated. At Wat Nahoob, there was a rough concrete box on the edge of the forest that contained the body of the village headman's mother. The body had been there for a couple of years because the headman didn't want it cremated until he had saved sufficient money to ensure the funeral was as grand as possible.

In rural areas, the body is usually kept in a coffin in the family home, but in cities is more likely to be taken straight to a monastery. The body will be washed and then dressed in the dead person's best clothes. The hands will be folded across the chest, with a flower and joss sticks clasped between them. The body is then placed in a cheap plywood box that is itself then placed in a very elaborate coffin. The outer coffins, which are very expensive to buy and not burned in the cremation, are usually borrowed from a monastery, or sometimes hired from a specialist shop. At Wat Nahoob, we had a choice of two outer coffins that could be borrowed by villagers – a white and gold one, or a red and gold one.

After the death, nine monks are invited to take breakfast in the house of the deceased each morning for seven days. Before breakfast, the monks chant for about half an hour and then, after eating, chant a short Pali verse about the impermanent nature of life. The verse translates as: 'Alas, transient are all compounded things. Having arisen, they cease. Being born, they die. The cessation of all compounding is true happiness.' That might sound a little bit odd but in fact it contains the essence of the Buddha's teaching: that there is no phenomenon which has any permanence, that all things must end and clinging or attaching to impermanent phenomena must eventually bring suffering of one kind or another.

The verse is chanted while the monks hold a length of 'sacred' white cotton string called *sai sin*. The string is tied to the coffin and is then wrapped around a Buddha image and then through the hands of the monks. It is traditionally believed that the string helps the dead person continue contact with the suttas and blessings being chanted on his or her behalf. On each of the six evenings preceding the cremation, four monks will go to the house to chant passages from the *Abhidhamma*, their faces hidden behind ceremonial fans. Although these passages and all other suttas and blessings are chanted in Pali, the Thai people are usually aware of their meaning and they genuinely seem to help the bereaved cope with their grief. Seven days after a cremation, the family of the deceased will invite monks to take a meal at the house, or sometimes at the monastery, and again on the fiftieth and one hundredth days.

The first time I was invited to take breakfast at the house of a bereaved family in Nahoob, I stood in absolute amazement at the sight that greeted me. The family was quite poor and the house was little more than a large, ramshackle shed on stilts, but it was like walking into an Aladdin's cave of colour and light.

In the main room was an enormous, three-feet-deep, wooden coffin, painted white and with masses of gold plastic decoration. The coffin was set on a stand about five feet high and surrounded by dozens of brilliantly coloured bouquets of huge polystyrene flowers, with wreaths made of towelling folded into the shape of peacocks and butterflies. A large photograph of the deceased stood on a stand at one side. In front of the coffin stand was a small table on which stood a brass bowl containing a single massive incense stick and two candles. Everything, including the coffin, was draped in flashing, multi-coloured fairy lights and the whole display was back-lit with green neon.

The room was quite small and contained not only the coffin and accessories but also a five-piece brass and percussion band, nine monks and dozens of villagers. As more villagers arrived at the house, each approached the coffin and knocked a few times on one end, the head end, and I noticed that a small tray of food had been placed at that end of the coffin. We ate our breakfast sitting on the floor with the eight-feet-high flashing coffin towering over us, while the band played a very mournful dirge. Although I was able to control my outward expression, I got a fit of internal giggles during breakfast when I suddenly recognised the music the band was playing. It was 'You are my Sunshine' but played rather badly at about one-third speed. I've since often heard the same dreadful tune played at other similar occasions, so I suppose it has become adopted as traditional funeral music in Thailand.

Although I found the whole scene in the house quite bizarre, it was not at all undignified. The lights and colour were, I think, a reflection of the Thai people's very pragmatic attitude to death. It is a time for grief but the bereaved try to make the atmosphere as bright and cheerful as possible because it is not necessarily an unhappy time for the deceased who, hopefully, is on his or her way to a better rebirth.

On the seventh day of that particular funeral, several other monks and I went to the house to escort the coffin to the monastery's crematorium. It is an old tradition that the dead should not leave the house by the normal route. Since it is usually impractical and undignified to hoist the coffin through a window, the stairs are sometimes covered with cloth or banana leaves to make the usual route a little different.

Once down the stairs, the coffin was loaded onto a

buffalo cart that had been beautifully repainted for the occasion in black and white. There was no buffalo to pull the cart and instead it was pushed and pulled along the dirt track by some of the village men. Most of the mourners wore black, white or a combination of the two. The procession was headed by a villager scattering rice grains along the path and he was followed by the chief mourners, carrying the photograph of the deceased, and one of the giant incense sticks in a brass pot. Next came the band, playing 'You are my Sunshine', followed by the monks walking in single file, each of us holding on to a length of very thick sai-sin. The string passed through all our hands to the coffin, though we were not actually pulling the cart with the string. Behind the monks came half a dozen men and little boys who had ordained as novices for the day, then the rest of the mourners, all holding the sai-sin.

When we arrived at Wat Nahoob we were joined by about forty other monks who had been invited from nearby monasteries and we all assembled on a three-foot-high wooden platform that had been erected in one of the salas. The coffin was unloaded from the cart and placed to one side of the platform, together with the wreaths and the photograph of the deceased. There is no specific number of monks required to perform funeral rites. I have been present at a funeral with only a few other monks but have also taken part in a ceremony that involved more than two hundred. I think it largely depends on the family and how grand they want to make the occasion, though it also seems common to have the same number of monks as the deceased was years old; fifty monks for a person who was fifty years old, for example.

Ajahn Waow gave a thirty-minute sermon about death and impermanence but, unlike at funeral services in the West, there was no personal eulogy for the deceased. After the sermon the monks chanted for about twenty minutes and then each was presented by the chief mourners with a sabong, an incense stick and an envelope containing money. The monks were also given some white wood shavings that had been beautifully worked into the shape of a rose. The mourners did not hand these gifts directly to the monks. Instead, the gifts were placed across the sai-sin, which was laid along the platform floor in front of the monks, though still attached to the coffin. The monks took the gifts from the sai-sin so, in effect, it was the deceased who was making the offerings. After the presentation, the coffin was loaded back onto the buffalo cart and the whole congregation proceeded to the crematorium, where we escorted the coffin three times around the building in an anti-clockwise direction.

Unlike the functional and discreet crematoria of Europe, Wat Nahoob's was really quite colourful and pretty. Nothing about death is as grim in Thailand as it is in the West. The crematorium was on a high concrete base with steps leading up on three sides to a small chamber with a tall, thin chimney. Like most Thai monastery buildings, it was painted white with lots of red and yellow cast concrete decoration of heavenly beings, and with snakes and scrolls in every angle. On top of the newel posts were large, pink concrete lotus buds. Most Thai crematoria that I have seen are of similar style, though some are considerably larger and grander than Wat Nahoob's small building.

After circling the crematorium, the coffin was carried up the steps and placed on a low stand. The ornate outer coffin was dismantled in a few minutes, revealing the inner plywood box. The inner box is sometimes left open if the sight of the body is not likely to cause too much distress to the family or, perhaps, is not too badly damaged or unsightly. I have been present at funerals where the very young children of the deceased have been picked up so that they can look inside the box at their dead mother or father. Oddly, I have never seen a child upset by the sight. An acceptance and understanding of death starts very early in Thailand.

When everything was in place, the immediate family members placed sabongs on top of the body and a number of monks were invited to take them from the coffin. As they did so, they again chanted the Pali verse about impermanence. That tradition recalls the time from many centuries ago in India when monks used bits of cloth found in charnel grounds to make their robes. The rest of the monks then mounted the steps and placed their incense sticks and wooden flowers in the coffin, on top of the body. Friends and family followed to do the same, while the new novice monks scattered coins into the crowd, symbolising the deceased's final rejection of materialism.

The inner coffin was then loaded onto a metal trolley with wheels, quite a bit like a wheelbarrow. In the mesh bottom of this were placed layers of newspaper, cardboard and charcoal. These were lit and the trolley was rolled through the crematorium's heavy steel door and into the oven. The door had a small peephole so that the village funeral director could check on the progress of the cremation. There was also another small hole through which he could insert a long, forked metal rod to shift the position of the body from time to time.

Beneath the chamber was a trap into which ashes and small fragments of bone fell. They would be collected by the family the next day and would be kept in a small brass urn, a miniature of the huge stupas and chedi that can be seen in many Thai monasteries. The urn would usually be kept in the family home, together with the photograph. I have visited many homes that have had dozens of such urns on shelves, and photographs going back many generations lining the walls. If the family is wealthy, a small concrete chedi may be built in the monastery grounds, with the urn interred inside it.

I found my first experience of a Thai funeral extremely interesting, though at the time I was a little surprised at some of the crudity of the arrangements. Having people running around looking for old newspapers before the body could be burned seemed undignified, or at least disorganised, though I appeared to be the only one who thought so. No doubt that was a reflection of my Western conditioning. Having since attended many hundreds of funerals, both in rural and big city monasteries, I realise that Thai funerals can be very sophisticated indeed. One monastery in Nakhon Sawan City has recently built a multi-million baht electric-fired crematorium, where the business of loading the body into the oven takes place behind screens and floral displays and anything in the least bit undignified is kept out of sight. The cost of a funeral at that particular monastery is very high. I suppose rural people are less sophisticated than their city cousins, and usually less wealthy, but they do the best they can.

Although some of the rites at the first funeral I attended seemed strange to me – since I didn't understand them at the time – basically all people face the same problem or duty when a death occurs in the family; to dispose of the body. The Thais seem to do it with more ritual and ceremony than in the West but it also seems to be done in at least a semi-cheerful way. It has always been my impression that the moment the oven door is shut, the grieving stops and life for everybody else goes on. There has always seemed to be a calm and pragmatic acceptance of death; a natural understanding that this is how all lives end and that tears and hand wringing aren't going to change a thing. I have only very rarely seen anybody cry at a funeral in Thailand and I have never once seen the sort of hysterics that are common at funerals in the West. I think this pragmatic attitude shows a very profound understanding of the Buddha's teaching about the impermanent nature of all things. At the same time, perhaps this understanding is also at least partly responsible for the Thais' ability to enjoy themselves on a moment-to-moment basis, without worrying too much about what the future might hold. There is only one certainty in this life and that is that it ends.

I know that some of the rites and rituals I have a duty to be involved in as a monk are sometimes more closely related to Animism and Brahmanism than to Buddhism. At funerals, at least, that doesn't cause me any personal conflict as a Buddhist monk. I believe *anything* that helps people cope with their time of grief must be worthwhile, whether it be the Pali chanting or the flashing fairy lights.

Funerals for monks follow much the same pattern as those for lay-people. During my Pansa at Wat Nahoob, one of our monks died and was cremated at the monastery. Just before the Rains Retreat started, an old monk had wandered into Wat Nahoob and asked Ajahn Waow if he could spend the Pansa with us. The abbot had said he could. The old monk, Phra Ghin, was more than eighty, though he had been a monk for only about five years. I believe he had ordained so that he wouldn't be a burden on his family during his old age. His village was in the north-east of the country but he had spent several years wandering all over Thailand, staying each night in any monastery he found himself close to and the Rains Retreat in any monastery which would accept him.

Phra Ghin seemed to be a very nice but rather lonely old man and I occasionally sat with him in the forest.

He would chatter on in his Lao dialect and although I rarely had more than a vague idea what he was talking about, I would smile, nod or shake my head, whichever seemed most appropriate.

He started to complain of stomach pains and after a few days Ajahn Waow sent him off on the back of a motorcycle to Nakhon Sawan hospital, about forty kilometres away. About a week later, Phra Ghin died and was returned to us wrapped in polythene in the back of a pick-up truck.

When a monk dies, only other monks are allowed to prepare the body for cremation. Ajahn Waow asked for volunteers but most of the monks disappeared rather hastily, so Giant and I got the job of washing the dead body and then dressing it in Phra Ghin's robes before laying it into the coffin. I had never handled a dead body before and I thought I might find it distasteful or, at least, distressing, but, even though the dead flesh smelt very badly, I found I was totally able to accept that this was no longer the Phra Ghin I had known, however slightly, and the body had no personality at all. Handling the body seemed no different from the occasion when I'd found one of the monastery dogs dead and had dragged it into the forest to bury.

When we had the corpse laid out in the plywood coffin, Giant placed a single lotus flower on the chest and carefully folded the cold hands around it. To me, that was very touching and at that point, much to my surprise, I found I had a lump in my throat, though I had previously been quite emotionless.

We covered the corpse with Phra Ghin's spare robe. Before we nailed the lid of the coffin down, Yom My appeared with a very thorny branch he had cut from a bush. He laid it on top of the body. The reason, he said, was to prevent Phra Ghin getting out of the coffin in case he came back to life in some sort of zombie state. That is an old Animist belief which still seems very common amongst rural people, though Yom My seemed rather embarrassed to admit it.

Ajahn Waow had informed Phra Ghin's family and we delayed the cremation until they could make the long journey from the north-east, after which they took the ashes home with them. Life carried on as usual at Wat Nahoob and I don't think I ever heard Phra Ghin's name mentioned again.

Although Thailand is frequently known as 'The Land of Smiles', it can also be a very violent country, as one particular week at Nahoob was to show.

The week started off with the news that six people had been killed at the end of the track when their pick-up truck, driven by a drunk, crashed into a tree. None of the dead were from Nahoob village, so that didn't concern us too much.

Another violent death occurred a few days later. There was a man living at the monastery who occasionally helped out around the grounds. He was generally considered good for nothing and I rarely saw him sober. He was very unpopular in the village and I really don't know why Ajahn Waow put up with him. Compassion, I suppose.

One morning that week, I was woken up at about 2am by a monk banging on my kuti door. I couldn't make much sense out of what he was saying but it was obvious that he wanted me to go with him to the sala. I followed him and found a small group of villagers standing around the dead body of the man. He had been shot through the chest by his brother-in-law in the village following a drunken argument. It was not a pleasant sight. The bullet had exited through the man's back and had made a very large hole indeed. I was told that the police had already been and gone and that they had confiscated the gun. Money had changed hands and that was the end of it. We cremated the body the next day with the minimum of ceremony. Most of the villagers attended, in what I can only describe as festive mood.

In that same week, the monks were sitting in the sala eating breakfast one morning, surrounded by villagers. A man rushed in and blurted out what was obviously dramatic and exciting news. All the villagers hurriedly left. The monks continued eating without comment and I was totally mystified as to what had happened.

It turned out that a village woman had cut her husband's throat with a machete. I never knew why and I never knew the outcome, but it was cause for yet another quick and discreet cremation.

18

I lived at Wat Nahoob for more than a year and during that time I was able to observe and participate in most of the annual Thai religious and cultural festivals.

Thai people love to celebrate. Some will celebrate almost anything, even events adopted from the West that they often know little about and which play no part in their own traditions or culture. St Valentine's Day, Hallowe'en and Christmas may all play a part in the festival calendar, especially for young people in the cities who are increasingly influenced by anything Western and are easy prey to department store marketing.

In rural areas, festival celebrations are perhaps not particularly sophisticated by Western standards, though they follow much the same pattern. Some very loud music, lots of simple food, alcohol and plenty of friends and neighbours dropping in are all the ingredients necessary for *sanuk* – having fun. The Thai calendar is full of special cultural and religious dates and almost every month seems to bring an excuse for people to get together, either for making merit at monasteries or simply for having a good time at home.

My personal favourite when I lived at Wat Nahoob was *Songkran* the Thai New Year festival. The date of the opening of the New Year is 13 April but the occasion is celebrated over three days. Since 1941 the official New Year date has been 1 January, but Thai people still celebrate the traditional period with considerably more enthusiasm.

Mid-April is quite a logical time for farming people to celebrate a new year because it comes at an important change in the seasons. The very hot, dry weather is just about over by then and the theoretical beginning of cooler and wetter weather is not far off (although the rain may still be some months away). The change in the environment at about that time is considerable, something like the change in Europe from winter to spring, when new leaves and buds start to appear on dry and apparently lifeless trees and shrubs. The period also comes at the end of the rice-growing cycle, when one rice harvest has been gathered in and the new crop has not yet been planted.

Originally, Songkran was concerned with the anticipation of rain and included Brahmanic rain-invoking ceremonies. It is still all about water – throwing it over everything and everybody. To walk down any street in any city, town or village in mid-April means getting wet; perhaps a few drops of water poured over the hands, a bucket-full poured over the shoulders, or a total soaking with a hosepipe. It doesn't matter who you are or what you are wearing, you are expected to smile wetly and join in the fun. For three days, everybody is constantly dripping and the water used must run into millions of gallons. This boisterous and sanuk side of Songkran has developed from the more restrained practice of paying respect to one's elders by pouring a little scented water over their hands.

My first experience of Songkran was when I was travelling in north-eastern Thailand with Phra Maha Laow, before I became a monk. We had stopped at a little roadside café so that he could eat lunch. The café was empty of other customers, apart from a policeman sitting at another table. Usually in Thailand, at even the most modest roadside stalls, a glass of water will appear on the table even before the customer has ordered anything to eat or drink. On this occasion, a woman appeared with two glasses of water. She respectfully placed one in front of Phra Maha Laow and then slowly, and very deliberately, poured the other one over my head and shoulders. Phra Maha Laow and the observing policeman thought this was hilarious and burst out laughing. Although I knew about Songkran in theory, I wasn't terribly happy to have this first unexpected and practical experience of it.

'Smile,' said Phra Maha Laow when he saw the look on my face. 'At Songkran everybody can expect a soaking. It doesn't matter who you are, except monks and royalty . . .'

I picked up Phra Maha Laow's glass of water and walked over to the laughing policeman. 'Smile,' I said, and poured it down the back of his neck. I walked back to our table.

'. . . and policemen,' added Phra Maha Laow.

Oh.

Unsmiling, the policeman got up from his table and dripped his way over to us, looking quite sinister in his reflective dark glasses and with one hand resting casually on his gun holster. He stood for a tense moment looking down at me. '*Sawatii pee mai*' – 'Happy New Year' – I stammered nervously, with the biggest and falsest smile I'd ever managed in my life. The policeman burst out laughing and sat down to join us for lunch.

Besides pouring water over each other, the idea of cleansing out the old year and welcoming the new is also observed in the home. The house gets a good spring clean and everything is prepared for the new beginning. House parties go on for days and almost every province has a parade through the city streets, with school bands, floats and, a recent addition, a Songkran Queen.

Many people will also go to their local monastery, where the main Buddha image is given a ritual washing as each person pours a little scented water onto it from a small silver bowl. Traditionally, people may also take clean sand to the monastery to spread around the grounds.

I was at Wat Buddhapadipa in London getting my knee fixed during my first Songkran as a monk. The festival has no particular significance in Buddhism but the monastery allows the grounds to be used for celebrating Thai cultural festivals. On that day, there were many thousands of visitors enjoying displays of Thai classical dancing, Thai boxing and a wide range of Thai food from a market that had been set up in the monastery's car park.

The main Buddha image in the Bote was too big to be moved, but water cannot be allowed in the building anyway in case the murals get accidentally splashed and damaged. A smaller image was set up on the marble steps outside and that was ritually washed by many hundreds of people.

The monks also got a ritual washing. We all sat on our mats in the shrine room in the house, with our hands held over small silver bowls. Dozens of lay-people filed past on their knees and each poured a few drops of scented water over our hands. Very respectful and restrained and not a bit like the celebrations at Wat Nahoob the following year.

At Nahoob, the village people celebrated in the monastery grounds and visitors from miles around came to join in the festivities. They included a band playing traditional north-eastern or Lao music amplified to ear-splitting volume, whilst at the same time an outdoor movie screen showed a Chinese kung fu movie, also at ear-splitting volume. There was much eating and drinking and some graceful and gradually not-so-graceful ramwonging. Everybody was madly throwing water about but frequently the recipients were too far gone to even notice.

Of course, the monks didn't take part in any of that and Ajahn Waow closed his eyes to the amount of alcohol being consumed in his monastery. The monks' part came towards the end of the afternoon when the bell was rung and we all assembled in front of the Bote, where a line of chairs had been set up on the grass.

I was expecting much the same as I had experienced at Wat Buddhapadipa the previous year but when country people celebrate they do so with great enthusiasm. Within seconds, I was soaked from shoulders to feet, though the people were careful not to pour water over the monks' heads.

Hundreds of people filed past in two lines, one in front and one behind the chairs, and absolutely drenched us from cups, buckets and a hosepipe. The temperature was in the nineties so that was quite enjoyable for me, even when several children slipped ice cubes down the back of my robe. For about forty-five minutes we sat while gallon after gallon of water was poured over us, until our chairs started to sink in the mud.

The Thai monks accepted all that with unmoving expressions, keeping their eyes fixed firmly on their folded hands. But Thai happiness is infectious and how can one ignore hundreds of excited, smiling faces? I couldn't and within seconds I was smiling back at them, exchanging a sincere 'sawatii pee mai' with each person that passed in front of me and occasionally flicking water at faces I recognised.

By the end of the day the lawn was a quagmire and everybody was soaked, but the people had really made the most of it. I think I enjoyed it as much as they did.

At the other end of the year, in November, is the *Loi Krathong* festival. That is also concerned with water, but whereas Songkran is primarily about having a boisterous good time and letting off steam, Loi Krathong is a gentle and beautiful festival, concerned more with inner reflection.

Loi means 'to float' and a *krathong* is a small boat. The little boats are usually circular and about nine inches across. The base is a slice of banana palm, cut straight across the stem, and then banana leaves are used to make the sides of the boat. In the centre each carries a candle, an incense stick, flowers and sometimes a small coin.

On the day before Loi Krathong, I sat with some of the village children and watched for hours while they made their little boats. Like most Thai people, they were extraordinarily gifted with their hands, deftly bending and shaping the leaves and flowers and carefully folding and mixing tiny petals into complex coloured patterns. I tried making a krathong, but it was quite hopeless. When I tried it out in a bucket of water to see if it would float properly, it immediately turned bottom up and all the decoration fell off, much to the amusement of the children.

Some krathongs are very elaborate and may be several feet across and in height. Many cities hold competitions between schools, businesses and institutions to see who can make the best-looking krathong. I've seen huge ones in the shape of galleons, fantastic sea creatures and peacocks.

One explanation for the festival is that it is a way of making offerings to *Mae Kong Ka*, the goddess of water, to thank her for allowing the donor to make use of the water in various ways over the past year. The gifts of light, incense and money also atone for any pollution the donor may have caused to the water. As the krathong floats away, the sins of the donor are carried away with it. Another explanation is that the gifts atone for boating or swimming over Buddha images which may be lying on the riverbed. Yet another explanation is that it prevents death by drowning.

The origins of the festival are as obscure as its meaning. I have read that it came from, or was inspired by, similar ancient festivals in India and China, but I have also heard that it originated in the old Sukhothai kingdom about 700 years ago. According to that story, a beautiful lady of the court, named Nang Noppamas, made the very first krathong in the shape of a lotus flower as a gift for the King. The King was pleased and lit the candle and floated the little boat on the palace lake.

The festival has no place in the religious calendar, so I was quite surprised when a group of teachers from a local school came to the monastery to present me with a krathong they had made. It was beautifully decorated and at first I thought it was a cake. On closer inspection the decoration proved to be hundreds of red, yellow and green chillies, so it was just as well I didn't eat it.

214

That evening I joined some of the village people at the monastery pond, carefully lit my candle and gently launched the little boat. There were several dozen krathongs moving lazily on the pond in the evening breeze, each with its candle flickering and being reflected in the dark water.

Later that evening, Giant and I and several other monks went into Banpot town and watched many hundreds of krathongs of all sizes bobbing past on the fast-flowing Ping river. The town was packed with people, most carrying krathongs. Some shops had stayed open late for the sale of ready-made krathongs, many of them, sadly, made from polystyrene. There were bands and parties on every street corner and in the grounds of the main monastery, Wat Somciel, a concert and film show were running simultaneously and very noisily. The monastery itself was brightly lit with thousands of fairy lights. As monks we had to keep a distance from the festivities, but it was very nice to see so many people enjoying that special night.

The religious calendar starts in May and the full moon day of most months has some special significance, though only four are widely celebrated. These four, *Visakha Puja, Asalha Puja, Khao Pansa* and *Magha Puja* are all national holidays in Thailand.

Visakha Puja in May commemorates the Buddha's birth, Enlightenment and passing away. Many people go to their local monastery on the night of *Visakha Puja* to take part in a *wien tien*: a candle-lit procession that circles the Bote three times.

215

On *Visakha Puja* at Wat Nahoob, the monks assembled on the high balcony of the Bote at dusk to await the arrival of the villagers. They came in procession from three different directions and each person carried flowers, incense sticks and a candle. They joined us on the balcony and, with the monks in the lead and also carrying candles and flowers, we circled the Bote three times. During the circumambulation, the monks began to chant softly and the chanting was taken up by the villagers. After the third time around, the candles and incense were placed in holders around the balcony and we entered the Bote to pay our respects to the image there and to lay our flowers on the altar tables.

The whole ceremony only lasted about thirty minutes. Although low key, it was very beautiful and gave the opportunity for reflection on the Buddha's life. Afterwards, as I walked back through the forest to my kuti, I looked back at the Bote. It looked quite dazzling, lit up by hundreds of tiny points of light.

Asalha Puja is in July. It commemorates three important events: Prince Siddhattha's renunciation of his princely lifestyle, his first sermon as the Buddha, and the First Council, the coming together of his monks three months after he passed away. July is also the beginning of the Pansa (*Khao Pansa*) when many young men ordain for a few months.

There was an incident in the Buddha's life when he left his monks and, tradition says, lived alone in the forest with only the animals to care for him. That occasion is remembered in September. At Wat Nahoob, the sala became a forest for the night, with whole cut banana trees tied to the pillars and likenesses of monkeys and elephants lurking in the shrubbery. Throughout the night, until dawn, the abbot read traditional stories of the Buddha's previous lives to about fifty villagers. These beautiful and inspiring stories are much loved by all Thai people and they seem never to tire of hearing them. The abbot read from a high pulpit that had been fantastically decorated with tiny flowers woven into curtains resembling lace.

Wan Ork Pansa marks the end of the Rains Retreat and on that day the lay-people make special offerings to the monks. At that time, many young men who ordained just for the Pansa disrobe (though some stay as monks for another month). In the village, the noisy celebrations went on through the night as families welcomed their sons home.

In the period between the full moons of October and November, the *Tot Kathin* ceremony takes place. A *kathin* is a wooden frame on which cloth is stretched for cutting and sewing. At the time of the Buddha, the kathin was used by the monks to make their own robes from scraps of cloth found in charnel grounds and forests. Later, people who wanted to make merit started to leave pieces of cloth so that they could be found by the monks, then later began to leave complete robe-lengths of cloth. Over the centuries, the practice has slowly developed so that in modern times, people present complete sets of ready-made robes to monks who have completed the Pansa.

Magha Puja in February is an important religious festival. It marks the occasion, about three months before the Buddha passed away, when 1,250 *Arahants* (monks who had reached the final stages of perfection) gathered together without previous arrangement. All these Arahants had become monks at the invitation of the Buddha before the introduction of the lengthy ordination ceremony. Then, the Buddha would invite a person to join his following simply by saying '*Ehi-passiko*' – 'Come and see'. It was at that spontaneous gathering of the Arahants that the Buddha first recited the rules of the monks and also announced that he would pass away in three months. Magha Puja is celebrated in the same way as Visakha Puja, with a candle-lit procession.

All these festivals, both cultural and religious, were enjoyable to me and I understood their background, but I found myself becoming increasingly involved in other ceremonies that sometimes seemed inexplicable. Although I didn't understand them, they didn't worry me particularly at first. Everything was still very new to me, so when a pick-up truck arrived to take the monks to someone's house for breakfast or lunch, or whatever, I just got in and went along with the crowd. Often, I hadn't the faintest idea of where we were going, or why, or what we would do when we got there. But slowly, and unknown to me at the time, a doubt was beginning to form; shapeless and nameless, but gently simmering away at the back of my mind . . .

19

Doubt, according to Buddhism, is one of the major obstacles to spiritual progress and understanding. Together with lustful desires, ill will, hatred, anger, sloth, torpor, worry and restlessness, doubt must be faced, examined and cleared away before progress can be continued. At Wat Nahoob, I found myself becoming increasingly concerned about the small doubts and uncertainties that were beginning to form in my mind.

Before I ordained I had travelled through many different parts of Thailand, usually staying in monasteries and taking every opportunity to observe religious services and customs. This was to be my future life, so it was important to me to learn as much as I could. Sometimes I would see an activity that I didn't understand and I would always try to find out what aspect of the Buddha's teaching the ceremony was concerned with. When I once asked a very senior English-speaking monk about the relevance of the sai-sin – the 'sacred string' – and the realities of transferring merit to dead people, he told me, 'It's Buddhist metaphysics.' Many of the ceremonies I observed didn't seem to be concerned with Buddhism at all, at least not as I understood it. Then, 'It's Thai custom' was frequently the answer to my questions. At the time, I accepted that some of the odd ceremonies I saw were all part of the richness of Thai Buddhism.

Later, when I became a monk and had to be involved in some of these ceremonies myself, that remained my attitude, at least at first. Although I couldn't see the relevance of some of the rituals, that didn't mean they weren't right. It was more likely to mean that I simply lacked sufficient understanding. They seemed perfectly harmless and at the time I gave them little conscious thought. I had no strong opinions but slowly and quietly I was becoming uneasy and later began to question whether I really ought to be involved at all. Some of the ceremonies seemed quite bizarre to me.

In my first week at Wat Nahoob, all the monks and others from a nearby monastery were invited by a layman to take breakfast in a field. A pick-up truck arrived at the monastery early in the morning and we all piled in the back. We were trundled along miles of bumpy tracks and then cross-country to a paddy field. A small, three-sided, blue-and-white marquee had been set up in the field. Inside the marquee was a long, makeshift platform for the monks to sit on. The platform was about three feet high and the whole thing looked exactly like a stage for a very amateur dramatic performance. Sitting expectantly on the floor in front of the marquee were about fifty people, most of them from a nearby village.

The nine monks climbed a step onto the platform and I really felt we should break into a song and dance routine. Instead, we sat down and the other monks chanted for about thirty minutes before we were presented with breakfast.

Stretching all around us were miles of paddy fields with not a single tree in sight, except one; a very tall palm tree about eight metres from the marquee. The tree, it turned out, was the reason we had been invited to the field. It had apparently been struck by lightning, though I could see no sign of damage, and the farmer wanted it blessed. After breakfast, Ajahn Waow unrolled a length of sai-sin, one end of which was tied around a small Buddha image and then round a brass bowl filled with water. A beeswax candle was fixed to the rim of the bowl and the melting wax dripped into the water. The string passed from the bowl, down the line of monks and through all our hands. The end was tied around the palm tree. We chanted briefly and then, using a small brush, Ajahn Waow splashed the lustral or holy water over the tree, as well as over the audience. Each monk was presented with a lotus flower and a small gift of money and we were driven back to the monastery.

On another occasion, a man drove into Wat Nahoob in a huge cattle truck. It was new and the owner wanted it blessed, presumably so that it wouldn't break down or crash. After a bit of chanting, Ajahn Waow used his finger to daub a magic symbol on the truck's bonnet with white paste and then liberally splashed truck and driver with lustral water. We were each presented with a gift of money and the truck driver, no doubt now convinced of his invincibility on the roads, drove off happily at high speed. The truck would probably never be taxed or insured, but at least it had been blessed.

I have been with a chapter of nine monks when we have carried out a similar ceremony on a new motor-cycle and once on a whole fleet of trucks and pick-ups. There were many such occasions, sometimes several times each week. One of the most bizarre for me was when we were invited to take lunch at a house in order to bless a new washing machine. The head monk daubed some symbols on the machine and splashed it with lustral water while the rest of us chanted, holding on to the sai-sin which was tied around the washing machine.

That was exactly what the householder wanted but I came away (clutching my envelope of money) feeling distinctly uneasy, with the words hocus pocus upper-most in my mind. What exactly was I doing, and why? From where, or from whom, I asked myself, did our power or authority come to enable us to dispense blessings on trees, trucks and washing machines? Was I a Buddhist monk, or was I becoming a Brahmin priest? And yet I had seen photographs of the Supreme Patriarch, the head of the Thai Sangha, performing exactly the same type of ritual for Thai Airways on a new aircraft. I had as much respect for the Supreme

Patriarch as any Thai monk. If he performed such rites, who was I to question or doubt them?

I had even been present at an exorcism. I am sorry to say that it took place at Wat Buddhapadipa in London. I was not a monk at the time but I watched as a chapter of monks chanted whilst holding the sai-sin, one end of which was tied around a Buddha image and the other to a corner of a large, white tablecloth. The cloth was draped over a woman who lay on the floor of the shrine room, writhing and loudly screaming. After about ten minutes she became silent, then got up, gave the monks their white envelopes containing money, and left, presumably exorcised. I have also seen the white cloth treatment used a couple of times in Thailand for people who simply felt they were going through unlucky periods, as well as for someone who was frequently ill. I was quite willing to accept that if the exorcism or the ceremonies for the banishment of bad luck or illness actually worked for the people involved, if they really believed they had been exorcised of their personal demons, then it had some validity. But was it Buddhism? Was it even 'Buddhist metaphysics'? Or was it just superstitious rubbish?

I had no particular criticism of Thai Buddhism. One cannot criticise or praise a thing until one knows for oneself absolutely that it is wrong, or right. Even if I found that these curious rites and rituals were not strictly Buddhism as I understood it, I would still not have any criticism for the way Thai lay-people practised their religion. At Nahoob, few or any of the villagers were interested in meditation or in the psychological or metaphysical teachings of the Buddha. They were simple farming folk, descended from generations of simple farming folk. Their lives were hard. They were naturally more interested in the things that had an obvious and direct bearing on their lives; in the seasons and in whether they would get a good harvest that year. Although on the whole they followed the simplest aspects of Buddhist philosophy, such as in keeping the Five Precepts, many of their religious beliefs owed much more to Animism. Over many centuries the two had become jumbled together into a hybrid. That was okay; it suited them and their way of life. I had no right to say to them, 'You should practise only this way, or that way.' The laity of all faiths take from their religion whatever they personally require of it to suit their particular circumstances. As a group, they frequently add to it for the same reason.

But can that be valid for Buddhist monks? For them, surely there can be only one way of practice – the way the Buddha taught. Presumably we had all become monks so that we could follow and practise the teaching. Any doubts I had were reserved for the way we, as monks, were practising and, more specifically, for the way I seemed to be expected to practise. The Buddha pointed the way to true freedom, happiness and liberation from suffering. He said that it was up to each of us to make the effort to reach those goals. Lay-people make the effort to the best of their individual ability and in their own way. Monks also make the effort to the best of their individual ability but for them, whatever their personal ability or understanding, they must follow the philosophy taught by the Buddha and live their lives within the framework of the rules of the monks. Where did the idea come from that monks – even the newest of them like me – could dispense blessings, perform exorcisms, banish bad luck and heal the sick?

I had often seen very senior monks blowing on the heads of sickly children. The parents seemed to believe that this would cure the child. What the parents chose to believe is up to them, but do the monks who indulge in that sort of practice also believe that they have miraculous or spiritual healing powers and can cure sickness with their breath? Maybe they had, I just didn't know. Even I had been stopped on the street and had been presented with a spotty baby so that I could blow on its head.

Every country and culture has its own superstitions and traditional beliefs. In England, there are old wives' tales about black cats, walking under ladders, pinches of salt and that sort of thing. Some of these superstitions stem from pre-Christian pagan religions, just as many of those in Thailand stem from old Animist beliefs. That's fair enough and I believe they add colour to the culture of the people. But we were Buddhist *monks* following what I had always considered to be the most scientific and logical of philosophies; a philosophy based on wisdom, not ignorant superstition.

A story about the Buddha often sprang into my mind during this time. He was speaking to a group of people who were confused about the conflicting religious philosophies they were hearing from various teachers who passed through their town. They asked the Buddha for his opinion. Although the Buddha's reply was concerned specifically with religious philosophies, it seemed to me that his advice could be applied to many other situations as well. He said, 'Do not be led by reports, or tradition, or hearsay. Do not be led by the authority of religious texts, nor by mere logic or inference, nor by considering appearances, nor by delight in speculative opinions, nor by seeming possibilities, nor by the idea "this is our teacher". But when you know for yourselves that certain things are unwholesome, wrong and bad, then give them up. And when you know for yourselves that certain things are wholesome and good, then accept them and follow them.'

I didn't *know* for myself that these blessings and the paraphernalia that went with them were wrong or merely empty rituals, but they didn't seem to fit in with what I *did* know. They didn't feel right to me, but no doubt they felt right for the lay-people involved. They were simple and harmless little ceremonies but they seemed to be the only thing the people demanded from the religion and from the monks – and they seemed to be the only thing that many monks were able to offer. They were planting seeds of doubt in my mind. Not about Buddhism itself, but about what Buddhism seemed to have become.

These were not just the opinions of a new, know-nothing monk. Several of Thailand's most senior and revered monks were saying or writing much the same thing. In one of the last books he wrote before he died, the greatly revered Phra Ajahn Buddhadasa said that Thai Buddhism had hit 'rock bottom'. Another greatly respected Thai scholar monk, Dr Phra Maha Chanya, wrote in his book *Introduction to Buddhism*: 'The role of the Buddhist monk is being changed from the holders of Dhamma light to performers of rites. They change their role from spiritual leaders to civil servants. No one can deny that the majority of Buddhist monks give the people what they want, even if it sometimes contradicts the real Buddhist truth.'

I was once present at a lecture when a very senior Thai monk was telling junior monks how they should behave in front of lay-people. The lecture was in Thai but was translated for me sentence by sentence. The senior monk said, 'It is the monk's job to know how to chant and to be a good actor in front of the laity.' Was it? Were we, then, merely *pretending* to be monks? Acting out a part in our costumes and chanting our lines and blessings for the benefit of the paying audience? Is that why the Buddha had set up the Sangha all those centuries ago? Is that what I had given up my life in England for?

I was hardly conscious of it at first, but my sense of sabbai was disappearing and I found myself becoming increasingly cynical and unhappy. Rather than face my doubts, I decided to push all such thoughts aside. That was a mistake. The seeds of doubt had taken root and were to come to fruition in a most dramatic way.

20

I have not often been really angry in my life. As a child, I was prone to what my parents called temper tantrums and I think in my mid-teens I was a bit sulky, always claiming that nobody understood me. In adulthood, I could be easily irritated and had sometimes given a show of anger, but the emotion had rarely been very deep and was always soon forgotten. I don't think I really knew what true anger was until one day at Wat Nahoob I suddenly and unexpectedly found myself in a rage. It was an emotion of an intensity and completeness that I had never experienced before. It blinded me to all reason and later led me to question whether all my hundreds of hours spent in meditation, seeking some understanding and control over my mind, had been a waste of time and whether my apparent developing equanimity was a thin veneer.

It began with the howl of a dog. At Wat Nahoob we had half a dozen mangy dogs that hung around the place looking for scraps. Most dogs seem to have a hard time in Thailand, especially in rural areas, because they are not generally seen as pets in the same way that Westerners view their dogs. Even if someone ties a piece of coloured string around a dog's neck, thereby claiming ownership, the unfortunate animal may still be subjected to abuse. Cats fare better. I have heard that they are believed to be naughty novice monks, reborn in cat form.

There was a man living at Wat Nahoob who had been there for many years as a sort of general handyman. He was educationally disadvantaged, which wasn't his fault. His parents had been too poor to provide any sort of education for him at all and he had never been to school. He had grown up as a temple boy in a series of monasteries, unable to read or write. Despite his academic failings, he was quite well liked in the village because of his apparent knowledge of herbal medicines and traditional Thai massage. I thought he was a bit strange and the village children told me he was *tingtong* – the equivalent of barmy rather than clinically mad. The children seemed not to like him and tended to stay away from him, though it was some time before I understood why. He usually had a lovely smile on his face and I certainly didn't dislike him, though we could not communicate in any way.

His sister lived in a nearby village and she offered to sponsor him to become a monk so that she could make merit. He ordained at Wat Nahoob and built himself a tumbledown shack in the forest about twenty metres from my kuti, whilst waiting for his sister to have a more permanent structure built. His nearby presence caused me no problem at all but I started to become increasingly disturbed by his treatment of the dogs.

When it came to dogs and, as I later observed, small children, he seemed to have a vicious and bullying streak in him. Frequently I would see him beating a dog, or even a tiny puppy, with a bamboo cane, or firing stones at the dogs with a catapult. At those times his smile turned into an ugly and perverse leer. That sort of behaviour is not particularly unusual in Thailand, even in monasteries, but I always tried to ignore it. I reminded myself constantly that I lived in a society where many attitudes were quite different from my conditioned Western ones and that I should not use my personal values or habitual responses to become judgemental about other people.

One day I was sitting on my kuti steps reading when a dog howled in pain. The sound of a dog being hurt had become commonplace in that part of the woods, but that particular howl was quite different. It was a scream of agony. I looked across at the monk's kuti, for I knew he had to be the cause. He was. He had one of the male dogs tied down to a bench and was castrating it with a machete. Any ideas I might have had about remaining aloof and non-judgemental disappeared in an instant.

I made no conscious decision about whether I should be involved or not. In fact, my mind didn't seem to be functioning logically on any level. I only recall that I suddenly arrived at his shack. Somewhere in my blind dash along the way, I had uprooted a sapling that I now held in my upraised hands above my head. I brought it crashing down across the monk's back. The machete went flying into the bushes somewhere, which was just as well. I don't know if I was making any sound at all but, if I was, I doubt if I would have been heard above the dog's howling and the monk's screams of outrage. I seemed to have no control at all and continued to beat him about the head and shoulders until he fell to the forest floor, trying to crawl away from me. I wanted him to know what pain and humiliation was and, if the machete had still been handy, I'm sure I would have castrated him so he would know exactly what it felt like.

Although my anger seemed to totally consume me, it probably lasted no more than a minute or so and was snuffed out as quickly as a candle flame. One moment I was in a rage and in the next it had totally disappeared. I was left trembling uncontrollably and the sapling dropped from my hands to the forest floor. The monk lay on the ground staring up at me in fear and shock. I just stood, trying to control my trembling body as well as my mind, as full realisation of what I had done swept over me, almost causing me to faint.

At that moment the dog was forgotten, the beating was forgotten, the man at my feet was forgotten. I was horrified and I watched my faith and belief in myself as a monk, as a *meditative* monk and a strict follower of the Buddha's teaching, evaporate. I was left feeling empty and desolate. I had neither learned nor understood anything. It all suddenly seemed to have been a waste of time. I turned and walked slowly back to my kuti.

I was able to put the dog's agony out of my mind easily. The damage was already done and there was nothing I could do to correct it. I did look for the dog in the monastery grounds that day to see if I could care for it in any way, but I couldn't find it. I never saw the dog again. The monk suffered no damage and later the same day was telling the other monks and villagers about the Phra Farang's extraordinary behaviour. The incident had already become a joke for him. In fact, I had broken an important Vinaya rule by attacking another monk, but that didn't bother me too much. Whether I had done right or wrong was not my immediate concern and I felt no particular guilt about the attack itself. It was all secondary to what then seemed to be the main issue.

What was the main issue? I had, probably for the first time in my life, totally lost control. That was something I'd never even done *before* I started my meditation studies. Why did it happen? How was it possible? I had to find the answer.

I meditated hour after hour, day after day, night after night. In my kuti, outside in the forest, walking, sitting, standing, lying down, getting absolutely nowhere. I tried using mantras: *Bud-dho . . . Om Mani Padme Hung*. Nothing. I tried counting the breaths, I watched the breath at the nose tip, I watched the abdomen rising and falling. I tried every meditation posture and technique I knew of but it was all a total waste of time. Although my initial rage had completely disappeared, a new anger and bitterness was growing inside me like a tumour. I could find no reason for it. I could hardly eat and was sleeping only a couple of hours at night. I became more and more frustrated and slipped into a deep depression. My thoughts even turned to leaving the monkhood.

On about the seventh night after the incident, way past midnight, I left my kuti and walked through the dark and silent monastery grounds to the Bote. The building was always kept locked but the key was left lying on a ledge just outside the door. I let myself in, pulling the heavy door shut behind me. I stood for a few minutes just inside the door, in total darkness and silence, wondering why I had come. There was nothing here, I told myself, it was just a building with a big bronze image of a man who had died centuries before. There was nothing here to console me; nothing that could help me understand my own feelings or motives. There was no refuge here from my anxiety and confusion. There was no Buddha here.

I walked slowly to the altar. I lit the two candles that had been placed there earlier in the evening in preparation for morning chanting. They did little to lighten the darkness of the small hall but they faintly illuminated the larger-than-life image on its plinth about five feet above me. The white enamel eyes, half-closed, reflected the light and seemed to stare down at me.

I lit three incense sticks and carefully placed them

in the brass, sand-filled container between the two candles. The fragrant smoke drifted upwards in the warm, still air, catching the candlelight and flowing around the image.

I knelt on the floor, sitting on my heels, simply looking up at the image. I made no bows. I wasn't at all sure what I was doing there or what I expected to find. Any answers could only be found on the inside, in my own mind, not in this building, nor anywhere else.

I felt overwhelmingly lonely and close to tears of despair. And yet, there was some comfort in simply looking at the image. I realised how much I loved and respected this man and everything that he was, everything that he became. I felt in some ways that I had not only let myself down, but I had let him down as well. He had devoted most of his life to teaching the Way, teaching people like me, but I hadn't really listened. I had listened with my ears, but not with my heart.

It was childish and illogical, I knew, but at that moment I didn't want him to have been just a man. I wanted him to be God. I *needed* him to be God. I needed a cosmic shoulder to cry on. I didn't have the strength to 'be my own refuge', as he had taught. I needed something else, someone else, to whom I could bow down and pray; from whom I could beg for help, or guidance, or forgiveness, or sanctuary. I didn't have the courage or strength to travel this path alone.

For a time I wallowed in self-pity. Tears quietly flowed and I let them flow, continuing to stare up at the image.

I stayed there for a long time, several hours. I hadn't made any conscious decision to meditate but my mind became focused on the image and I seemed to be slipping in and out of meditation almost naturally, as though it was beyond my control. The tears stopped and I felt the concentration level of my mind increasing, building up to a degree of focus that I had never experienced before. The self-pity evaporated, the need for a God evaporated, even the concept of 'Buddha' evaporated. Only the teaching remained.

The admonition of every meditation teacher I had ever known or read constantly passed through my mind: 'Let go . . . let go . . . let go. That's all there is to it. Just let go . . .'

Watch the emotions arise, bring them into full consciousness, observe and examine them dispassionately, see their ultimately delusory nature and let them go.

It all came slithering to the surface. I saw my earlier rage and realised it was just a front, an easily recognisable emotion obscuring much more complex issues. I saw beyond my anger, to my disappointments and frustrations. I saw the fixed views in my mind that led to those frustrations. I saw the ill will they had generated. I saw my doubts and I saw an intense and bitter resentment. And there lay the cause of my earlier outburst. Not resentment against the dog-beating monk in particular; this was resentment on a much bigger scale that just happened to condense into that man.

I resented Thai Buddhism. That was the truth of it. I had no resentment against the Thai lay-people at all, or the way they practised their religion. I resented that the teaching of the Buddha had lost its original purity and that the monks had not only failed to prevent it but through their own ignorance, superstition and greed had seemed to be party to it. Over the centuries, the teaching seemed to have been undermined and subtly altered. It had become so tainted, so corrupted, that it was now frequently hardly recognisable.

I resented what I saw as Thai Buddhism's non-Buddhist practices – the Animist and Brahmanist rites and rituals, the chants and magic charms, the 'sacred' string and 'holy water'. I resented what seemed to be its superficiality and the constant emphasis on 'making merit'. Developing generosity is perfectly in keeping with the Buddha's teaching, but 'making merit' to the lay-people now seemed to mean only making gifts to the monks and monasteries, encouraged by the greedy monks themselves. I resented that there seemed to be so little effort by most monks to teach the lay-people at anything more than the most superficial level, as though the Thai people were too stupid to fully understand anything but the simplest teachings. And I resented the empty and hypocritical blessings from so-called 'holy men'; men whose secret behaviour sometimes made a mockery not only of the Vinaya but of everything the Buddha taught. There had been many cases of highly respected monks who had been caught out and forced to disrobe for serious offences, usually of a sexual nature. The damage they had caused to the Sangha, to Buddhism and to the faith of the people was immeasurable. I had been a monk for only a short time, but as a layman I had stayed in dozens of monasteries all over Thailand and I had seen for myself.

Before I ordained, I thought the rites, rituals and superstitions of Thai Buddhism were merely 'icing on the cake' and that beneath the icing the real teaching of the Buddha remained intact. But I was beginning to suspect that Thai Buddhism was all cultural icing and had no cake at all.

I believe the Buddha taught the perfect philosophy. Presumably all other Buddhists believe the same. If we, as Buddhist monks, accepted that his teaching was perfect, how could we allow even superficial changes to it? If it was already perfect, it could not be made better, it could only be made less than perfect and therefore something different from what the Buddha taught. Was Buddhism enriched by these rituals and superstitions, or was it degraded?

All this resentment and doubt was writhing inside me like a venomous snake and I knew I could never make any personal progress, neither as a monk, nor in my meditation, while such feelings remained. I didn't really know if my doubts had any solid foundation and, even if they did, I knew I could do nothing about the situation. Perhaps at some time in the future, if I was ever skilled enough and understood enough, I would be able to teach Dhamma myself, but such a time was a very long way off.

But, I asked myself, if I resented Thai Buddhism so much, why did I live in Thailand? Why not just take

myself off to some other country where I wouldn't *see*?
I didn't leave because the country wasn't a problem and
the people weren't a problem. I was a Buddhist monk
and therefore, as far as I was concerned, I should be
able to live and practise what the Buddha taught
anywhere. I certainly wasn't going to run away from the
country and people that I loved just because their way
of practice was often not the same as mine. My resentment had little or nothing to do with the people and
was concerned only with our practice as monks.

But I also recognised that although I felt Thai
Buddhism had reached, in Ajahn Buddhadasa's words,
'rock bottom', my own thinking was also off course.
I wanted everything to be perfect in my little world. I
wanted everybody to practise the way I thought they
should practise. I wanted perfect monks in perfect
monasteries practising the perfect teaching in a perfect
way. And wasn't there some ego here as well? Was I
perhaps subconsciously thinking of other monks: 'You
don't practise correctly, therefore I am better than you?'
This needed deep investigation, but I had to face it all.
It wasn't something I could run away from. One can
run away from external conditions, but not from one's
own mind or the delusions and problems it contains.
They're always with you, wherever you go.

After hours of concentrated thought my mind was
reeling, but I had to let it all come to the surface. I had
to acknowledge and examine my doubts and resentment as dispassionately as possible before I could let
them go.

But to realise, to understand at an intellectual level, *what* I resented was not really the issue. Things are always as they are. To resent or approve makes no difference to the conditions themselves. The conditions were not affected, changed or improved by my resentment or approval. Only I suffered. I had to let go of this resentment. Easy to say, but how does anyone just let go?

Was letting go the same thing as *mai bpen rai* – 'it doesn't matter'? Perhaps, in an ultimate sense, nothing matters, but as a relative truth '*mai bpen rai*' was frequently just an excuse for apathy.

The candles had long burned away. I was sitting in total darkness and felt as though I was faced with a Zen riddle. 'Let go.'

'But how do you let go?'

'You just let go.'

'But how . . . ?'

The more I thought about it, the more difficult and paradoxical it became. Now my resentment, either as a fact or as an emotion, was no longer the issue. The letting go of it was the problem.

I realised I was actually clinging on to the idea of letting go. This was madness. I had been taught the mechanics of meditation, of letting go, but I didn't know how to do it. Had any of my teachers actually managed it? Yes, one certainly had. The man whose image loomed above me in the darkness. But many of my teachers had spent their whole lives in the robes studying, practising and teaching meditation. Ajahn Amara Thera was probably one of the most knowledgeable meditation masters in Thailand. It was demeaning to him to suggest that he hadn't taught me anything. But there was actually no way of teaching how to let go; there was no method and there were no words to adequately describe it. It had to be intuitively realised for oneself through meditation, rather than learned or taught.

So what had I been doing in all my hundreds of hours of meditation? It hadn't been a complete waste of time because I had learned many things, but I understood now that much of it was of relatively little importance. Yes, through my meditation I seemed to have cultivated some of the qualities that the Buddha taught should be developed: universal love, compassion, joy at others' happiness and even, until the incident of the dog-beating monk, equanimity. But I saw that to an extent I had only been fabricating those qualities. They weren't real, they weren't deep. I had, partly at least, not only been wrapping Peter Robinson in a robe but also encasing him in a shell. Beneath the surface, much of the same bitterness, frustrations, ill will, anger and petty jealousies, some of which I had never consciously recognised, were still boiling away like a volcano. And, like a volcano, they were sure to break out one day, destroying both the volcano and everything around it. This was no good at all. It had to stop.

I decided to rethink everything I believed I had learned about meditation and to start again. To find my own path. 'Look within,' said the Buddha, 'for thou art Buddha.' Look within. Yes, I would look within. I would look as deeply as I possibly could and I would continue looking until I had some answers, until I *knew* for myself.

The Buddha's final words came to me, as he lay dying under a sal tree in India more than 2,500 years ago. 'Monks, I address you now. Transient are all conditioned things. Strive on with diligence.' Strive on. The Buddha himself said that he only pointed the way and that it was up to each of us, up to me, to work out my own emancipation, to liberate myself. To strive on with energy, determination and conviction.

Several hours had passed and I was worn out. I was too tired to think any more and I decided to put all this aside for the moment, put it entirely out of my mind. Now I would go back to my kuti and make some coffee before I had to ring the morning bell. I started to get up from my kneeling position . . .

My mind let go.

I actually fell back to my knees. It felt as though someone had thrown a bucket of clean, cold water over me. Not over my physical body, but over my mind. For just a few moments, my mind seemed to empty itself of all the conflict and rubbish that was in there. Not just from the past week, but all of it, all forty-odd years of it.

I cannot adequately describe the feeling, but in those few moments my mind had seemed to be totally silent, totally still, totally *pure* and I had an overwhelming Insight into how things could be, how they were meant to be. This was not a spiritual or religious experience, nor any sort of enlightenment, at least not with a capital E; it was just a natural result of my practice. But, for the briefest moment and for the first time, I saw the potential goal. For the first time I knew what meditation was about.

Like an idiot, I tried to hold on to the feeling, so it disappeared as quickly as it had come. Nothing whatsoever should be clung to. For a while, I continued to sit in the darkness, before the darker shape above me. I examined my emotions, poked about in my mind. It was still all there, but different, like the sloughed-off skin of a snake. I could recognise the snake from the discarded skin, but the serpent had slithered away. I found I had no anger and no resentment of any kind, just a wonderful sense of peace and of *knowing*.

I think from that very moment, the rites and rituals of Thai Buddhism, and the activities and antics of some of the monks, ceased to concern me. I realised I was becoming too self-righteous and far too serious about it all. That was hardly the way to develop equanimity! But I saw that none of it really mattered, either relatively or ultimately. How others chose to practise needn't affect the way I practised. Each of us must follow his own path. Let it be . . .

I lit two new candles and three incense sticks and placed them mindfully on the altar. At some time in the past few hours my robe had slipped off. I carefully adjusted it, sat back on my heels, and intoned three times:

Namo Tassa Bhagavato Arahato Samma Sambuddhassa.
Homage to the Exalted One, Perfectly Enlightened
by Himself.

I bowed three times, with total conviction, and
quietly let myself out of the Bote.

The days, weeks and months that followed were to
see new energy and determination in my practice.
Although it is against the advice of most teachers, I
dropped the idea of sitting at specific times of day or
for specific periods. I had no formal meditation time
because I didn't want my practice to start becoming
routine or habitual; something I might take for granted.
I meditated instead at the times when I felt it would
be most productive for me and sat only until my meditation came to a natural end, whether that was a few
minutes or a few hours. Although I was determined, I
was equally determined that I wasn't going to force
myself to practise. I would not sit with clenched teeth
waiting for the time to pass simply so I could log up
more meditation hours. I also made much more effort
to make ordinary, routine little activities more a part of
my meditation, with the result that everything in my
life started to take on new meaning.

I probably spent less time in formal sitting meditation than before, but I believe it was time more
productively spent. I made no conscious effort to
regain the seemingly perfect stillness that I had briefly .

243

experienced in the Bote, but I did re-experience it on several occasions, always just as briefly and just as unexpectedly. I tried hard not to cling on to the feeling, nor to actively seek it, but was simply willing to accept that it was one result of my practice.

For a time I thought about leaving Wat Nahoob and going to one of the international forest monasteries in the north-east of Thailand, where most Western monks live. I had visited the monasteries before and they seemed more suited to the farang temperament than Thai monasteries. Monks at the international monasteries follow a stricter discipline than is found in most Thai monasteries and I believe the monks have considerably less contact with lay-people, nor the ceremonies they need and demand.

But to change my dull red robes to the brown of the forest tradition would only be that – a change of outside colour. The 'work' had to be done on the inside, regardless of the colour of the robe. I felt I could do that just as well at Wat Nahoob as anywhere else, perhaps better in some ways. Although at one of the international forest monasteries I would certainly find other monks who were practising well and who would be good examples to me, I didn't want to run the risk of subconsciously merely copying someone else's practice. That would only be cloaking myself in outward form. I genuinely wanted to come to grips with the defilements in my mind and, in a way, by placing myself in the more difficult environment of a 'normal' monastery, my defilements and hindrances became more obvious.

My resentment had been forced to the surface by my religious environment. What I resented was not the issue in the long term. It was the fact that I was capable of resentment on any issue that needed to be faced and dealt with. To live in a sort of meditative paradise with other Western monks, and with little contact with the lay-people would, I felt, be detrimental to my progress in some ways. I decided to stay where I was for the time being (though I did briefly allow myself the vanity of wearing the brown robes of a forest monk!).

My feelings of sabbai quickly returned at Wat Nahoob and the incident of the dog was soon forgotten. Strangely, the dog-beating monk became quite respectful to me after the incident and I never saw him hurt an animal again. Perhaps he had also reflected on his actions and motives, so maybe we both learned something. I learned to accept what was going on around me, though not in an apathetic way. Since there was nothing I could do to change things, any action or 'mind movement' became superfluous and I was determined that my equanimity should become genuinely deep.

The ceremonies that I sometimes had to be involved with were undoubtedly frequently Animist or Brahmanist in origin, but they didn't affect me. They were my duty; they weren't my personal practice. Perhaps that's how many Thai monks viewed them as well. I never capitulated and if I could get out of being involved with them, I would, but that didn't stop them happening. If anything, my own practice became better because of them. I started to watch myself much more closely, constantly looking for signs of wayward practices or the development of bad habits. But I had let go of my resentment.

That was all there was to it, really – just letting go.

21

As part of Giant's final year at the Buddhist university, he had to undertake social or teaching work in a rural area. That was what had brought him to Wat Nahoob in the first place. He had the idea of starting an English language school for the village children.

Most of the older children in the village attended the local high school. Although the curriculum included English, the standard of teaching was really quite poor. It has never ceased to amaze me how many students manage to graduate from Thai universities with Bachelor degrees in teaching English but are unable to speak more than a few words of the language. They usually know everything there is to know about English grammar, often more than many native speakers, but frequently they cannot hold even the simplest conversation. It is quite a problem in Thailand and is at least partly responsible for the number of private language schools that specialise only in teaching conversation skills. The problem is not only due to the poor standard of many English teachers, but also to prevailing government and social attitudes.

For many years, successive Thai governments have had, in theory at least, an 'equal education for all' policy. In practice, the big schools in the cities usually receive more financial support and better equipment, therefore attracting the best and most ambitious teachers. Socially and culturally, the majority of children in rural areas – certainly the majority of the boys – are not greatly inspired to break free from their rural environment. Although I think only a minority wanted to work on the land, most of the students at Giant's school were resigned to becoming rice farmers, just as the male members of their families had done for generations. Some of the girls had quite a different attitude, possibly because they had seen enough old ladies permanently bent double from the backbreaking work in the paddy fields. They often seemed more determined not to follow the traditional lifestyle.

The Thai government acknowledged in the mid-1990s that its approach to English teaching had been wrong. The government had stressed the importance of reading and grammatical knowledge and few high school curricula included speaking skills. The university entrance examination did not require students to speak, only to read, write and answer multiple choice questions, so most high school teachers had concentrated on teaching those aspects of the language. Students who graduated from university often found they then had to take private English lessons to learn how to converse before they could get a decent job. Most major companies in Thailand now insist that their employees, at management level anyway, are fluent in both spoken as well as written English. I once spoke at length with the head of the English department of a rural secondary school with more than 4,000 students. Receiving just nods and grunts in reply to my questions, I finally asked him how long he had been teaching English. It sounds like a joke, but he looked at his watch and said, 'Half past twelve.' The man had been an English teacher for sixteen years and could not hold even the simplest conversation.

Giant had it in mind that his language school would concentrate on communication skills – my job – while he would teach conversational grammar. The school was rather grandly to be called 'The Wat Nahoob Languages Centre'. Languages was plural because Giant planned that the school would also teach Thai. I would be the only student, albeit a reluctant one.

Giant set up the school in one of the monastery's open-sided salas, with a large whiteboard at one end and with desks and chairs borrowed from a local primary school. On the school's opening night we started our lessons with a class of more than forty students, ranging in age from five to thirty years old.

It was very hard and time-consuming work, especially for Giant. Besides giving his own lessons for two hours a night, five nights a week, he also had to attend my weekend communication classes to translate and explain my model conversations.

Most of our students could already read very well and I was initially impressed, until I realised that few understood a single word they were reading. I got hold of a textbook used in teaching English at the local high school. The book was full of mistakes and the very limited number of conversational exercises included such useful subjects as 'My holiday in New Mexico' and 'The history of the Apache Indians'. I was really quite appalled. By chance one day, I met an English teacher from the school and told her so. Me and my big mouth. It was to lead to me having 900 students in my conversation class, though not all at the same time, of course.

Unfortunately, the Wat Nahoob Languages Centre was not a resounding success, either at teaching English or Thai. Both Giant and I tried hard but, for various reasons, attendance started to decline. Some students stopped coming because they thought learning English would be fun, which we tried to make it, but it was also much harder work than they expected. Some stopped coming because after spending all day at their regular school they were too tired to spend all evening in study as well, or they had household or farming chores to do. If it was raining, *nobody* would show up, not even Giant. Frequently he had to be away from the monastery in the evening for six consecutive nights to chant at houses where there had been a bereavement. When he was away, I couldn't handle his classes on my own because the students and I had little mutual language, so I was unable to clearly explain the points Giant wanted to make.

The school drifted to a close after seven or eight months but it led to other things. The abbot of the main monastery in the district, Wat Somciel in Banpot town, decided to build a school for monks and novices where, besides learning the traditional subjects of Pali and Dhamma, the students would also be taught a normal school curriculum. That was an excellent idea. Many young novices, some of whom later become monks, are from very poor families. The families sometimes cannot afford to keep the children at home and often the boys have had little or no formal education beyond primary school. Few of them want to become novice monks but neither they nor their parents have much choice. To help the novices finish their six years of basic study and gain their high school certificates at least gives them the option of disrobing and finding some sort of work.

Teachers of Thai, maths, geography, history and science from various local schools volunteered to give lessons at the Wat Somciel school. Giant was invited by the abbot to be the headmaster. That meant he had to move from Wat Nahoob to Wat Somciel. I taught English at the Wat Somciel school for a while but my own teaching schedule was becoming so busy that I had to stop.

The teacher to whom I had voiced my opinions about the textbook came to see me at Wat Nahoob with several of her colleagues. She asked if I would give the occasional talk about Western culture to fourth, fifth and sixth formers at her school, since few of the students had ever met a Westerner before. I was happy to do so but, almost before I knew it, my occasional talk became a weekly event and then turned into a daily conversation class. Finally, I was teaching all day, five days a week – more hours than any other teacher at the school. (I was not, of course, being paid.) At first I didn't mind this heavy schedule at all. It was enjoyable and I have always been conscious that I rely totally on the kindness and generosity of Thai people for my food, shelter, robes and everything else in my life, so I was happy to be able to return something to them.

I prepared a teaching manual which set out what I thought were relevant model conversations for young people. Never mind the American Indians, I based my conversations on typical boy meets girl situations and similar subjects, using vocabulary which I thought was relevant and useful in my students' daily lives.

I had great fun but I soon discovered how difficult and demanding teaching in a classroom setting is. I started each of my new classes by trying to ascertain how much English each student already understood. That led to some quite hilarious and bizarre conversations. One of my favourite students, a little fat boy, was a particular trial to me. When I first met him, I asked, 'Can you speak English?'

'A little,' he replied in Thai. He added, 'I learned from watching American videos.'

Encouragingly, I said, 'What have you learned? Try to speak to me in English.'

'Fug you,' he replied.

Oh, I see. Arnold Schwarzenegger videos. We obviously

had to work on his pronunciation a little and an improvement in his vocabulary wouldn't go amiss either.

As my schedule and workload increased, I found that besides teaching in the daytime I was spending every evening preparing my lessons for the next day. I was also giving extra tuition to a few particularly keen students who would visit me at my kuti. I realised I was meditating and studying less and less and, at one point, not at all. Although on the one hand I was happy to teach, and thoroughly enjoyed it, a more selfish voice inside had started to ask whether I had really given up everything and travelled 10,000 kilometres to live in a garden shed and be an unpaid teacher. I began to question just how far my social responsibilities as a monk extended. By chance, Ajahn Amara Thera was in Thailand at that time. I went to Bangkok to pay my respects and took the opportunity to put the question to him.

He was quite adamant that I was doing too much English teaching and that my real duty as a monk was to increase my knowledge of Dhamma and meditation. If I wanted to continue teaching, he advised that I should find a middle way between my own studies and my teaching schedule. I agonised for a long time. I wanted to help my students but at the same time needed to make progress as a monk. Finally though, the decision was taken out of my hands. The school director decided that English conversation was not a useful subject for his students and that they should concentrate on the requirements of the university entrance examination. My course was dropped.

His decision caused something of a fuss at the school amongst the more progressive teachers, as well as some of the students, but I was happy to accept the situation. The best students, as well as some of the teachers, continued to practise their conversation skills at weekends at my kuti. I actually preferred that to teaching in the classroom. In all my many classes at the school, there always seemed to be a small rowdy element who simply didn't want to learn or who had resigned themselves to being rice farmers. They saw no practical use in speaking English. The rowdy element made it difficult for me to teach and caused problems for those students in class who really did want to learn. Maybe I'm just not cut out to be a schoolteacher.

The students who came for lessons at my kuti were very keen and usually already had a good standard of English. Whilst talking to the students on a one-to-one basis, I got to know some of them very well.

I was greatly saddened by some of the things I learned about them. All my students were very bright, the brightest at the school, and they all wanted to continue their education at a higher level. Unfortunately, because of their parents' poverty, few of them had any chance at all of going on to universities or colleges of higher education. Even if they passed the entrance examinations, they would still not be able to take up their deserved places. It seemed such a waste, and so unfair, that potential graduates should be forced to work in the paddy fields or in mundane jobs just because of their poor backgrounds. I very much wanted to help, but I had little money of my own left, no income, and no way of raising funds to help them.

The top student in the school was named Seckson and his was a particularly sad case. He lived at the school full-time because his parents couldn't even afford his daily bus fares. The school had an old house in the grounds where half a dozen very poor students lived, doing odd jobs around the school to pay for their keep. Seckson was a night watchman. One of his teachers was generously paying his school expenses and Seckson's classmates gave him any cast-off bits of uniform they didn't need any more. Seckson wanted to study for a degree in physics and there was no doubt in anybody's mind that he would pass the university entrance examination. His dream went further than just a Bachelor degree – he wanted a PhD – but he knew it was just a dream. He had resigned himself to following a different career when he finished high school at the end of that term: somebody had offered him a job in a petrol station, cleaning car windscreens.

Ajahn Amara Thera had made it clear to me that a monk really should not involve himself to any great extent in the affairs of the lay-people, but I was determined that Seckson should not throw his potential future away. I didn't know at the time that it was a decision that was going to have far-reaching effects for hundreds of students.

'No,' I told him. 'You are going to university.'

And I was going to London.

22

My reason for going to London again so soon after my first visit was not specifically to seek help for Seckson. I'd received a letter from a friend telling me that my stepfather had suffered a heart attack. After my mother died some years before, my stepfather had lived alone. Since he was in his seventies, I felt I should do whatever I could to help him. Unfortunately, I left it too late. Unknown to me he died about a week before I arrived in England.

It was late February, England was blanketed in snow and it was bitterly cold. For me, coming from the beginning of the hot season in Thailand, the change in the weather was so extreme that I quickly became unwell. I had little money and could not travel to see my friends, most of whom now lived outside of London. I stayed in the monastery most of the time, helping the other monks and talking with my old friend, Phra Maha Laow.

I was very happy to re-meet some of the Thai and

European lay-people who devoted so much of their time in supporting the monks and monastery. During my conversations with some of them, I mentioned that I was now teaching English and that I was concerned about the future of one of my students. Within hours of my arrival at the monastery, various lay-people had pledged not only sufficient money to ensure Seckson's university education, but also a surplus to establish a small trust fund to help other disadvantaged students in similar circumstances. The fund, the Students' Education Trust, grew from there and was later to become supported by generous and compassionate people from all over the world. (At the time of publication of this edition, 1000 students are receiving scholarships or other support.) With the trust fund's continuous support, Seckson completed his Bachelor degree in physics and went on to gain his Master degree too. He later became a university lecturer and, using his own financial resources, studied for a PhD in Nuclear Physics – good progress for someone who once saw his future as cleaning car windscreens.

Whilst staying at Wat Buddhapadipa I had a quite extraordinary experience which I really can't explain. If anybody else told me this story, I would be able to explain it away, finding all sorts of logical alternatives to what the storyteller thought they saw. But I am convinced: I saw a ghost.

I use the word 'ghost', although that to me implies a sort of rather pathetic white-sheeted, chain-rattling apparition that lurks in dark places and floats out crying 'boo!' to frighten little children. I'd never believed in such things and still don't, but it wasn't like that at all. I saw something that I cannot explain and, whatever it was, it scared the life out of me.

Several of the monks at Wat Buddhapadipa claimed that the main house was haunted. Phra Maha Laow told me that on many occasions, late at night, monks had heard something moving and snuffling outside their bedroom doors, followed by a soft tapping on the door. None of them ever saw anything though, or had the experience that I had.

The house has three floors. On the ground floor are public rooms, on the first floor are the monks' bedrooms and two bathrooms, and on the floor above are what were originally staff rooms, now also used by monks. It was the middle floor that the monks claimed was haunted. That floor has a long corridor running down the middle, with rooms either side. On one side, the rooms overlook the rear grounds while those on the other side overlook the road. At both ends, the corridor turns a corner and leads to a bathroom and there is a staircase at each end leading to the other floors. Above each stairwell is a window, the only natural source of light for the corridor. At night, the corridor is poorly lit by only one small electric light which is usually not turned on anyway.

I was staying in Phra Maha Laow's room, which was at one end of the corridor, but we used the bathroom at the other end, a distance of about twelve metres or so.

At about 9pm one evening, I walked down the almost

dark, unlit corridor to the bathroom. After I'd show-ered, I came out and turned the corner to walk back down the corridor to the bedroom – and stopped dead. At the far end of the corridor, slightly illuminated by the light from the window, was a very large, very black shape. The shape was more than two metres tall and almost round, but with a slight bulge on top, like a head that was half-absorbed into the body of the thing. The shape was fat and almost filled the corridor from side to side but I had the impression it wasn't solid, or perhaps only as solid as thick, oily smoke. There was no question of calmly trying to analyse logically what the image might be – a shadow, a trick of the light or even a person – I just *knew* it was none of those things and I was instantly terrified.

The thing didn't move for about thirty seconds, but then soundlessly started to move very slowly down the corridor towards me. It had no arms or legs that I could see and seemed to be drifting just an inch or so above the carpeted floor. I stood almost paralysed in the middle of the corridor as the thing got closer and closer. Though terrified, I knew that I was directly in its path and felt that was not the best place to be. I moved quickly to one side of the corridor and pressed myself into the wall as the thing continued its approach. It drew level with me. I ought to be able to say at this point that I felt the air turn icy cold or smelt rotting flesh or something, but there was nothing like that at all. The apparition simply passed within inches of me and drifted around the corner. The instant it was out of sight, I ran down the corridor without looking back and flung myself into Phra Maha Laow's room, slamming the door behind me and almost scaring the life out of him. I leant against the door as my legs gave out, and I slid to the floor.

And that was it. For the next few evenings we were both quite nervous of going to the bathroom and always turned the corridor light on, but I didn't see the thing again. But I saw it, I *know* I saw it.

Besides seeing a ghost, I also had a surprise reunion. The very first time I visited Wat Buddhapadipa I had met a young man, John something, who told me he was soon to leave England to ordain as a monk in Thailand. I saw John briefly at the monastery a few more times and then not again. I forgot all about him. During that trip to England, John turned up at Wat Buddhapadipa wearing the purple and yellow robes of a Tibetan monk. We recognised each other immediately and he told me of his time in the orange robes of a Theravadan monk in Thailand.

Many of John's experiences reflected mine exactly. In his case, he reached a point where he became so disillusioned with Thai Buddhism that he disrobed. But he never had any doubts about the Buddha's teaching and was determined to find a teacher from whom he could learn what he called the 'real' Dhamma. He found his teacher in Scotland, at the Samye-Ling Tibetan Buddhist Centre, and he ordained as a novice monk in the Tibetan tradition. That was a coincidence, because I was also at that time finding an interest in other forms of Buddhism besides Theravada. I had recently been reading a book about Chinese Zen and found it fascinating, though much of the teaching seemed so paradoxical it was beyond me.

John and I sat chatting in the garden of Wat Buddhapadipa for hours and it was a lovely meeting, but I remember thinking what a bizarre picture we must have presented. Me in my orange robes and John in his purple and yellow, sitting on a wall in a snow-covered English garden. I had to tell John, or Dav as he was now named, that I really didn't like his purple shoes very much. He didn't answer, but merely looked at my bright yellow, rubber sandals.

Some time later, after I returned to Thailand, Dav sent me a note in which he included a Tibetan teaching about impermanence: 'Like stars, mists and candle flames, mirages, dew drops and water bubbles. Like dreams, lightning and clouds. In that way will I view all composite phenomena.' I liked that very much and found a large, beautifully-shaped piece of wood, worm-eaten but still with the bark on one edge, smoothed and polished it and asked Giant to paint the words on the wood. (Giant's English handwriting was much neater than mine.) I hung the board on a tree over my meditation platform in the forest.

Because I was feeling generally so unwell, I decided to stay in London only a short time. If I had known how ill I actually was, I would probably have sought medical help in England. I returned to Thailand, happy that I was carrying good news for Seckson but feeling very ill indeed. Once back in my little kuti at Wat Nahoob, I took an aspirin, went to bed, and stayed there.

My illness continued for a couple of weeks, I think, until one afternoon I woke up and found myself in Banpot's tiny hospital. I was in a private room and Seckson was asleep under the bed. He had been living in the hospital for many days, taking care of me while I was treated for 'food poisoning'. He was actually my nurse, for Thai rural hospitals are frequently very short-staffed and it is often left to the family not only to feed the patient but also to change their bedding, and even to see to their various drips, of which I seemed to have plenty.

The only resident doctor at the hospital was very nice and very young, just out of medical school and repaying one of the terms of his government study loan by working up country for a couple of years. I think he was a little nervous about treating such a rarity as a Phra Farang, as though my internal organs might be different from other people's. After a few days, he decided I didn't have food poisoning at all and started treating me for bronchitis. I actually had pneumonia. Happily, a few weeks later, by which time I was in the province's main hospital in Nakhon Sawan City, my pneumonia had largely cleared up.

I was staying on the top floor of the hospital in a ward reserved for monks. On the first day that I felt strong enough to get out of bed, I took a short stroll around the ward and some of the corridors outside.

From one of the windows I could see the top of a huge, ancient, brick chedi and the multi-tiered roof of a very grand-looking Bote. On the top of a tree-covered mountainous hill behind the monastery gleamed a gigantic, golden Buddha image, staring out across the countryside, though the impressive effect was somewhat diminished by five very tall red and white transmitting aerials nearby. I asked a nurse what the monastery was called. 'Wat Khao Kob,' she said. I knew immediately that the Monastery of Frog Mountain would be my next home.

Why should I want to move from the pleasant and quiet environment of Wat Nahoob to what was obviously a big and important monastery in the middle of a noisy city? Partly, at least, because of a passing comment Dav had made in the gardens of Wat Buddhapadipa. He said that after a couple of years as a monk in Thailand I might find myself becoming complacent. I made no reply but his words set off alarm bells in my mind. Complacent. The word is actually anathema to me and throughout my life, whatever situation, environment or relationship I have found myself in, I have always been careful to watch out for this state of unreasonable self-satisfaction.

Lying in my hospital bed, I had taken the opportunity to look objectively at my life at Wat Nahoob and I'd realised I *was* becoming complacent. I was also sabbai, but that was quite a different thing.

At Wat Nahoob I had everything I needed: a delightful little kuti in a beautiful forest setting, I admired and respected my abbot and I got on well with the village people. I had all the food I needed and all the time I needed. I was slowly beginning to learn some of the more important chanting and I had cleared away my doubts. All those things helped create my feeling of sabbai. The complacency was really the other side of the same coin, the darker side of sabbai, and for me it was a definite danger, a potential hindrance, for it could lead to torpor and apathy. A monk should always be satisfied with things and situations just as they are but not to the point where his mind becomes stagnant.

I liked Wat Nahoob and everything and everybody connected with my life there, but I felt no clinging or attachment for it and was quite prepared to move if, by doing so, I could make progress, or stop myself regressing.

Even before I saw the roof of Wat Kob's Uposatha Hall, I knew it would soon be time to leave Wat Nahoob, but I had no idea at all about where I should go. Back to Bangkok? No, my physical health wasn't really good enough to subject it to the capital's noxious fumes. A big monastery or another small one? Country or city? It didn't matter, as long as I shattered my complacency. The Frog Temple would do as well as any other.

As things turned out, it did very well indeed.

23

Wat Kob's official and modern name is Wat Worranatbanpot but most people know it by its original name. For about 700 years, the monastery has been a place of pilgrimage for those with the energy to climb the 437 steps leading to the hilltop and who want to pay respect to the ancient images and footprint of the Buddha that reside there. Since 1991, Wat Kob has been a Royal Monastery, one of many that are supported by HM the King.

The main part of the monastery is now at the base of Khao Kob and the upper part is occupied by only a handful of monks who want to be isolated from the busy city far below. During the Rains Retreat, there may be as many as one hundred monks and novices living in the lower part of the monastery. A visitor could easily think that they are two quite separate monasteries. A large area of land at the base of the mountain has been used by the provincial authority to build a massive town hall and offices, thus effectively cutting the monastery in two.

Wat Kob is big, covering an area of more than forty-six acres, though most of that comprises the mountain. It is an important monastery and always has been. An engraved stone was found there which records how a group of Thai monks brought two stone Buddha 'footprints' from Ceylon in about 1220, a gift from the government of that country in gratitude for Thailand's help in re-establishing Buddhism there. The right foot-print is at Wat Trapang Thong in Sukhothai and the stone records that the other was placed on the moun-taintop of Pak Phra Bang, which was the old name for Nakhon Sawan. The stone is now in the National Museum in Bangkok.

Of course, the 'footprints' are not actually the Buddha's footprints. The Buddha is believed to have had curious designs or whorls on the soles of his feet. Natural rock formations, sometimes of very large size, are occasionally found which resemble these designs. Alternatively, footprints may be cast in concrete and covered in gold leaf.

Another engraved stone found at Wat Kob records that the monastery was originally built by Phraya Ban Muang, a ruler of the kingdom of Sukhothai, in memory of his brother who died on the mountain. When he established Wat Kob, Phraya Ban Muang built chedis, viharns and Buddha images and the monastery was surrounded by a lotus-filled moat, bamboo groves and Bo trees. The bamboo groves and moat are long gone, but some of the ancient buildings and relics remain.

The chedi that I had seen from the hospital window

is from the Sukhothai period and contains the relics of the brother of Phraya Ban Muang. The chedi is about thirty-two metres high and was originally covered in plaster. The plaster has almost all fallen off now, revealing the dull-red bricks of the chedi's construction. The chedi looks in imminent danger of collapse; it seems to have twisted about halfway up and now leans at a definite angle. In an ancient viharn nearby is a magnificent thirty-eight-feet-long wooden reclining Buddha image from the Sukhothai period. The wood is petrified and the image is believed to have been carved from a single piece of teak, then covered in plaster and gold leaf.

There's an odd superstition surrounding the image. It sounds laughable but many local people take it seriously. Apparently, about fifty years ago, a woman claimed that she left her baby nearby while she paid her respects to the image. When she had finished her bows, she discovered that her baby had disappeared. She concluded that the image must have eaten it. Although the story seems somewhat unlikely to me, local people have told me that pregnant women and mothers with very young babies generally won't go anywhere near the image.

The monastery's huge new Uposatha Hall dwarfs a 600-year-old tiny Bote that stands nearby. The old Bote looks like a small English village church and inside is a frieze of delightful mural paintings showing scenes from the Buddha's life. The murals were added only about a hundred years ago and were painted in a particularly naïve style, as though by a child. Even the old

Bote is not the original Uposatha Hall of Wat Kob. In another area nearby are older stone arches that mark the *sima,* or consecrated ground, of an earlier Bote, probably the original one. Nothing else of the building remains.

Despite the monastery's obvious importance, little is known of its early history. It was deserted for many centuries but nobody seems to know why. Its buildings and images, already centuries old, became ruins overgrown by shrubs and trees. Until Luang Por Tong arrived.

Luang Por Tong must have been an extraordinary monk. He was born in 1856 and became a monk when he was twenty-one. In 1882 he was wandering around the country and visited the ruins of Wat Kob. The people of the town asked him to stay there for one Pansa and he agreed. He stayed for fifty-nine years until he died in 1941, aged eighty-five. Luang Por Tong made it his life's work to begin the restoration of Wat Kob and it is largely due to him that the remaining ancient buildings are in such good condition.

Legends have grown up around Luang Por Tong's name and even when he was alive many people believed he had supernatural powers. He was a very strict and devout monk, always wearing robes taken from a coffin just before the funeral pyre was lit, always living at the base of a tree and never failing to walk on alms round. Even when he could no longer walk unaided, he had a samlor to take him on his regular alms route each morning.

There is a story that he was on a scaffold repairing

the very top of the old chedi when he fell thirty metres to the ground. He was completely unharmed and immediately climbed back up the scaffold. Another story relates how he could miraculously shorten distances. He was seen on alms round in villages many miles from Wat Kob, though it was quite impossible for him to have got there by any normal means. Yet another story says that he could not be photographed – the film always came out blank. There is only one known photograph of him, for which he gave permission, and that is today on the abbot's sermon seat.

Just outside Wat Kob's present boundary wall, on what was once presumably the monastery's land, there is a very large, deep pond full of enormous old turtles and huge catfish. There is a story that Luang Por Tong dug this pond himself, using his alms bowl to carry the earth away.

Luang Por Tong left another small mystery, two in fact, named Ta Kob and Yai Khiat. They are the life-sized stone figures of a grandfather (Ta Kob) and grandmother (Yai Khiat). They are really very strange indeed and originally sat in small shelters in front of the old Bote, though they have recently been relocated to shelters near to the chedi. They seem to have come to represent everybody's ancestors, especially for the Chinese population of Nakhon Sawan. On festival days, lay-people leave gifts of food, tobacco and betel nuts for them. Keeping up with the times, someone has recently presented grandfather with a pair of spectacles (and more recently, a gold Batman mask!) but there is no record to show who the figures actually represent or why Luang Por Tong had them made. It seems likely that they represent the original owner of the land on which Wat Kob stands. It is recorded that his name was Kob, so possibly his wife was named Khiat.

Even today, many local people attribute supernatural power to anything associated with Luang Por Tong. In the new Bote is a display case with Luang Por Tong brass and bronze images for sale, as well as amulets to be worn around the neck. These amulets, some claim, can protect the devout wearer from bullets. Laughable, of course, but there is a series of twelve photographs in the Bote taken in 1994 that show the arrest of a gunman after he shot a rival in Nakhon Sawan City. Other photographs show a doctor removing several bullets from the victim's chest. The victim is smiling and proudly showing his Luang Por Tong amulet, bent by the assailant's bullets, and he appears to have been only superficially injured . . .

The ashes of Luang Por Tong are now enshrined in the Bote, together with a painting of the old monk. In the monastery grounds is a shrine with an almost life-sized image of Luang Por Tong and many people go there every day to pay their respects to his memory.

Luang Por Tong is the first recorded abbot of Wat Kob. The second was Phra Khru Thammakhun (abbot from 1942–1963), but it is with the third and present abbot that the modern history of Wat Worranatbanpot begins. As Luang Por Tong saved Wat Kob from total ruin, so Phra Suthee Thammasopon has not only carried on his predecessor's work, but has also built upon it, to make the monastery the important religious centre it is today.

When Luang Por Suthee became abbot in 1964, he saw in the spacious grounds the opportunity to create a modern, working monastery which retained the traditions of the past but with all the facilities that a modern monastery needs. His vision included a full-sized school for monks and novices, where they could study Dhamma, the Vinaya and the Pali language. He saw the need for modern accommodation, simple and functional and befitting the monks' lifestyle, but clean and easy to maintain. He wanted to build a new sala to accommodate thousands of people, and a new Bote, big enough for the large number of monks and novices who would eventually live at the monastery. With the willing support of the lay-people he has achieved it all, and more.

The new Uposatha Hall was completed in 1990 and has something of the grandness of a small cathedral. It is one of the tallest Botes I have seen, though its outside dimensions are misleading. Half the height of the building is attic space and inside it seems considerably smaller than from the outside. The outside decoration has all the ornateness usually seen on Thai Botes but, again, that is misleading and inside it is simpler than most. The floor is of grey, polished marble, much of it raised about eight inches to make a higher level for the monks than for novices or lay-people. The walls are painted cream and are unadorned by murals. The main Buddha

271

image is large and modern and the altar decorations are simple and subdued. There are lots of candles and flowers but, unlike in many Thai Botes, the altar is not cluttered with all sorts of strange religious artefacts.

The present abbot was also responsible for the building of the monastery's crematorium, the first I had ever seen with a double oven. Funerals are an important source of revenue for any monastery in Thailand and one the size of Wat Kob needs a huge income just for its maintenance and upkeep. Although the monastery relies greatly on the income, the abbot has made a deliberate policy of charging as little as possible for funerals. Consequently, neither oven in the crematorium gets much chance to cool down and the building, although only about twenty years old, is already in need of replacement.

A large, air-conditioned library has also been built and contains not only the monastery's collection of religious books, but also books of a more general nature too. Thailand doesn't have much of a network of public libraries, so the abbot decided to open the monastery's library to anybody who wanted to use it.

Luang Por Suthee also has his own ideas about the environment.

Unfortunately, many monasteries in Thailand are simply not clean or tidy. A few are beautifully kept but others are like rubbish tips. Luang Por Suthee was determined that his monastery would not go the same way and it hasn't. I have visited many hundreds of monasteries in Thailand in cities, towns and villages. Wat Kob, although not exactly beautiful, is one of the cleanest and neatest of them all. It even has its own skip for rubbish – the only one I have seen outside of Bangkok – and it is changed every week.

Luang Por Suthee has carried on Luang Por Tong's work by having the old Bote renovated and the viharn containing the reclining Buddha has been rebuilt to give better protection to the ancient image. He has established a walled meditation garden, thick with mango trees, with a few small kutis for monks who want to live in isolation from the main part of the monastery.

I didn't know any of that as I stood staring out of the hospital window. I only knew that I wanted to live at the monastery. Doing that wouldn't be a certainty until I paid my respects to the abbot and asked his permission. A visit was in order.

Mit, one of my students from Nahoob, studied at a high school in the city and stayed at a friend's house close to the school during the week. The house was in a lane that ran along one side of the monastery, so Mit was quite familiar with the layout of the wat.

Mit's English was very good and after I was discharged from the hospital I asked him to accompany me on a visit to Wat Kob to act as interpreter, in case the abbot couldn't speak English. Mit told me that the monastery was sometimes locally known as 'the frog that eats people', on account of the number of cremations held there.

We walked into Wat Kob and by chance met the abbot almost immediately. I made a respectful wai but, before Mit or I could say anything, the abbot asked, 'Are you better now?'

'Yes, thank you,' I replied, wondering how on earth he had known I had been ill.

It transpired that the abbot already knew just about everything about me, at least as a monk. For many years, Ajahn Waow had been the abbot's *looksit*, or attendant, when they both lived at Wat Somciel in Banpot town and the two were close friends. I also didn't know at the time that the abbot is a very high-ranking monk indeed, with the title *Chao Khun*. I have heard this title translated as 'Lord', or 'Excellency', so I guess it's a bit like an English knighthood. In recent times, the abbot has also been promoted to the rank of *Chao Canna*, 'Lord of the Province', with overall responsibility for all Nakhon Sawan's monasteries – more than 600 of them.

I asked the abbot if he would allow Mit and me to wander around for a while and he gave his permission. I made another wai and said goodbye.

We had only been walking around for a few minutes when a monk approached us and, speaking in English, invited us to his room for a chat. His name was Phra Maha Sutont and at that time he had been a monk for about twenty years, so he was quite senior. His English was very good but, well, a bit odd sometimes. He had cleverly taught himself by listening to the BBC World Service on the radio and from a couple of very old books of idioms, one English and one American. He would occasionally call me 'my dear fellow', or exclaim, 'shucks!', sometimes in the same sentence, but we initially got on well. On that very first meeting he suggested I should consider living at Wat Kob. We could be 'buddies', he said.

During the next couple of weeks, I made several visits to the monastery and on a couple of occasions stayed overnight in one of the new kuti blocks, in a room next to Phra Maha Sutont's. These two-storey buildings look much like modern apartment blocks and each of the four buildings contains sixteen single rooms, as well as communal showers. The rooms are large and each has parquet flooring and mosquito screens at the doors and windows. They also have security grills, which are unfortunately very necessary in Thailand, even in monasteries.

It was about a month before the beginning of the Pansa. Many of the new Rainy Season monks had already ordained and were living in the kuti blocks, together with their stereos, TVs and radios. I had no objection to that but I thought the noise level at night was sometimes inappropriate for a monastic environment. In fact, it was horrendous. I knew I wouldn't be happy staying in the new block long-term but I had already made up my mind that I would live at the monastery. I asked Phra Maha Sutont if we could request the abbot's permission.

That was a little bit awkward for me because I hadn't yet told Ajahn Waow I would be leaving Wat Nahoob. I wasn't sure which step should come first. I didn't want to offend Ajahn Waow by telling him that I had already made new arrangements without his prior knowledge, but at the same time also didn't want to tell him I was moving before I had a new place confirmed, just in case the abbot of Wat Kob said no. These situations can be quite difficult in Thailand, where one always has to consider the 'face' of others.

Phra Maha Sutont and I went to the abbot's kuti and I made my request. After a few moments' deliberation, the abbot said I was welcome and that I could live in one of the kuti blocks, or in the mango garden, or choose some other empty kuti in the monastery grounds. I already knew exactly which kuti I wanted. At the back of the monastery and fairly isolated from the main areas were three large, old wooden kutis, all very ramshackle and in need of repair. The kutis stood quite high above the ground on concrete legs and the space beneath each had been walled up to make three small rooms. Two of the kutis were occupied but the middle of the three had apparently been empty for several years. Later, I found out why. One of the former residents, a novice monk, had fallen down the steep stairs leading to the upper part and had died after his head split open on the concrete below. That was enough to ensure that the other residents moved straight out and nobody would ever live there again.

Despite the fact that the old kuti was falling to bits, I thought it looked charming and I was sure it would be quieter than a room in one of the kuti blocks. The abbot and Phra Maha Sutont tried to dissuade me from the idea because many temple boys lived in the tiny rooms under the three kutis and, said the abbot, they were very noisy indeed. I doubted that they could be noisier than some of the new monks, but didn't say so. My mind was made up; the old kuti would be my new home.

During my chat with the abbot, I explained that I was worried Ajahn Waow might be offended because I hadn't told him of my planned move from Wat Nahoob. I didn't want to appear to have been under-handed. The abbot told me not to worry and that he would telephone Ajahn Waow to explain. He did later telephone and although Ajahn Waow never mentioned anything about it, I think he was a little offended. On my last day at Wat Nahoob he wasn't around, so I never even had the opportunity at the time to say goodbye, or to thank him for his great kindness to me over the previous year. That was probably the only thing that saddened me as my few belongings and I were driven out of the monastery in a villager's pick-up truck.

It was to be several years before I made a return visit to Nahoob. I'm not sure why; it's only about forty kilometres from the city and it isn't a difficult journey to make. On the day I left Nahoob, many villagers had made me promise to return often. I said I would and I sincerely meant to. At that time, I even had the thought that I would probably end my days at Wat Nahoob. Maybe I will. Anyway, the fact is that I was to become so absorbed in my life at Wat Worranatbanpot that I somehow never got round to going back for a long time.

When I eventually did make a return visit, it was for the funeral of Phra Sert, the monk who had beaten the dog. In retrospect, I was quite grateful to Phra Sert. That whole incident with the dog had forced me to take a very objective look at some things that were going on in my mind at the time and had helped me straighten myself out. Phra Sert died from stomach cancer and, from what villagers told me, had endured more than a year of suffering with great fortitude.

In the years I had been away from Wat Nahoob, I'd heard only a little news about the monastery and village. I hadn't seen Giant at all during that time, though I knew he was still the headmaster of the school at Wat Somciel, and was very highly regarded for the job he was doing. Although working at Wat Somciel, he had returned to live at Wat Nahoob and about twenty of his novice students had gone with him, so the community at the monastery had grown considerably.

The occasion of Phra Sert's funeral was to be the last time I met Giant as a monk. He disrobed soon after and got married, though he continued to live at Nahoob and remained the headmaster of Wat Somciel's school.

When I arrived at Wat Nahoob for the funeral, I was very surprised at the changes in the little monastery. The old kuti block in which I had originally stayed had been demolished and a rather grand new one had replaced it. Sadly, most of 'my' little forest had gone as well, to make way for even more kutis. Besides the large number of novices in residence, about ten monks were also living at the monastery, so space was at a premium. My old kuti was no longer screened by the forest and I could see it clearly from the crematorium, but I didn't go over there to have a closer look. I've never been one for maudlin sentimentality. The Uposatha Hall had been repainted and there were many other small changes and improvements. Even the ladder in the bell tower had been replaced with a new and safer one.

One thing that hadn't changed was Ajahn Waow, except that he had become even more widely respected and well known in surrounding districts. He welcomed me in a very friendly way and I felt a great surge of affection for him.

I would like to have had the opportunity to stroll around the village but there wasn't time. Anyway, almost all the villagers were attending the funeral so it wasn't really necessary. Without exception, the villagers seemed genuinely pleased to see me again and I was delighted to be received so warmly. Many asked when I would be returning to live at Wat Nahoob. The only person who wasn't in evidence was my old friend, Yom My. I met his wife, Noi, who told me that My was drinking very heavily and spent most of each day sleeping. I sought him out and found him lying flat on his back under a tree. He was so drunk he couldn't even get up to greet me.

Despite the fact that I was revisiting Wat Nahoob for a funeral, I had a very pleasant few hours there. Being back in the little monastery, I realised how important a part it had played in my life as a monk and how much I owed to Ajahn Waow, Giant, and the village people. Even though I may visit only rarely, I will never forget my year at Wat Nahoob. But I have moved on.

24

When I moved to Wat Kob, I spent my first two weeks living in the kuti block, in the room next to Phra Maha Sutont's. I couldn't move straight into my chosen kuti at the back of the monastery because it really wasn't habitable. I needed to spend a couple of weeks working, simply to get it clean.

Within days of arriving at Wat Kob, I realised that Phra Maha Sutont had a few problems that were apparent in some rather odd behaviour. None of the other monks seemed to like him much and he seemed determined to isolate me so that he would be my only friend. He was in and out of my room every five minutes and just wouldn't leave me alone. At first I thought he was just being friendly and welcoming, but I soon realised that he had his own agenda for me. I even found a notice that he had written in Thai and pinned to my door, telling the other monks that they weren't allowed into my room. The note had apparently been signed by me.

Even within my first couple of weeks at Wat Kob, I felt that some of the other monks were not very happy with my presence. Some seemed to actively dislike me. That wasn't Section 5 paranoia again. I was to find out some months later, when I did succeed in making a friend, that Phra Maha Sutont had been telling the other monks that I didn't think they practised well and that I considered them no better than buffaloes. That's a major insult in Thailand. Not a word of it was true, but it doesn't matter now. I survived, Phra Maha Sutont didn't.

It had also become very obvious to me that Phra Maha Sutont was extremely nervous of being in the abbot's company. He almost seemed to be frightened of the abbot. Whenever the abbot and I needed to meet, with Phra Maha Sutont as translator, he would be sweating and visibly trembling, though I couldn't see why at all. To me, the abbot seemed to be quite a jolly fellow. I described him to a friend in England as being a bit like Father Christmas, though without the hair and beard, of course.

I wasn't at all sure how I should relate to the abbot. We were at extreme and opposite ends of the Sangha hierarchy. I was a new and very junior monk and he was very senior and held high religious office. I'm not being critical of Thai people when I say that they seem to be very impressed by titles, uniforms and social status. I'm not impressed by such superficialities and, probably like most Westerners, I believe respect has to be earned. I have met many senior monks and have always gladly shown the correct level of outward respect for them, triple bows and all that, as befitted our relative stations, but that was only outward form. I didn't know them. Before ordaining, I'd learned a hard lesson from a very well known, greatly respected and much-loved monk named Phra Yantra. At the time, he seemed to be the epitome of what a Buddhist monk should be. He fooled me, and millions of Thai people too. He turned out to be a liar, a cheat and a womaniser and was forced to flee to America. I won't make that mistake again. I have no more pedestals.

Soon after I'd settled into my new kuti, the abbot made his first visit, accompanied by Phra Maha Sutont to translate. The abbot lowered himself into a rickety old chair I'd found, while Phra Maha Sutont and I sat on the floor. The abbot regarded me silently but benevolently for a minute or two and then said, 'You're very thin.'

That is true. I looked pointedly at his rotund belly and replied, 'And you, Venerable Sir, are very fat,' equally truthfully.

Phra Maha Sutont began to quiver nervously.

'I'm not fat,' said the abbot, and pulled up his ungsa to reveal a very round belly hanging over the top of his under-robe.

'Yes, you are,' I said, and poked his belly with my finger, causing both it and Phra Maha Sutont to shake violently.

I'm sure Phra Maha Sutont wasn't used to hearing the abbot spoken to in that way and he looked about ready to fling himself off my balcony. The abbot roared with laughter. I think he might have found it quite refreshing to be spoken to so plainly.

From that moment, my relationship with the abbot seemed to be established. He frequently tells people that I am not a 'normal' monk, though quite what he means by that, I'm not sure!

Since that first meeting, I have gradually developed a very great deal of respect and affection for the abbot and make a point of showing it with a triple bow whenever the opportunity arises. I enjoy it because I genuinely think he deserves respect, not because he is the abbot and my boss, nor because he is a *Chao Khun* or Lord of the Province, but because of what I believe he really is inside, underneath the titles and the robes. He's not perfect, but none of us are. He has his funny little ways, some of which can be irritating. I'm sure some of my own funny little ways irritate him just as much. I don't place him on a pedestal and I don't worship him, but I like him enormously. He's only about fifteen years older than I am but in a way he's like a father to me. He's not always jolly and although I have never once seen him angry, or heard him raise his voice, I have seen him turn wayward novices to stone merely with a look.

Sometimes when we're walking on alms round, or even chanting in the Bote, he'll turn round and glance at me and smile. Sometimes he even bursts out laughing. I'm not sure what the joke is, though I suspect it's me, but I always respond with a smile and, whenever I see him, I want to poke him in the belly.

Although we both tried, in my first year or two at Wat Kob smiling was about the only type of communication we had, unless I called in an interpreter. The abbot once, quite inexplicably, said 'hot water' to me, leaving me unsure whether he wanted some or whether I was in it, but that's the only time I have heard him speak English. On the rare occasions when I need to ask or tell him something, I carefully look up the required vocabulary in my English-Thai dictionary and write out what I want to say, paying particular attention to the tones.

It is the tones that prevent many foreigners from ever speaking Thai well. There are five tones and every word needs to be pronounced in the correct one, otherwise a completely different word to the one intended may be used. Some words which are phonetically the same may have four or five quite different meanings when used with different tones. The words for 'near' and 'far', for example, are perversely phonetically identical – both *klay* – but one is spoken with a low tone and one with a falling tone. I've suffered with tinnitus for many years and sometimes have great difficulty hearing any tones at all. That's sometimes resulted in me walking miles to some place that I thought I'd been told was 'near', or waiting an hour for a bus to take me to a destination that was 'far' but which turned out to be about fifty metres away. Apart from not being able to hear the tones very easily, when speaking I also invariably pronounce my words in entirely the wrong one and frequently come out with the most bizarre and

sometimes embarrassing statements. I once quite inno-
cently asked a rather grand Thai lady if she had ever
eaten penis!

The best opportunity to speak to the abbot is directly
after evening chanting. I start to approach him, my
carefully rehearsed lines running through my head. A
look of panic appears on his face and his eyes dart from
side to side, seeking an escape from what he knows is
going to be a mystical and mystifying experience. The
little novices who have started to get up from their
places at the back of the Bote immediately sit down
again, nudging each other with excited and expectant
whispers of 'the Phra Farang's going to speak Thai', and
giggles sweep over them.

I approach the abbot and, with my hands held in a
respectful wai, state my piece: 'The roof of my kuti has
a leak.' He looks at me blankly for a moment, seeking
some sense in whatever it was I actually said, and then
says something like, 'Have you been to the doctor?' I
frequently misunderstand what he said too, so my reply
to his question might well, and usually does, add to the
absolute gibberish.

When I finally decided to get the roof fixed myself,
I called in a couple of workmen. That made me late
for morning chanting. When the abbot asked me why
I was late, I told him it was because I had two elephants
on my kuti roof – merely the difference between a
falling tone and a high tone, but enough to further
my reputation as being somewhat weird and prone to
hallucinations.

I once told him I wanted a plastic mat for my kuti. He asked me in amazement what I was going to do with it. I said I wanted to sit on it, of course. He told me that the monastery storeroom didn't have any, as far as he knew, but I protested that I had seen hundreds of them, all over the place. He simply looked at me very strangely and sympathetically before hurrying back to his kuti for a lie-down. I'd told him I wanted a plastic tiger to sit on.

We can go on like this for several minutes, our conversation doing justice to a book of Zen riddles, until finally one of us gives up. He usually gives a non-committal grunt, I respectfully wai, the roof of my kuti continues to leak and I don't have a mat. As I walk out of the Bote, the little novices stare at me in fascinated awe.

The worst, or perhaps best, example of our lack of communication came after our head novice was disrobed for taking drugs. Drug addiction, especially to amphetamines, is quite a problem amongst young people in Thailand. Although not unknown amongst monks and novices, it is rare in monasteries. Monks and novices usually don't have sufficient income to sustain a drug habit and anybody found to be using drugs is immediately disrobed. I think the few addicted monks and novices who are occasionally caught were probably already drug users before ordaining. Some may even have ordained in the hope of curing themselves. In our head novice's case, that hadn't worked.

The abbot was naturally very shocked and disturbed

at the discovery and ordered a questioning of all the monks and novices, and a search of the rooms and kutis. None of the other monks or novices were found to be involved with drugs in any way but we all seemed to be under suspicion for a while, especially me because, well, because I'm farang.

In the same week that the novice was kicked out, and while the abbot was still in a prickly mood, I discovered I had a problem with the fishpond in my kuti compound. The small pond contained only a few very ordinary goldfish that people had given to me, but it gave me a lot of pleasure and I always took care to ensure that the water was clean and the fish healthy. One day, I discovered the water had become green and cloudy and a few fish had died. I guessed there was some fishy disease in the water. Besides changing the water, I decided to buy a chemical medicine that could be added to the water to cure any of the remaining fish that might be sick.

There was a fish shop not far from the monastery and the owner recommended a medicine imported from America. I bought one of the tiny phials of bright blue liquid. When I arrived back at the monastery, I met the abbot. '*Pai nai mar?*' he enquired – 'Where have you been?'

Considering the prevailing circumstances, my reply was classic: '*Pai sue yar pla mar,*' which was supposed to mean, 'I've been to buy fish medicine,' but which actually came out as, 'I've been to buy amphetamines.'

I knew even as the words came out that I'd made a

ghastly mistake and the abbot's look of horror confirmed it. 'What! What did you say?' he demanded loudly, in disbelief at what he had heard.

I tried to correct my mistake by repeating the words '*yar pla*' in assorted stammered tones, whilst twitching and sweating under the abbot's glare exactly like someone going through withdrawal symptoms. In the end I smiled madly and scurried off, but I didn't even make it back to the safety of my kuti before the abbot's deputy, probably urgently warned by the boss, jumped out on me from behind a tree.

'Have you got fish medicine in your kuti?' he demanded.

'No, the drugs are in my bag,' I gabbled. After a couple of minutes of this madness, I took the tiny bottle out of my bag and showed it to him, realising as I did so that the label had come off the bottle and that there was nothing to identify what it contained. Presumably speed doesn't come in bright blue liquid form and he was eventually satisfied that I wasn't about to drink this stuff or inject it into my veins. The medicine was a total waste of money anyway, and all my fish died.

Although at times I seem to manage to push the abbot close to the edge, he is usually a very calm person and has great presence of mind in emergencies and unexpected situations. I've seen several examples of that. One of the most striking occurred one evening as the assembled monks were chanting in the Bote. It was during the rainy season, when in the early evening the nightly storm is often preceded by a very high wind.

Along two sides of the Bote are twelve six-feet-high, unglazed windows, each of which has two huge, heavy wooden shutters. The shutters open on the inside and are kept closed by sliding wooden bars.

As we were chanting, the wind started to get up and blew with great force right through the Bote from one side to the other, causing the carpets to lift off the floor and drape themselves over the kneeling monks. A few monks hurriedly closed all the shutters. The chanting continued, but suddenly there was a great crash as the shutters on a window directly adjacent to the high altar were flung open by the strength of the wind.

When the wind hit the altar, dozens of brass candle sticks and several china vases full of flowers were blown off, crashing down onto the abbot who was kneeling on the floor directly beneath the altar. His head and shoulders were soaked with water and strewn with flowers, bits of broken vase surrounded him and dribbles of melted wax solidified on his bald head. I expected him to jump up from his place and call a halt to the chanting while the mess was cleared up, or to react in some dramatic way – at least to mutter a few un-monkish words. But no. He never moved, never even twitched, but just carried on chanting as though absolutely nothing had happened. In fact, we all carried on chanting as though nothing had happened, which I thought was pretty cool.

Unfortunately, Phra Maha Sutont didn't really seem to have the same measure of control and our relationship never did develop into becoming buddies. His behaviour in the first few months that I lived at Wat Kob became very eccentric indeed. I'd started to avoid him by then so it didn't concern me too much, but he upset just about everybody. He became more and more weird until, one day, he simply wasn't there any more. I never knew exactly why, or where he had gone, but I learned much later that a group of other monks had suggested that he should leave the monastery. They had even kindly helped him pack his bags.

There were some moments in my first few months at the monastery when I thought I should move on too. When I examined those thoughts objectively, I realised that Wat Kob was as good as anywhere else, so I stayed put.

At those times, I remembered a story about the late Phra Ajahn Char, the much-revered teacher of many Western monks at his international forest monastery, Wat Pah Nanachat in Thailand's north-east. Ajahn Char was talking about a monk who was always going from one monastery to another, looking for the ideal environment. Ajahn Char likened him to a man with 'shit on his sandals, always looking for a place that didn't smell and not realising that he carried the smell with him'. In another teaching in a similar vein, Ajahn Char told his monks to watch the monastery dogs and to notice how they would sit down in a place, scratch, move to another place, scratch and move again, always scratching and moving and looking for a place without fleas, not realising that they carried their fleas with them wherever they went. The point was that we all carry our problems with us in our minds, so moving from one place to another is not going to solve them. The work has to be done on the inside, regardless of the outside environment.

My own 'fleas' were never too bothersome but they occasionally caused me to stop and think objectively about my life at Wat Kob, and even sometimes about my life as a monk.

Alms round at Wat Kob gave me food for thought as well as food for my stomach, and for a time I started each day feeling guilty and greedy. On my first day of living at the monastery, the abbot invited me to walk on alms round with him and about six other monks. The abbot is one of the most disciplined senior monks I've ever met regarding alms round. He very rarely misses. (A few years ago, in a particularly wet rainy season, the river that runs through Nakhon Sawan overflowed its banks. On our alms round route, the water was several inches deep on the first day of the flood. We walked on alms round as usual. On the second day, it was more than twelve inches deep, and we walked as usual. By the third or fourth day, it was nearly two metres deep in places. I think the abbot would still have insisted that we walked if not for the fact that a number of crocodile farms along the riverbank had been flooded. Dozens of crocs had escaped and were seen swimming down some of the streets on our route. The abbot only then decided that we would find a new route on higher ground).

Our route is a fairly long one and takes about an hour, passing through residential, commercial and market areas. The people in Nakhon Sawan are very generous and many offer food. Each person puts a couple of large spoonfuls of rice in our bowls and then adds a plastic bag containing a serving of curry or dessert and so on. As soon as the food is put into the monk's bowl, a temple boy takes it out and transfers it to a carrier bag, leaving just the rice in the bowl.

At several points along the route, we're met by a motorcycle onto which the boys load the carrier bags, by then full, and collect new empty bags for the next stage of the round. By the time we return to the monastery, the bags have been delivered to each monk's kuti. Every day, I finish alms round with four or five full carrier bags of food, plus about eight pounds of rice.

From all that food, I take only a small bowl of rice and curry for my breakfast and sometimes put an apple or some other fruit aside for lunch. I give the rest to the three students who live beneath my kuti. That's part of the deal: they do odd jobs around the kuti in return for free food and accommodation. Even after my three looksits have taken all the food they need for their breakfast, and put some aside for their evening meal when they return from college, there may still be two or three carrier bags of food left over. That's all thrown away. Every day.

When that much food is multiplied by the number of monks and novices who go out on alms round, it adds up to a very great deal of food wasted daily (though not every monk walks on alms round over such a long route, or for such a long time).

Besides being a useless waste, the food is sometimes offered by poor people who may give the monks better food than they eat themselves. Additionally, the food is given in good faith and, I thought at first, the people presumably expect the monks to eat it. Or had alms round become merely a symbolic gesture concerned more with making merit than actually feeding the monks?

I wasn't happy about this situation for a while. Some years before ordaining, I had worked voluntarily as director of a UK charity that raises money to help very poor children in north-east Thailand. Many of the children are malnourished, or at least undernourished. Although it was an illogical sentiment, I felt guilty that I wasted more food every day than some of them ate in a month.

I turned to the Vinaya or, more specifically, to the definitive commentary on the Vinaya rules, written by the late tenth Supreme Patriarch. In the commentary he explained every rule in a relatively modern context. The late Supreme Patriarch wrote: 'A *bhikku* (monk) is prohibited from accepting alms food above the top edge of his bowl, because to accept more would be to show greed. According to the traditions of the present day, to accept much on the basis of greediness is censurable, while to accept much on the basis of *Metta* (loving-kindness) is not censurable.'

If a monk personally feels he is collecting too much food, the answer would appear to be simple – not to walk on alms round for so long or so far. But if the monk only walks on alms round close to his monastery, lay-people who live further away may be deprived of the opportunity to offer food. It can take only a few minutes for the bowl to be filled, but if a monk walks for such a short time, is he really getting any spiritual benefit from the experience, or is he merely nipping out of the monastery to collect his breakfast?

Despite the late Supreme Patriarch's commentary, my social conscience was still pricked each day. Eventually I put some of my questions about alms round to a few teachers who visited me at my kuti. I asked them, at what point should relatively modern traditions be allowed to compromise the monks' lifestyle and whether the culture should outweigh the monks' rules, as laid down since the earliest days of Buddhism.

Somewhat to my surprise, there was general agreement amongst the teachers that the monk *should* accept as much food as the people wanted to offer, even though most of it would be thrown away. The teachers said that the donors were usually fully aware that the monk couldn't possibly eat all the food, but the point was in the giving, not in the receiving. They agreed that the monk should show Metta and allow the people to make merit. Okay. My questions were answered and I continued to go out on alms round with the abbot – according to the traditions of the present day.

Another small incident also made me think quite hard for a time. When I first moved to Wat Kob, I decided I would start teaching English again, though not to the same extent that I had been doing at Nahoob. Wat Kob is only a short walk or bus ride from all the important colleges in the province, including the teacher-training institute. I had taught or lectured at most of them on an ad hoc basis but as they were more than an hour's bus ride from Nahoob it had never been very convenient to do so regularly.

Some of the teachers from the vocational college visited me and asked if I would teach a communications skills course. I readily agreed but explained that I would not allow teaching to interfere with my meditation or other studies. I suggested they draw up a timetable, which they did, and when we had all agreed on the shape and content of the course, I rather belatedly suggested that they should formally ask the abbot for his permission. They went to see the abbot and he said 'No'.

I couldn't believe it and I went to see him one evening, determined to change his mind. Why, I asked, would he not allow me to teach? I explained that the students would benefit from being taught by a native speaker and that I very much wanted to teach so I could return something to the Thai people for their many kindnesses to me. The abbot was adamant. He told me that a monk should be above the world and the problems of the laity, whilst remaining compassionate for them.

He went on to explain that if I was teaching Dhamma or meditation, that would be acceptable. To teach English was too much like a job, regardless of whether I was being paid for it or not, and that a monk should not work for the laity. That seemed to be the exact opposite of Ajahn Waow's view. He had not only actively encouraged me to teach at the local high school but had also offered my services to other schools in the district. (I have never, incidentally, accepted money for teaching.)

I thought about the abbot's words for a long time, even wondering briefly if perhaps I had made a mistake in coming to live at a monastery with such an unreasonable and old-fashioned abbot. I finally told the teachers to tear up the schedule. I think if the abbot had left it to me to make my own decision after his little lecture, I probably would have taught, but I would never have been sure if that was the right decision.

As is often the case, things turned out quite well in the end. The abbot had no objection to people visiting me at my kuti and I began teaching, or really just having conversations, with teachers. Some had never had the opportunity to talk with a native speaker before so in a way that was more productive and far-reaching than actually teaching students.

Although it's not a question that plays on my mind or raises any doubts, I do sometimes wonder how far the monks' social responsibilities should go in modern times. Theoretically I believe we have none at all and yet, using education as an example, prior to about 1930, before the government started building new schools, nearly all schools in Thailand were in monasteries and the teachers were mostly monks, teaching all subjects, not just Dhamma. In 1931, eighty-seven per cent of schools in Nakhon Sawan Province were in monasteries.

My own work with the Students' Education Trust involves me in meetings with college principals and heads of departments, interviews with students, meetings with donors, presentation of scholarships at colleges and universities and producing a fund-raising newsletter for supporters. I don't think my abbot would whole-heartedly approve of any of that. In many ways I would have to accept that his disapproval was justified, because I sometimes feel I have one foot in the monastery and one in the streets and, perhaps, have wandered a little off the monks' main path. But I believe the Trust's work is both constructive and important, since it enables many disadvantaged and impoverished Thai students to study at universities and colleges to gain degrees or vocational qualifications. Without SET's help, most of the supported students would have had to drop out of higher education and return to work in the family rice paddies, or would never have the opportunity to study in the first place.

I don't do that work because I am a Buddhist monk, nor even because I am Buddhist; I do it because I believe it is the *right* thing to do, the compassionate thing to do. I am in a position to help and I consider it my social responsibility and my duty – not as a member of the Thai Sangha but as a member of the human family – to give what help I can. I think SET's own supporters worldwide feel the same way. Few of them are Buddhist, but regardless of their religious or philosophical beliefs, all of them believe in practising compassion and generosity towards those less fortunate than themselves. That seems to me to be perfectly in keeping with the Buddha's teaching, as well as with the teachings of all great religious leaders.

It's easy to develop a sort of theoretical compassion if one isolates oneself in a cave or forest, or even in a big city monastery, where one doesn't have much contact with the world and its problems and suffering. But how deep, how genuine, can such compassion really be? I personally believe that genuine compassion can only develop through a deep and genuine understanding of people's problems, not by being above the world and the problems of the laity. To develop compassion means getting your hands dirty and caring in a practical and immediate way for those who are suffering; for the sick, for the old, for the needy.

Some monks obviously do feel that they have social responsibilities. I have visited a nearby province where the abbot has turned his isolated monastery into an AIDS hospice. I believe when it opened, it was the first such hospice in Thailand. The monastery is still a monastery but now has many hundreds of patients, some of whom live at the monastery and others who go for daily treatment. The abbot has also raised funds to build a sixteen-bed hospital at the monastery for those in the final stages of the disease. He now receives help from the government and both praise and condemnation from other monks. I was immensely impressed by the work he is doing and I believe him to be a very compassionate man, but I couldn't honestly say if it is right or wrong of him to be doing it *as a monk*.

25

Towards the end of each year, I start looking at the calendar in an increasingly dejected mood. It's visa renewal time again and that usually means hassle.

Once you know the procedure it's fairly straightforward, but it still involves a lot of to-ing and fro-ing to various official departments in Bangkok, with the associated nightmare that travelling anywhere in Bangkok brings. It's also a lot more difficult and complicated for a monk to renew his visa than it is for an ordinary applicant, though there are good reasons for that.

For visitors to Thailand who simply want to extend their stay by a few more weeks, the procedure is relatively simple. Go to the Immigration Department visa office, fill in a form, pay the fee and get the passport stamped. Other foreigners who need an extension for three, six or twelve months face more difficulties and waiting time but the process is still relatively straightforward – though judging by the number of frustrated-looking foreigners I have seen at the visa office, there might be some who would disagree.

Foreign monks are usually issued with a twelve-month visa but that's by no means automatic. The first time I needed to renew my visa, I thought the monks' high status in Thailand would make the procedure fairly painless and free of difficulties, but at the Immigration Department everybody is just a foreigner and all are treated equally, regardless of what they are wearing or their social status. I'm sure the officers in the visa department don't deliberately put up any barriers to make life awkward for Western monks, but they seem to be a bit more cautious before banging away with their innumerable rubber stamps and handing out the very desirable twelve-month extensions. That caution is entirely justified. It isn't unknown for young foreign men, at the end of not only their visas but also their money, to suddenly get religion and try to ordain as monks.

I had encounters with such people myself when I was staying at Wat Mahadhatu. Occasionally, I would be called to the Section 5 reception desk to meet and talk with young Westerners who claimed they wanted to attend a residential meditation course, or even that they wanted to ordain as monks. Sometimes they seemed quite genuine and we tried to help them as much as we could. Just as often, they were obviously not. The crunch always came when they were told that before going any further we would need to see their passports to check their status in Thailand. Usually their visas had already expired, or were about to do so.

After I moved from Wat Mahadhatu, I heard that there was such a case when a young European was accepted for ordination. Like me, he was ordained by the abbot and was, I believe, only the second Westerner to have had that honour. He was given help in applying for a twelve-month extension so that he could continue his Dhamma and meditation studies. As soon as he had his new visa, he simply walked out of Section 5 wearing the jeans and t-shirt he had arrived in, leaving his robes in a pile on the floor of his room. Within the Sangha, that was a shocking thing to have done and something that no Thai monk, no matter how insincere, would ever do. The Section 5 monk who told me the story said that the abbot was far from happy, which I don't doubt for a moment, and that in future the monastery would be far more cautious in its dealings with Westerners.

I had originally arrived in Thailand with an ordinary tourist visa which was due to expire soon after my ordination. Phra Maha Laow and Ajahn Amara Thera had both returned to England by then, so I had nobody to advise or help me. I knew the first step was to go to the Religious Affairs Department, which is part of the Ministry of Education, and get a special form for non-Thai monks. The form asks forty questions, helpfully written only in Thai, and I had to find a translator to help me complete it. Once completed, the form had to be signed three times: by my Upachaya, by the religious governor of Bangkok and by the religious governor of the province. In my case, my Upachaya and the governor of the province were one and the same, and I made an appointment to see the abbot of Wat Mahadhatu to request his two signatures.

I had to wait a couple of days for an appointment. There was no problem about the abbot signing the form as my Upachaya, but he said he couldn't sign as the provincial governor until the district governor had first signed. Fair enough, so I made an appointment with the district governor, who at that time was the abbot of Bangkok's Wat Po. I waited a couple of days until he was available and got the form signed. Then back to my Upachaya, another day or so of waiting, and he signed for the second time.

I returned to the Religious Affairs Department and handed over the form and a photocopy of my passport. 'Where's your letter?' asked the official.

'What letter?' I replied.

'The letter from your Upachaya to say why you want to extend your visa.'

In fact, that is exactly the information that is already on the form that was signed by my Upachaya. Never mind, back to my Upachaya who by then had gone away on official business to another province for a few days. On his return, he had his secretary-monk prepare the necessary letter, which I then delivered to the Religious Affairs Department. They told me to return in seven days for a letter from them to the Immigration Department requesting the twelve-month extension.

I waited a week and returned as instructed. My file had been lost and I was told to come back the following week. By then I was becoming a little concerned because by that time my old visa had expired and I was theoretically an illegal alien. I naïvely hoped that my status as a monk would make that unimportant, but civil servants are the same all over the world. When I eventually arrived at the Immigration Department, clutching my various bits of paperwork, it was politely pointed out to me that before any progress on the new visa could be made I would have to pay 2,000 baht for my overstay, as well as 500 baht in advance for the new stamp.

I had only recently become a monk and there was still very much more Mr Peter Robinson in me than there was Phra Peter Pannapadipo. I found myself in both a potentially confrontational situation and an embarrassing one, since I didn't have 2,000 baht. I really try to avoid confrontations as much as I can but I could feel my European hackles rising at what seemed to be the injustice of the situation. That's conditioned response, of course.

The young officer was very pleasant, very polite and just doing his job, but I was about to point out to him in no uncertain terms that (1) I was a monk and that therefore (2) the Vinaya rules prevented me from dealing with money or buying and selling and (3) that it was the inefficiency of another Thai government department that had caused me to overstay and (4) as far as I was concerned, such mundane and worldly matters as visas and passports were of no importance whatsoever. All of which would have undoubtedly fallen on deaf ears and just goes to show how pompous and naïve I was then.

I was just getting my righteous indignation nicely worked up when happily the no doubt one-sided potential confrontation was avoided when another officer came into the room. We recognised each other immediately. We had met very briefly years before in a railway station when Phra Maha Laow and I were about to board an overnight train for a visit to Sisaket Province in the north-east. The officer had been Phra Maha Laow's looksit many years ago.

I presume he was senior to the officer I was about to unfairly lambaste. He took me aside, looked through all my papers and asked me to wait. He left the office but within ten minutes returned to say that the head of the visa section had not only waived my overstay fine but had also paid my 500 baht visa fee himself. Added to that, he had given me 100 baht for my taxi fare back to Wat Mahadhatu.

I felt not only immensely grateful at this generosity but also very humbled. Even though I had not actually confronted the young officer with an indignant, ridiculous and typically Western outburst, I was embarrassed that I had even considered it.

After that, my dealings with the visa office on that application went very smoothly. I was issued a temporary new visa and told to return the following month, by which time my application would have been considered and either rejected or approved. The following month I collected my twelve-month visa.

Unfortunately for me, Phra Maha Laow's ex-looksit transferred to another department soon after, so in following years I had to manage on my own. It isn't a problem. I know the routine now and since that first time it has become progressively easier, additionally helped by the visa section itself and the introduction of a simpler system of application. There's still lots of to-ing and fro-ing, especially now that I live in a province that's more than five hours' bus and taxi ride away from the monasteries and offices I need to visit, but my dealings with the Immigration officers are always cordial and good-tempered.

When making my application a few years ago, I discovered that not only my visa but also my passport was about to expire. That necessitated a nightmare of journeying between Nakhon Sawan and Bangkok, the British Embassy, the Religious Affairs Department and the Immigration Department, as well as the abbots from whom I needed signatures. You can't get a visa without a valid passport and you can't get a passport without a valid visa; a Catch 22 situation only resolved by a very helpful Thai lady at the British Embassy.

Whilst at the Immigration Department I have met, or at least observed, many other Westerners applying for visas of various durations. I have occasionally been absolutely appalled by the behaviour and attitudes of some of them. At the same time, I have much admired the Thai officers' continual politeness and good humour when dealing with these wretched people. Some visitors seem to have made no effort whatsoever to understand what constitutes polite or impolite behaviour in Thai society. In their manner of speaking, acting and even dressing, they constantly insult their hosts – maybe not deliberately, but simply out of ignorance of Thai ways.

I notice that on the streets as well. Because few Westerners visit Nakhon Sawan, most of my time is spent surrounded by Thai people. I am sure I have gradually and unconsciously changed and have adopted many Thai norms of behaviour, as well as monk norms of behaviour. When I occasionally visit Bangkok, I quickly realise that I now see Westerners, at least partly, in the way that Thai people see them. I am frequently embarrassed by what I see.

Once when I was staying at Wat Mahadhatu, I was asked by an angry group of Thai people to tell a Western couple to leave the monastery. The couple, a man and woman in their early twenties, were sitting on the floor of the Bote, wearing the skimpiest shorts I had ever seen, with their legs stretched out and their feet pointed at the main Buddha image. I politely explained the basic rules of conduct when visiting a Thai monastery and was told in no uncertain terms to, well, to go away. But at least they left the Bote soon after. I was very embarrassed and apologised to the Thai lay-people, but happily the incident, once over, fell into the *mai bpen rai* category.

Perhaps that was an extreme case, but I often see examples of less obviously bad behaviour that I know causes offence to many Thais, particularly those who don't have much contact with Westerners. It is, of course, easier to be objective and judgemental about the behaviour of others than it is about one's own. Perhaps I also still make many stupid errors in my behaviour, but I'm sure the Buddha's teaching about mindfulness, about being aware of one's actions and speech from moment to moment, has helped me a lot in that respect. Sometimes though, I wonder if some of the tourists who visit Thailand have even taken the trouble to read a guidebook to the country. The books invariably explain the most basic social dos and don'ts, but the attitude amongst some visitors seems to be the wrong side of *mai bpen rai*: a sort of 'I'll do whatever I want to do and it doesn't matter' attitude, which is very sad.

One silly mistake I made was to cause intense embarrassment to another monk. After Phra Maha Sutont was persuaded to leave Wat Kob, there was only one monk remaining who could speak English. Because it was thought I was close to Phra Maha Sutont, this monk, along with most of the others, had previously avoided talking to me. After Phra Maha Sutont's departure, that situation quickly changed and the monk and I became good friends. His name was Phra Suthee and at that time he had been a monk for about five years. He was very small and looked much younger than his twenty-six years – in fact he looked like a schoolboy and had a sense of humour to match. We got on very well, though we occasionally came to verbal blows when we discussed our differing views of what constituted real Buddhism.

I'd once conducted a survey amongst my students at the school in Banpotphisai, in which I asked them what their hobbies were. To my surprise, at the top of the list came 'sleeping', followed by 'visiting Fairyland'. Fairyland is a department store in Nakhon Sawan City. I was interested to visit this emporium to find out what the great attraction was for my students, as it seemed an odd hobby. I asked Phra Suthee if he would like to go with me.

He was horrified at the idea of a monk going into a department store, which quite mystified me. He explained that it was acceptable for a monk to go to an ordinary little shop if he needed to buy something, but that he shouldn't go to a big store. That was somewhat lacking in logic to me (Western logic, that is), because I had grown up in a country where department stores were on virtually every high street and were simply considered as convenient places to shop. I didn't like to tell my friend that whilst living in London, I had frequently escorted Thai monks from Wat Buddhapadipa around such 'shops' as Harrods and Fortnum's, which they seemed to love visiting even though they rarely bought anything.

I could see that despite his objections, Phra Suthee was really quite excited by my rather naughty idea. He eventually agreed to go with me. Having about 20 baht between us, we weren't intending to actually do any shopping, but nevertheless we set off with the feeling of going on a great adventure.

Fairyland is modelled along Western department store lines, with cosmetics on the ground floor, clothes on the second, electrical goods on the third and so on. We walked through the main doors and with my huge strides I was halfway through the first department before I fully realised where we were. Phra Suthee, hurrying to keep up with me, suddenly stopped dead in his tracks. I had never seen a Thai person's face go red with embarrassment before, but my friend's face did just that. 'Oh . . . oh . . . oh . . .' he said in a little strangled voice, as he found himself completely surrounded by displays of plastic female torsos wearing only knickers and bras. We had come in the entrance that led directly to ladies' underwear and lingerie.

Poor Phra Suthee seemed to be paralysed, his eyes glued to the floor as though his life, his honour and his purity depended on it. 'Oh . . . oh . . . oh . . .' he kept saying. A lady customer nearby picked up a black, frilly thing from a counter and held it against herself. 'Oh . . . oh . . . oh . . .' Unfortunately, I burst out laughing at his obvious embarrassment, as did several young lady customers. Finally, I had to take hold of his arm and lead him through the department since, by that time, his eyes were tightly closed. He didn't open them again until we were safely out of moral danger in the stationery department.

As it turned out, Fairyland was a very ordinary, average-sized department store, but I realised that for my mostly very poor students it was aptly named. The store was full of Western or Western-style consumer goods, TVs and videos, home computers, beautiful clothes, furniture and all the rest; the things that most of my students could only dream about, but few would ever own.

I don't think Phra Suthee ever quite forgave me for taking him to the store but, in a roundabout way, he did get his own back.

The visit became a standing joke between us and we would often make schoolboy-type references to his reactions in the underwear department. One evening soon after the visit, I was sitting on the balcony of my kuti when a little novice arrived with several cartons of milk, a gift from Phra Suthee, he said. My friend and I often shared the small gifts of 'special' food that lay-people offered. I told the novice to thank Phra Suthee and to tell him I looked forward to seeing him in ladies' underwear again soon. The novice looked at me as though I was very strange, though there was nothing new in that, and off he went.

Next morning I met Phra Suthee on our way to the Bote for morning chanting. 'Thanks for the milk,' I said.

'What milk?' he asked, quite mystified.

'The milk the novice delivered last night. He said it was from you, from Phra Suthee.'

'Oh,' replied my friend, as realisation dawned. 'He meant from Phra Suthee Thammasopon, the abbot.'

The abbot. THE ABBOT! I had sent a message to the abbot to say I wanted to see him in ladies' underwear? Aaarrgh!!!

26

During my second year at Wat Kob, the cool season lasted only about a week and the following hot season was very much longer and hotter than usual. The quite phenomenal heat was to lead to a curious madness in the monastery, or at least to a wave of eccentricity.

I'm not sure if it's true, but I have been told by many people that Nakhon Sawan is the hottest province in Thailand. That year, the daytime temperature reached forty-four degrees Celsius and remained near that level for a couple of months. The nights weren't much cooler and I found it almost unbearable. I was constantly soaked in sweat, suffered from frequent headaches, prickly heat rashes (as well as a prickly temper) and felt generally debilitated for weeks.

Quite apart from the physical discomfort, from which the Thai monks seemed to suffer as much as I did, that hot season saw frayed tempers, misunderstandings, petty arguments and some very odd un-monk-like behaviour.

In view of the oppressive heat, that was mostly under-standable and forgivable and as far as I know there weren't any serious repercussions from any of the incidents. Almost every day saw a new drama unfold. I was fascinated, especially as I usually didn't have a clue what was happening, but I was quite happy to observe from the sidelines. On one occasion, follow-ing some especially bizarre incident, I had a message from the abbot to tell me that Wat Kob wasn't usually like this and please not to run off to some saner monastery! I wouldn't have dreamed of it anyway, because I was always too intrigued to see what might happen next.

After a few weeks of the relentless heat, I was aware that my friend Phra Suthee seemed to be very on edge, as we all were to some degree, but then there was a very odd incident involving a bag of sugar.

Somebody gave me a couple of one-kilo bags of sugar, each wrapped in brown paper. I decided to share the gift with my friend. Phra Suthee lived in the mango garden, but when I got there I found his kuti locked and deserted. The sugar was well protected from ants in its wrapping, so I left the package on his kuti steps, knowing he would find it when he returned.

About an hour later, the serenity of the monastery was shattered by the sound of sirens, as several army jeeps came tearing down the small road that leads through the grounds. Nakhon Sawan has a huge mili-tary base just outside the city and the jeeps had obvi-ously come from there. The jeeps disappeared into the mango garden but emerged a short time later, much less dramatically. I strolled over to see what the fuss was about. I found Phra Suthee sitting on his kuti steps, looking dejected and embarrassed and surrounded by spilt sugar. I asked him what had happened.

He said that when he returned to his kuti, he saw a suspicious-looking package on the steps and assumed it was a bomb. Well, naturally, one would. So he called the bomb disposal squad at the local barracks and they responded immediately. After prodding at the bag with an official stick, they declared it to be harmless. I asked my friend why on earth he should assume the package to be a bomb. Glancing conspiratorially around the garden, he lowered his voice and said, 'They're out to get me.'

'Who? I asked. '*Who* is out to get you?'

'Them,' he replied.

He refused to elaborate, but made me promise not to leave any more packages on his steps.

My friend's kuti was close to the monastery's back wall, on the other side of which is a lane. About a week after the unexploding sugar incident, Phra Suthee told me that his kuti was under attack at night, being bombarded by rocks thrown over the wall from the lane. It was 'Them' again. In fact, his kuti was directly beneath a mango tree and when mangoes fall and hit the roof at night they make a very loud noise. I know, because a mango tree also shades my kuti and I am often woken up at night by the same thing. I pointed this out to my friend, but he wouldn't accept it, preferring to believe that the mysterious 'Them' were attacking. Happily, my friend's paranoia about 'Them' quickly disappeared when the temperature eventually started to fall, but his odd behaviour lasted for a couple of months.

Another weird incident might have had serious repercussions, but since no action was taken either by the abbot or the police, I assume there was some justification or, at least, attenuating circumstances, apart from the heat. There was a monk of about fifteen Pansas living at the monastery. Everybody, including myself, liked and respected him very much. From my own observation, he appeared to be an excellent monk in every way. He was very quiet, very calm, and always smiling, whatever the circumstances. He was a large man and quite fat and I think he probably suffered badly in the heat that summer. Certainly it didn't seem to do his usually unshakeable equanimity any good.

One afternoon, all the monks, except him, were assembled in the Bote for the twice-monthly recitation of the Vinaya, or rules of the monks. Unusually, he hadn't turned up. The novices don't have to attend the recitation, but they join the monks in the Bote afterwards to listen to a lecture from the abbot about how monks and novices should behave. The recitation was nearing its end and the mostly very young novices were gathered outside the Bote doors, waiting to come in.

Suddenly, the monks were startled by the sound of terrified novices screaming hysterically and scattering in every direction. We all looked around and there, looming massively in the huge, open Bote doorway, silhouetted in black against the sunlight like a horror movie poster, was the missing monk. In the crook of one arm he held a policeman's head. Happily, it was still attached to the policeman's body, but probably only by chance, since in the other hand the monk was holding a large axe. Well, what would you expect?

There seemed to be a joint holding of breath for a moment. Then the abbot heaved himself from the floor with a sort of, 'Oh gods, what now?' groan (it had been a particularly bad week for bizarre behaviour) and strolled almost casually over to the doorway. The abbot has enormous presence and great calm. He said a few very quiet words to the monk, who dropped the axe – narrowly missing removing some of the abbot's toes – and released the policeman. The policeman fled the scene. The monk fell to his knees before the abbot, his hands in supplication, and the abbot calmed him down before instructing a very reluctant novice to escort the monk and his axe back to his kuti.

Amazingly, while this drama was unfolding, the monk who was chanting the Vinaya never even paused in his recitation, despite the sudden loss of interest amongst his audience. The abbot came back to his place and we carried on as though nothing unusual had happened. The only real, and welcome, difference it made to our day was that the abbot didn't bother giving his usual two-hour-long lecture about monks' behaviour. I never discovered what the incident was about, but it didn't seem to affect the amount of respect or affection that everybody, including me, held for the axe-wielding monk.

My feelings nearly changed about a week later. I was walking through the monastery quite late in the evening, on my way to visit Phra Suthee, and I passed in front of a group of trees in front of the axe-monk's kuti. It was very dark under the trees and I very nearly had a heart attack when the monk suddenly jumped out and grabbed me round the neck. He quickly released me and apologised. When I told Phra Suthee about it afterwards he said that the monk was standing guard over his kuti. I asked him whom he was guarding it from. 'Them,' he said. Oh, 'Them' again.

The next incident was equally as weird. There were two monks living in the monastery, each with about ten Pansas. They were both large and tough looking, but they were also very genial and pleasant individuals. What I didn't know at the time was that before they ordained and reformed, they were leaders of rival street gangs. There remained some old animosity between them, though that never showed and their behaviour as monks seemed beyond reproach.

During that hot, hot summer, old animosities seemed to boil over. I've never seen monks fighting and I am sure it is a very rare occurrence. I have heard of it happening, but I believe it is usually no more than a petty squabble between young monks who sometimes don't have a great deal of discipline. That hot season, however, we were living in unusual and interesting times.

The fight between the two monks took place in the street, directly in front of the monastery, very late one stiflingly hot night. One of the monks was in a house, talking to some lay-people, though he shouldn't have been at that time of night. For some reason, the other monk went looking for him. Discovering him in the house, he threw a handy cauldron of rice through the glass window. That's odd enough behaviour for a monk anyway, but odder still was that the rice-throwing monk was wearing a quilted anorak and a knitted bobble hat. The monk in the house came running out, wielding a length of wood, and the two started circling each other. Neighbours, hearing the ruckus, came out of their houses to see what was going on. Several ran into the monastery to get help, while others telephoned the police.

Only a few harmless blows were exchanged, but the bobble-hatted monk seemed to think he was the victor. He started doing a little jig in the street, whilst chanting in a language that onlookers claimed they had never heard before, leading to later speculation that he was possessed by spirits. The police quickly arrived and spoke with both monks, but decided to take no action and instead released them into the abbot's care. Next day, the monks disappeared in different directions from the monastery. After a few weeks, when both the weather and tempers had cooled off, they returned to the monastery, where they resumed their pre-hot season behaviour of politely ignoring each other.

It wasn't just some of the monks who were affected by the heat. During part of that hot season, I had a Western layman staying in the monastery for a meditation retreat. One afternoon, I returned to my kuti to find the man sitting on my balcony, white as a sheet and trembling uncontrollably. He said that ten minutes before he had been sitting in the mango garden talking with a monk about Buddhism. At the very moment he was thinking how peaceful the monastic setting was, and how calm he was feeling, a young Thai man suddenly jumped out of the bushes and tried to stab the monk in the arm with a huge knife, and then ran off. Although there was a lot of blood, the monk suffered little more than a scratch. The monk claimed not to know his attacker, nor of any reason for the attack. The incident was just put down to more heat madness and was considered so trivial, at least in comparison with some of that summer's other events, that the police weren't even informed.

There were many other bizarre incidents that hot season and it quite amazed me that the abbot, who had responsibility for all the monks and novices in the monastery, didn't have some sort of breakdown himself. I think on several occasions I managed to push him a little closer to the edge, though my oddness had been accepted within the wat since I arrived, and wasn't particularly blamed on the heat. Of course, I don't consider myself odd at all, but sometimes I find it easy to understand why the other monks should think so.

The heat certainly affected my mental processes that summer and I also indulged in a little eccentric behaviour. In my case that usually manifested itself as a total loss of mindfulness.

One afternoon, trying to keep cool, I took a shower in the bathroom behind my kuti. That was really a waste of time because the temperature in the windowless room was higher than outside. By the time I finished drying myself off, I needed another shower. Afterwards, I left the bathroom, shut the door and clicked the padlock shut. Unfortunately, I had entirely forgotten to put my robes on and suddenly realised I was stark naked. The key to the padlock was on my belt, which was in the bathroom, as were all the keys to my kuti.

I had long before hidden a spare set of keys to my kuti under a flowerpot in my garden, and I frantically started turning over about fifty pots, looking for the right one.

My neighbour, an old monk in his eighties, chose that moment to look out of his upstairs window. He nearly fell out of the window in amazement. I quickly picked up a small flowerpot and clasped it to myself. 'What are you *doing*?' asked the old monk, incredulously. My mind went totally blank and my Thai language and powers of explanation completely failed me. Looking down at the flowerpot for inspiration, I calmly said 'gardening', and carried on looking for the keys, as though that was perfectly normal behaviour for a farang.

27

For anybody who plans or needs to stay in Thailand for longer than just a holiday, it is essential to learn how Thai people reckon time. In my own experience, most Thais really don't have much sense of time at all and are nearly always late for appointments, sometimes by several days, and rarely understand why many Westerners find that irritating. In Bangkok, of course, the traffic can usually be blamed, and is – frequently with good reason.

I decided I had to learn to tell the time Thai-style following an experience which cost me greatly. I wanted to meet a very highly respected Thai meditation teacher and I received a letter at Wat Kob informing me that he would be at a certain monastery in Bangkok on a particular date and that he would be expecting me. The letter had been delayed in the postal system for nearly a week and the appointment was for that very day.

At that time, I had a looksit who could speak fairly good English, but he had the habit of thinking in Thai and then translating word for word into English. His manner of speaking was consequently sometimes extremely odd, extremely funny, occasionally very misleading or, sometimes, all three at the same time. In other words, exactly how I speak Thai.

On receipt of the letter early in the morning, I threw it and a few changes of under-robes into a bag and my looksit and I dashed off to the bus station, forgetting that it was a special holiday and that all the buses were therefore fully booked. We jumped into a taxi and went to a private coach company, but they were also fully booked. Another taxi took us the several miles to Nakhon Sawan railway station and we arrived there at about 10.45am.

The railway system in Thailand is generally very good and I was sure trains to Bangkok were frequent. I sent my looksit off to the booking office to enquire about the time of the next train. When he came back, I asked him what time the train would arrive in Nakhon Sawan. He thought for a moment and replied, 'Five o'clock.'

'What!' I exclaimed in disbelief. 'I haven't got time to wait that long!' and without giving him the chance to say anything else, I swept out of the station, impatiently demanding he find me an aeroplane or, at the very least, a taxi.

Nakhon Sawan doesn't have an airport but the taxi we had arrived in was still parked outside the station. I negotiated a price for the 240-kilometre ride to Bangkok. That was about twenty times the rail fare, plus a bit extra because I was a foreigner, of course. I was desperate to get to Bangkok and had no alternative but to agree to the price.

When we were finally on our way, I managed to get both my irritation and my hunger under control. I hadn't eaten breakfast and by then had missed lunch as well. Seeing that it was reasonably safe to speak, my looksit asked, 'Why was Respected Father hot heart (impatient) to wait for the train?' Thinking the boy was an idiot, I slowly and calmly explained that we arrived at the station just before 11am, the train was due at 5pm, and therefore we would have to wait six hours. Thai trains, even those mysteriously called 'Express', are sometimes incredibly slow and the journey from Nakhon Sawan to Bangkok can take six hours; nearly twice as long as the bus. So, I explained, by the time we'd also got across Bangkok we would not actually arrive at the monastery I needed to go to until about midnight, or even the next day.

He was quiet for a moment while he absorbed this logic and then said, 'But we only needed to wait ten minutes.'

I looked at him in astonishment. 'Ten minutes? But you told me the train was at five o'clock!'

'Yes, that's right,' he said. '*Har mong* five o'clock.' I belatedly understood. *Har mong* in Thai does indeed translate literally as 'five o'clock', but five o'clock to the Thai is 11am by Western reckoning!

Thais split the clock into four periods and start counting from six. 6am Western time is also 6 Thai time, but 7am becomes 1, 8am becomes 2, 9am becomes 3, 10am becomes 4, 11am becomes 5 and 12 is noon, but can also be 12. Similarly, in the evening quarter, 6pm is 6, but 7pm becomes 1, 8pm becomes 2, and so on. There is an additional word after the number to make it clear which part of the day is meant, but the word is often omitted in speech if it seems obvious. The Thai system of telling the time does have its own sort of logic but it takes a while to get used to. It always seems especially odd to me that most Thai clocks have Roman numerals, but a Thai asked the time will still look at the clock, on which the hour hand is quite clearly pointing at nine, and say 'three'.

My lack of understanding of all that cost me about 4,000 baht for taxis and I decided then that it was time to learn to tell the time Thai-style. It actually cost me more than 4,000 baht. In my impatience to get out of the station and into a taxi, I left my bag behind on the platform, together with the letter that told me the name of the Bangkok monastery, so we never got there anyway. As soon as we reached Bangkok, we simply turned round and returned to Nakhon Sawan, arriving at about 7.30pm. Or was it half past one?

Time in most monasteries is still regulated to a great extent by the ringing of bells or the beating of drums; signals that advise, warn or command. At Wat Nahoob, I had the job of ringing the bell at the top of the tower for morning and evening chanting and a different bell – really, an old cog wheel – was rung to remind us that it was lunchtime. Another small hand-bell was rung to call the monks to special services in the Bote, such as ordinations.

It is a tradition in many Thai monasteries that during the Pansa period an additional call is made at dusk to warn any monks outside the monastery perimeter that they must return immediately, since a monk must be within his monastery boundaries every night of the Rains Retreat.

At Wat Nahoob, the new monks had the job of sounding this warning and it was done on huge old drums, kept in the sala. The idea at Wat Nahoob seemed to be to make as much noise as possible. The aesthetic value of the performance was of secondary importance. The few monks who were staying at the monastery for the Pansa would gather round the drums to listen or help, which made the exercise somewhat pointless since we were all very obviously already present. Nevertheless, the young monks enthusiastically beat not only the drums but also banged large saucepans together, and sometimes bits of wood, which culminated in the most terrible racket.

At most monasteries, I believe the evening call is one of two kinds, either similar to Wat Nahoob's or the straightforward, sonorous beat of a drum or ringing of a bell. At Wat Kob we are considerably more sophisticated than that. The novices who have the duty turn the evening call into a musical art form, albeit one that could only be described as 'free expression'.

Our two enormous and ancient drums are hung at the top of the bell tower, which also houses four bells of different sizes, all of them big. The bell tower is at least twice the height of Wat Nahoob's, ensuring that whatever sounds emanate from it are sure to be heard over the whole of the city.

The abbot of Wat Kob is usually a stickler for doing things by the book, but he seems quite happy to turn a blind eye, or at least a deaf ear, to the novices' nightly performance. It's usually a performance well worth hearing and one that I always look forward to.

It usually starts off without any warning, with a great drum roll. That lasts a minute or so, but then quite suddenly and unexpectedly stops. There may then be about a minute's silence, which builds up the suspense as to what might happen next. In fact, one of the novices told me that they use that silence to decide what to do next, since each evening's performance is always a bit different. A single 'ding' on one of the smaller bells often heralds the next phase. A drum beat, slow as a heart beat, booms out and after a few beats is joined by a bell, rung once between every half dozen or so drum beats.

Very gradually, the drum beat becomes faster and is then joined by another drum with a different tone. A second bell joins in and then, quite suddenly, all hell breaks loose at the top of the tower as the drum beats rain down at an incredible speed. A sudden stop and a long silence and then, again, the single 'ding' which heralds a second phase. The performance continues for about twenty minutes, each phase becoming faster and faster, until finally all the bells and drums are in use at the same time, making a noise that, although perhaps not best described as music, is certainly impressive.

Although the novices involved seem to have a fantastic sense of timing and rhythm, their sense of tone is somewhat lacking, or maybe it's just a warped sense of humour. There's one old bell that isn't used because it has a crack or fault in it. Just as the performance seems to have come to an end, there's often a single note struck on the faulty bell; a quite hideous sound unknown on any musical scale. It's as awful as fingernails on a blackboard and makes me both wince and burst out laughing every time I hear it! But any monk outside the monastery definitely gets the message: *come home*.

Bells are also used at Wat Kob during the Rains Retreat to waken the monks at 4am. Just before the Pansa starts, when the abbot is giving out various Pansa duties in the Bote to the assembled monks, he asks for a volunteer for the job of early morning bell-ringer. I've never seen so many monks trying to hide behind each other as the abbot's gaze sweeps around the Bote, looking for some likely candidate. Nobody, including me, wants to get up at 3.30am in the rain to climb the height of the tower to ring wet, brass bells. Usually there are no volunteers for the job, so the abbot has to appoint somebody, always some keen new monk, and the rest of us breathe a sigh of relief for another year. Although I was very happy with the duty at Wat Nahoob, I now have such a busy daily schedule that I begrudge losing even half an hour of sleep.

I don't think anybody who knows the Thais, nor even the Thais themselves, would dispute the fact that they have the most amazing ability to sleep. Any time, anywhere, on any surface and in any position. I once asked a European lady, on her first visit to Thailand, what her initial impression of the country was: 'Everybody's asleep,' she said. And when I ask students what their favourite pastimes are, 'sleeping' is invariably at the top of the list.

The most graphic example I've seen of this ability to sleep was when I observed a young monk paying his respects to the abbot of Wat Kob. Junior monks frequently bow three times to their seniors with what is known as a 'five point prostration'. The bow, or *graab*, starts from the kneeling position, sitting on the heels, and the upper part of the body is lowered until the elbows, palms and forehead are touching the floor. The abbot was sitting on his mat and the young monk approached on his knees, sat back on his heels and gracefully and mindfully made his first bow. He raised himself back to his kneeling position and then made the second bow, equally as gracefully. And then the third, but after the third bow he didn't raise himself up. He stayed where he was, his forehead resting on the floor, fast asleep. I was amazed, but the abbot didn't react at all. He sat for a few moments and then quietly got up and walked away, leaving the young monk to continue his sleep.

At Wat Kob we had a very nice young monk who was much like Giant at Wat Nahoob, not exactly fat, but big and soft-looking and with a lovely smile. He had the legendary reputation of being a very serious sleeper, even by Thai standards, and the other monks claimed that he spent more time asleep than awake. I didn't really believe that until I started to get to know him a little and observed him for myself. It was true. He slept through morning chanting, he slept through evening chanting, he slept through ordination ceremonies and through funeral services. I had even seen him sleep through lunch at a layperson's house. During services he would sit perfectly upright, his eyes closed, his hands raised to chest level with his palms together. Only his occasionally nodding head would indicate that he wasn't entirely with us.

Although it happened before I moved to Wat Kob, the other monks still laughed about an incident concerning the sleepy monk. Apparently there was a very long service in the Bote when the abbot and some forty or so monks and novices were sitting in a line on a specially-built platform, which raised them about a metre higher than the assembled lay-people. The platform was about a metre wide but the back of it wasn't against a wall. During the chanting, the sleepy monk, sitting with his legs folded to one side, hands in the prayer-like attitude, began to nod off. Gradually his body started to lean backwards, further and further. Suddenly, and with a great crash, he fell off the back of the platform and disappeared, much to the consternation of the lay-people, the horror of the abbot and the absolute delight of the novices, who collapsed in giggling heaps at this unexpected and welcome interruption to an otherwise long and boring service. I wish I had been there!

28

When a man ordains, he doesn't make a commitment to remain as a monk for a specified period. He is free to leave the Sangha, to disrobe, at any time. Some men do have a fixed period in mind, especially if they are ordaining for a short time to make merit for their family, or a departed loved one. That may vary from only a week or so, to several months.

The disrobing ceremony takes only about ten minutes but the first time I witnessed it I found it extremely poignant, probably due to the particular circumstances involved.

A young man of about twenty-five ordained at Wat Kob soon after his father died. The young monk was well educated and could speak some English. Unusually for a Thai, he was a very withdrawn and intense individual, but extremely likeable. We quickly became friends and I helped guide him in his meditation. It was clear that he took his ordination seriously, even though he knew it was temporary. He believed completely in the idea of transferring merit to the dead and had ordained in the hope that it would help ensure his father had a better rebirth. The company for which he worked allowed male staff three months' ordination leave, so he decided to ordain for that period.

I was present at his ordination and he was word-perfect in the Pali requests and responses. He was also one of the very few monks I have seen ordained who chanted the words, rather than just saying them. It was quite beautiful to hear. After his ordination, he walked on alms round with the abbot and me each morning and I also observed him frequently during the various ceremonies we attended together. Of all the short-term monks I have ever seen, and I have seen many hundreds, he was undoubtedly the most perfectly behaved. I believe his behaviour wasn't just 'show' or outward form. The Vinaya training rules about deportment and every other aspect of behaviour seemed to come perfectly naturally to him. His whole attitude towards his new status as a monk seemed to me to be one of total commitment and sincerity. That isn't always the case.

Many young Thai men who ordain short-term seem to do so with the attitude that it's something to be endured, almost like national military service. That's understandable within the context of Thai society and culture. Since they were little boys, they have known that when they reach the age of twenty or so, they would be expected to ordain and make merit, as a sort of 'thank you' to their parents for their upbringing. They accept ordination as part of their passing from youth to adult-hood. I don't think that's necessarily a bad thing, particularly if they ordain with a positive attitude and are prepared to learn from their time in the robes. Sadly, many are not.

In common with lay-people of all religions, many people in Thailand claim to be Buddhist without giving very much thought to what that means. They may often have no great understanding or interest in the religion beyond a few simple cycle of life ceremonies, or the most superficial and superstitious aspects of it. But I don't think there can be so much pressure on young men of other faiths to become so directly involved in their religion, whether they want to or not. Thai people generally, and young people in particular, are become increasingly more influenced by the West and by its materialistic attitudes, and hence decreasingly less inter-ested in spiritual matters. Most young men will still ordain for a short time, simply because of the social and cultural pressures on them to do so.

Frequently, when young men ordain they shave their heads and put on the robes, but those may be the only changes. Providing they can fill in the form, have no obvious physical or mental defects and have a guaran-tor, there is nothing to stop them from becoming monks and fulfilling their social or family obligations. Consequently, all types of young men ordain and they often bring into the Sangha all sorts of bad habits and vices, sometimes with no intention of giving them up, even for the short period of their time in the robes.

Judging by their behaviour some, I am sure, would benefit more from a few months in prison than in a monastery. In one Pansa at Wat Kob, we had about thirty young men ordain for three months. Within a week, four of them had to be disrobed. Wearing their robes, they had gone to a notorious house in the city to buy drugs and were picked up by police who happened to be watching the house.

The young monk who impressed me so much spent his three months studying Dhamma, the Vinaya and meditation and I was able to observe the changes in him even over a short period. He would frequently sort out the most senior monks at Wat Kob to talk about the Buddha's teaching and slowly his whole demeanour became one of confident calmness. Sometimes after a meditation period, his face seemed almost to glow with a radiance that came from inside. There was something about him that was definitely different from any other monk I have ever met. Others noticed it too and I had the feeling that he was exactly the sort of person who could not only greatly benefit himself by living within the Sangha, but could benefit the Sangha also.

On the day of his disrobement, twenty-two monks, including the abbot, assembled in the Bote. It is up to the disrobing monk how many other monks are present to witness the ceremony and I have never seen so many present for a disrobement before. Usually at Wat Kob, there are only five monks involved and sometimes the abbot does it alone. But the young monk had made so many friends and impressed so many of the other monks that we all wanted to be there to wish him good luck by chanting a traditional Pali blessing for him.

The monks sat in two lines, on the left- and right-hand sides of the abbot, forming a corridor through which the young monk approached the abbot on his knees. He bowed before the abbot and quietly chanted the Namo three times. He was then supposed to make a simple statement in Pali that translates as, 'I give up the training. May you henceforth regard me as a layman.' His voice faltered partway through. He stopped and looked at the abbot. The abbot looked kindly at him but did not intervene in whatever thoughts were going through the young man's mind. The thoughts in my mind were, 'Don't say it! Don't do it!' but nobody may interfere or try to influence another's decision in the matter. The young monk sat quite still for a few moments and the silence and tension in the Bote were almost tangible. I could imagine his mind torn between the life of a monk, which he certainly found deeply satisfying, and that of a layman . . . his family and friends, his career, perhaps a young lady waiting somewhere.

Finally, he continued the Pali stanza, sadly removed his folded sanghati and passed it to the abbot. The abbot directed him to leave the assembly of monks to change from his robes into ordinary clothes. When he returned, he requested the Five Precepts of a layman and the abbot splashed consecrated water over his head and shoulders, while the rest of us chanted a blessing wishing him good fortune in his new life. I, for one, meant every word, though I found the chanting difficult because of the lump in my throat.

I have heard many stories about long-term monks who for various reasons have decided to disrobe. For some, when it came to the moment, they were entirely unable to make the statement that declared their intention to return to lay life. They have stayed as monks.

I have also personally known of long-term monks who have disrobed and then almost immediately wished they hadn't. In some cases they have soon re-ordained, even though their disrobement nullified all the years they had already spent in the robes. A monk's seniority is measured by the number of Pansas he has lived as a monk in a continuous period. If a monk with, for example, twenty Pansas disrobed and then re-ordained, his previous twenty years would not count. He would be a junior monk again and even a new monk with only one Pansa would theoretically be his senior.

Once when I was visiting Wat Mahadhatu, a man came into Section 5 and smiled in recognition when he saw me. He was wearing jeans, a t-shirt and a leather jacket and it wasn't until he spoke to me that I realised he was one of my old teacher-monks from Wat Buddhapadipa. I had never seen him with hair or street clothes before and totally failed to recognise him, though I knew him well. He had returned to Thailand and disrobed but he was finding the life of a layman quite difficult. He had originally become a novice when he was about eight years old, ordained as a monk at twenty and remained in the robes for a further seventeen years. He knew little or nothing about the world outside the monastic environment, or how to cope with it. He was a Pali scholar and very skilled at chanting, but that isn't a lot of help when looking for a job. He was finding it difficult to get anything other than fairly menial work.

Besides the practical difficulty of being untrained and unprepared for living and working in the lay world, there is often another great difficulty for the long-term monk who disrobes. For many years, he has been in the highest social position in Thailand and may have become quite used to receiving great respect from everybody he comes into contact with; people prostrating before him, crawling around on their hands and knees and generally being at his beck and call. The monk, theoretically at least, is in a higher social position than HM the King. A monk does not bow to the King; the King bows to the monk. Once, when I was visiting Wat Buddhapadipa, I was invited with other monks to go to a house just outside London to chant for somebody's birthday, though I didn't know whose. On our arrival at the heavily guarded house, to my great surprise the young 'birthday boy' turned out to be one of His Majesty's four grandsons. All four Princes were in the house and all happily, and very properly, crawled on their hands and knees and bowed three times to me. Therefore, for the long-term monk who has become used to his high social standing, it must sometimes be extremely difficult to adjust to a new role: that of just another layman. In Thailand, people are frequently categorised socially and respected by others according to their wealth, standard of education and other outward forms of success. The long-term monk who disrobes may have none of those and finds himself suddenly at the bottom of the social heap, instead of on the top.

Many young Thai men ordain for two or three years and it is often they who really benefit from the Buddha's teaching. They have lived as monks long enough to understand something of the Dhamma and then want to continue a less reclusive life in the outside world, applying that understanding to their lives as laymen. But it doesn't always work out that way. At Wat Kob we had a young monk who was extremely handsome, though slightly less than bright. He had been a monk for two or three Pansas when he met a beautiful girl who said she was in love with him. He disrobed with the intention of marrying her, but as soon as she saw him in ordinary clothes, her passion dissipated and she rejected him! She only loved him as a monk. He re-ordained soon after and seemed to have lost all interest in women until, a year or so later, exactly the same thing happened again, with a different girl. That time, the abbot refused to re-ordain him at Wat Kob, declaring that it was about time he made up his mind what he wanted from life.

The second disrobing ceremony I attended affected me almost as much as the first, though in a different way and for a different reason. A week before the start of a Pansa, my good friend Phra Suthee decided he'd had enough and announced his decision to disrobe.

He'd been a monk for six years, but had never really wanted to be. Before ordaining, he had a good career with the Ports Authority of Thailand, he was halfway through an open university course for a Bachelor degree and, according to him, he had a very full and active social life. He told me that he was enjoying his life immensely, but his parents were having some difficulty with their own lives and felt they needed someone to make merit for them. They asked Suthee to become a monk. He reluctantly agreed, though without telling them of his reluctance. That may sound odd to a Westerner, but young Thais usually have a very high level of respect for their parents and for older people generally. They will usually follow their parents' instructions even when, as in Suthee's case, it goes against their own wishes.

Phra Suthee informed the abbot that he wanted to disrobe and the abbot set a date for a few days later that week. Nobody ever seems either surprised or disappointed when a monk announces his intention to leave the Sangha and I believe it is considered slightly impolite to ask why the monk reached that decision. My friend invited myself and three other monks to be present at the short ceremony in the abbot's kuti, which was set for 4am.

The day before the ceremony, Phra Suthee and I went into town to buy clothes for him. During his six years as a monk, his old clothes had long since been given away or thrown away. He needed trousers, shirts, underwear, shoes – everything, in fact.

337

Before ordaining, I really enjoyed shopping for clothes and would usually buy something new to wear almost every week. I didn't buy particularly expensive clothes, but they were always well designed, well cut and reasonably stylish. I liked clothes. I liked buying them and I liked wearing them. They were, I know, just ego props; a way of announcing to the rest of the world what sort of person I was, or at least considered myself to be.

The store that we chose to shop at had some very nice clothes indeed. As I helped Phra Suthee go through the racks of shirts and trousers, I totally forgot that I was supposed to be helping him choose and instead started to evaluate the various colours and styles for myself to wear. I usually don't have any money so even buying a pair of socks would be out of the question, but I could picture myself in that jacket, or this shirt. I rarely give a thought to my life before I ordained, but just seeing those lovely clothes led me to thinking about the sort of occasions that I might wear them, which in turn led me to remembering the enjoyment I used to have in my old life. A lot of it, probably most of it, was very superficial, but it was enjoyable nevertheless.

I started to become quite melancholy and, for a moment, found myself thinking about my own possible disrobement. When I ordained, I was sure that I would remain as a monk for the rest of my life, but I've learned enough to know that people change constantly, that we never know what the future might hold and that there should never be any regrets about the past, or fixed plans for the future. Only the present moment, right now, has any reality. Disrobing has never been on my agenda but the mind can constantly surprise with its fickleness, despite any attempts to train it.

My melancholy wasn't helped by suddenly catching sight of myself in a full-length mirror. It may sound strange, but I hadn't looked at myself in a mirror since the day I ordained. I use a very small, cracked, hand-mirror when I am shaving, but then I'm concentrating on the task in hand and don't see my face as a whole, and certainly not my body. Until catching a glimpse of myself in the shop's mirror, I had no idea what I looked like any more. What I saw in the mirror was a shock. A very tall, very thin, pale, bald and ageing man, wearing a hideously-bright orange robe which came only to his knees, with skinny arms and legs sticking out. It was not a pretty sight. Although I was shocked, I quickly reminded myself that any judgement based on my physical appearance was just vanity, ego, and really of no great importance. My life was no longer concerned, or should not be concerned, with such trivial matters.

Trivial matters . . . Phra Suthee was asking me whether I preferred the pale green shirt or the dark blue one, and was this tie suitable for that style of collar? A couple of laywomen, Phra Suthee's supporters, joined us at the store. We spent a couple of hours trying to decide whether slip-on or lace-up shoes were best, and then the style, then the colour, then the price. We went backwards and forwards between racks of shoes and sandals until I had a headache. I actually used to *enjoy* doing this? Just watching and listening to the three of them discussing, so seriously, how best to cover Phra Suthee's body with cloth and leather was a good reminder about how shallow so much of lay-life is. What would I do if I disrobed? Buy loads of clothes, stuff myself with pizza, party for a week – and then what? Thoughts of disrobing slipped away.

Mr Suthee came to visit me a couple of times after he disrobed. He had a job as a cashier in a petrol station. He seemed quite happy, though I couldn't really see how he could be. He didn't earn much money and had little time off and what free time he had was spent sleeping. It seemed to me that somehow his life didn't seem to have any point or direction any more. But he looked very smart.

29

I t is a fact that many Thai people simply don't take me very seriously as a monk. I have heard other Western monks comment that they have met with similar resistance. Despite wearing the same robes, shaving my head and following the same philosophy and rules as my Thai colleagues, I am still not considered to be a 'real' monk. That isn't a problem for me; if anything it is amusing, though mysterious.

When I have occasionally asked why I am not taken seriously, I've been told, 'You aren't Thai and you don't chant blessings.' I point out gently that the Buddha wasn't Thai either and, as far as I know, he didn't have a lot to say about the necessity or efficacy of chanting blessings. It doesn't make any difference. I've got used to the fact that to most Thai people I am an oddity and will probably always remain so. Thai people like to come and have a look at me and, although they always show the outward forms of respect and are very polite, it's obvious that they don't really know what to make of me. None of that stops me from getting on well with most Thai people that I meet, though.

Some of my Western visitors are much worse. I was sitting in my kuti one day when an elderly European man suddenly walked unannounced and uninvited into my room, accompanied by a young Thai boy. Without even greeting me in any way, the man theatrically flung out his arm, pointed at me and said to the boy, 'There he is! The Phra Farang!' I really feel sometimes as though I'm an exhibit in a zoo, especially when Westerners turn up without warning and say, 'I thought I'd come and have a look at you' – an opening comment I've heard dozens of times.

When I first went to live at Wat Kob, I felt that at least some of the monks also didn't quite know what to make of me. They were interested in this strange new species that had arrived in their midst but, although they knew that such beings existed, I don't think any of them ever expected to meet one.

At one time, there was a rumour circulating in the monastery that I was a spy for the Supreme Patriarch, though another version labelled me as a spy for the Pope! Sometimes, if I came upon a group of monks in deep discussion, they would fall silent until I had passed by, perhaps suspecting that I had a tape recorder hidden under my robe. Happily, we seemed to pass that stage after a few months and I think generally they do accept me now, or at least tolerate me.

Although to many Thai people I will never be a real monk in their terms, there are others who do take me seriously. Some make great effort to ensure I am happy and comfortable at Wat Kob, so that I can practise in my own peculiar Western way. Chief amongst these, luckily for me, is the abbot. If he didn't think I was serious in my practice, I don't think I would be welcome to stay, since I am probably more of a liability to the monastery than an asset. Although I never complain about anything, since I really have nothing to complain about, the abbot goes out of his way to ensure that I am sabbai at his monastery.

The students who live below my kuti think I'm a little weird, but we generally get along fine. They are noisy sometimes and I occasionally have to rebuke them about it, but that's not a great problem. One evening, I was sitting on my balcony talking with the head of the English department from the local teacher-training institute. She and her husband, a businessman, often visited me. On that occasion, I was helping the teacher with an English sociology course that she was preparing for her classes. Downstairs, radios were going full blast, doors were slamming and the students were laughing, shouting, singing and generally behaving in a perfectly normal manner for teenage boys.

The teacher asked me if I didn't find the kuti very noisy. I said that it was usually okay though the boys were sometimes a disturbance late in the evening, when I often did a couple of hours of meditation. Nothing more was said.

At that time, the old Bote was being renovated. It was to have a new tiled roof, a new polished marble

343

floor, ceiling fans, mosquito screens and a number of other necessary repairs. It could no longer be used for religious services, such as ordinations, because any monastery can have only one Bote and the old one had been 'decommissioned' when the new Bote had been completed some years before. It was a beautiful, cool and very peaceful building and its eighteen-inch-thick walls admitted hardly any sound. Despite that, the monastery really had no specific use for it.

Soon after the renovation was completed, the abbot came to see me and, to my great surprise, presented me with the keys to the building. He said that he had heard my kuti was sometimes too noisy for meditation and he was 'giving me' the old Bote as my personal meditation chamber. He added that, if I wanted, I could live in the old Bote and treat it as my kuti. He also intended having a shower and Western-style toilet built at one side of the Bote, for my use. I was quite overwhelmed by his kindness and, although I chose not to live in the old Bote, I use it frequently for my own meditation and for training others.

On another occasion, I decided to try to do something about the state of my toilet and shower, which are in a sort of concrete shed behind my kuti. The shed is divided into two tiny rooms, each with a shower and toilet. One room is for the monk's use and the other for the students living below the kuti. The tin roof leaked, the doors were hanging off and the shower rooms were very unpleasant, despite our efforts to keep them clean.

A friend in England had sent me a little money and I decided to use it to buy paint and some new corrugated tin for the roof. The abbot won't allow any alteration to any part of the monastery without his permission, so one evening as we were leaving the Bote after chanting I asked him if it would be okay to carry out this mini-renovation. 'No,' he said, and walked away.

I was quite surprised and assumed that, as usual, he hadn't understood me. I was even more surprised when builders arrived a few days later and completely gutted both toilet and shower rooms, and then entirely refurbished them.

I didn't know at the time that both the renovation of the old Bote and the rebuilding of the showers were paid for almost entirely by Khun Opas, the husband of the English teacher whom I had been helping with the sociology course. The abbot is much admired in Nakhon Sawan for what he has achieved at Wat Kob and I think his greatest admirer must be Khun Opas. For me, he epitomises Thai *jai dee*, good heart, and all that is most admirable in Thai people.

As I hadn't needed to use my friend's gift of money to renovate my toilet and shower, I decided to find out how much it would cost to have mosquito screens fitted to the doors and windows of my kuti. Mosquitoes have never been a bother to me, but whenever it rained the kuti would be invaded by literally thousands of flying ants, which were a nuisance. I hadn't a clue what mosquito screens cost or whether I had sufficient money, so I asked Khun Opas to arrange an estimate. The next day, a man came to measure up and the following day the screens were fitted. I was very embarrassed about that because I thought there had been a misunderstanding and I would now have to afford it, regardless of the cost. But no, Khun Opas had already paid the bill, and I never did find out what it was. I told him I wasn't too happy about that but he explained that he hadn't given the screens to me personally; they were for the kuti and for anybody who might live there. He was in effect donating them to the monastery, in which case I was delighted to accept them on behalf of all the monks who might live in my kuti in the future.

Every monastery in Thailand needs material support and every monastery has its supporters; people who either give of their own money or who are active in raising money from others. Khun Opas does both, but in a quiet way and, I believe, without conscious thought of making merit for himself. He does it simply because he has *jai dee* and a genuine and deep respect for the abbot. His *jai dee* doesn't extend only to lavish and obvious building programmes. Every Thursday, without fail, he will be waiting barefooted outside the monastery gates early in the morning, to offer food to all the monks as they pass by on their alms round.

I've been lucky enough to meet many good people like Khun Opas while living at Wat Kob. I don't deliberately cultivate such people, of course, but they are always welcome to visit me at my kuti if they want to practise their English conversation a little. Most of my visitors are associates or friends of teachers that I have

worked with, but I also have occasional visits from busi-
nessmen and even quite senior politicians. Once, the
Air Chief Marshal of the Royal Thai Air Force dropped
in for a chat, quite unexpectedly, although at the time
I hadn't a clue who he was. Unfortunately, I think the
social standing of some of my visitors has given me the
reputation at Wat Kob of being a bit of a snob, or a
'rich man's monk', not helped on one particular day
when, by chance, there were four brand new Mercedes-
Benz parked outside my kuti. (The one belonging to
the politician was obvious; it had gold-plated door
handles and diamond-studded window locks.) The
reputation is entirely unjustified because I also receive
dozens of 'ordinary' Thai visitors every week, but they're
just not so high profile on their mopeds or in their rick-
shaws. 'Important' or 'ordinary', I welcome anybody
who wants to call in. Most of my visitors are able to
speak good or very good English and some seem to
have quite a different attitude to Buddhism than the
majority of Thai people I have met.

A teacher and her husband invited me to lunch at
their house one Christmas Day. It was she who had
originally asked me to teach at the school near Nahoob
and we had kept in touch over the years. Unusually,
the invitation for lunch was for me alone, rather than
for a chapter of nine monks. I was delighted to accept,
though I nervously dreaded that I would have to chant
a solo Pali blessing after the meal.

My Christmas dinner was pizza, French fries,
Christmas cake and apples, eaten alone while the rest

of the family sat around the TV watching a video of the recently released *Jurassic Park*. I'd worked on the fringes of the film industry for a while and am a great admirer of Steven Spielberg, so I didn't know whether to mindfully eat my pizza or mindfully watch the dinosaurs. The pizza won, since I rarely have the opportunity to eat farang food. When I'd finished eating, I placed my hands together to give a blessing. 'Oh, don't worry about that,' said the teacher, 'we follow Buddhism as a philosophy, not as a religion.' I lowered my hands in amazement and instead of a Pali blessing, simply offered my very sincere thanks for their kindness.

Back at the monastery, I told my friend Phra Suthee about it and he was highly critical of me for not giving the usual blessing. He might well have been right, I really don't know.

I get on quite well with the other monks as far as I know, but in a neutral sort of way. Living in an isolated part of the monastery, I don't see that much of my colleagues anyway, except at morning and evening chanting. Few of us can communicate well, but the monks I particularly admire, generally the more senior ones, tend not to be especially communicative anyway. Some of them are like my old teachers at Wat Buddhapadipa in London and I learn a lot simply by observation.

One senior monk that I am especially fond of came out with a small pearl of wisdom that I've never forgotten. Nine of us were sitting in the back of a pick-up truck waiting to be taken somewhere or other, when a chatty new monk, trying to be friendly, said something to me in Thai which I didn't understand at all. He turned to the other monks and said, '*Mai ruu reuang,*' 'He doesn't know what's going on.'

The senior monk then said to him, '*Mai ruu reuang: sabbai,*' a Thai idiom meaning something like, 'When you don't know what's going on, you are content.' For me, that has really proven to be the case.

Monks are just people. Many are seriously trying to rise above what makes 'ordinary' mortals tick, but I think only a few succeed to any great extent. Any group of people, monks or laymen, adults or children, can become cliquey, especially when they live together in fairly confined quarters. Individuals squabble amongst each other, one bunch doesn't like the other bunch, they gossip about how bad that one is, or how well the other one practises. I expect that goes on at Wat Kob as much as anywhere else, but I don't know a thing about it and therefore am not involved. Nobody asks me for my opinion, I can't take sides in petty squabbles or personality conflicts and I'm not part of any clique. I am almost entirely isolated and that suits me just fine.

When I had my reunion in London with Dav, he told me of his own experiences in Thai monasteries. He said, 'If you want to survive in a Thai wat, you can be "one of" but you can't be "one-off".' My own experience has been quite different. I am 'one-off' because not only am I the only Phra Farang at Wat Kob, I am also the only one in the entire province. And I am not 'one of' because I choose not to chant blessings or splash holy water about and so on, as the Thai monks are expected to do. The other monks have slowly come to understand that I do not want to speak or socialise very much; not because I don't like my colleagues, but simply because I don't feel any need to. Hence, for a time, I had the nickname 'One man show'. I don't think that was an insult by any means, but was merely a reflection of my self-imposed, solitary status.

I understand enough Thai now to ask any questions I need to ask – there's a good chance that I might be understood – and to comply with any instructions I am given. And that's all I need to know. I enjoy the occasional chat in English with my visitors, but they also understand that I really don't want to socialise at any great length so they visit for short times and infrequently.

I get on with my own practice in my own way with, I think, my abbot's blessing. And that's all I do. I frequently haven't the faintest idea of what's going on. And I am sabbai.

30

Many years ago at Wat Buddhapadipa, Ajahn Amara Thera told me that after I ordained, I should wander around Thailand, 'looking in every cave and at the foot of every tree' until I found my spiritual guide.

Although the Ajahn had taught me, I think he knew from his long experience that he was not necessarily *the* teacher for me; he was not the teacher who would eventually led me to the goal of my practice. His great wisdom and experience had been the starting point, but if any student really wants to progress towards the highest reaches of meditation, he or she may often need a guide to whom the student can relate at a very deep and special level; an intuitive rather than an intellectual level.

The guide must understand the limits of the student and push the student gently – sometimes perhaps not so gently – in certain directions, with subtle advice that does not lead to expectations but instead allows genuine personal experience and understanding to arise at the Insight level. Often, these things can neither be put into words nor taught, but must be intuitively self-realised.

I haven't wandered around Thailand looking for my teacher-guide. As a consequence, I am sure I have made many mistakes in my meditation practice. Perhaps I am still making them. I know at times I have been side-tracked, but I believe I have usually managed to get myself back on the right course, or what I believe is the right course for me.

When I first moved to Wat Kob, I wasn't entirely sure if I was practising my meditation in the most productive way. I was still usually practising two or three hours of walking and sitting meditation every day but I was never forcing myself to meditate at pre-set times. That was generally satisfactory but I sometimes felt that the meditation itself was becoming almost routine. It is at such times that every meditator really needs a teacher-guide. Apart from some scholarly books, I didn't have a guide and had to rely on my own intuition about the direction I should take. I decided to break the routine and add new elements to my meditation; to push myself further and to experiment a little.

I first started to undertake continuous twelve-hour sittings and then later, on just two occasions, continuous twenty-four-hour sittings. I totally emptied one of the rooms in my kuti and had my then looksit, Banjob, lock the door from the outside. I couldn't get out of the room, so I couldn't eat, drink, go to the loo, or do anything else. I didn't sleep, I just sat in meditation. I wanted to observe the body and its physical and mental needs over a longish period and see what degree of control could be exercised over those needs. That wasn't particularly important, though it was interesting. At the end of the pre-arranged period, Banjob would open the door, massage some life back into my legs, and let me out. Those sessions were quite useful and although mentally I didn't find them too much of a strain, physically they didn't do me any good at all. During the second twenty-four-hour sitting, my knee cartilage was damaged again. Although that gave me the opportunity to meditate on acute physical discomfort, it marked the end of the marathons.

I also took to meditating inside the crematorium oven. Yes, I know that sounds weird, but I'll explain why I did it in a moment. For those who are as yet unfamiliar with such ovens, Wat Kob's is basically a brick chamber about seven feet long and two feet six inches wide. There are two such ovens in the crematorium, side by side and divided by a thick wall. In each, the walls curve upwards and towards each other to make an arch about four feet six inches high in the middle. Not high enough to stand up in, but I don't suppose many people need to.

Many cremations are held at Wat Kob, hence the need for two ovens, and rarely a week goes by without at least a couple of funerals being held. Sometimes both ovens are in use at the same time and therefore don't have much opportunity to cool down.

The first time I decided to meditate in the oven, I

almost gave up after a few minutes. Although neither oven had been used that day, the heat inside was almost unbearable. The bricks had retained heat from a cremation the day before and were actually hot to touch. Because of the narrow width, I was unable to sit facing the door and had to sit sideways, with my back against one wall and my knees pressed against the opposite wall. My back and knees were roasting within minutes and sweat was literally pouring from me.

The oven seemed to be airless, though some entered from the ash chamber beneath. The air was foul and stank of death. That may sound fanciful, but I have been close enough to burning corpses to recognise the smell; an oily and musty stench that catches in the throat and which not only seemed to cling to my skin but also permeated my robes, even after a short time.

The first night that I used the oven as a meditation chamber, I told Banjob to stand sentry on the crematorium steps while I was inside. He hated the idea. Like most Thai people, especially from the countryside, he was terrified of ghosts, but I needed him there to allay my own fears. I wasn't frightened of ghosts. I was worried that someone may have come and turned the big wheels that lock the thick, steel door, or even do a test firing of the oven, though why anybody should I cannot imagine.

I also needed Banjob to shut the heavy door after I climbed into the chamber and to open it at the end of the pre-set period of one hour. It is a feature of crematorium ovens that they do not generally have handles on the inside of the doors. I tested the door beforehand and found it extremely difficult to push open in the cramped quarters.

On the first occasion, I climbed into the oven and Banjob pushed the door shut. Then, rather than standing watch as instructed, he scarpered, too scared to stay anywhere near the crematorium at night. He ran back to his room, fully intending to return at the end of an hour but, in the nature of Thai people, fell asleep instead. I had no clock with me in the oven and it was anyway totally black inside, so I had no idea of the time. I eventually realised that considerably more than an hour had passed. I discovered later that I had been in there nearly three hours. With great difficulty, I squirmed about in the oven, covering my face and robes with soot as I did so, until I could get into a position to push the door open.

It was an uncanny piece of timing. At that very moment, an old Thai gentleman was walking past the crematorium and nearly died of fright when the oven door slowly opened and a pale, sooty zombie crawled out!

At first, I didn't tell any of the other monks that I was using the oven as a meditation chamber because they might conceivably have thought I was, well, mad I suppose. Of course, word about my latest weird behaviour eventually got around. Much to my surprise, several other monks wanted to join me for these 'bake-ins', as they became known.

I should explain that there was what seemed a genuine

purpose to this apparently bizarre behaviour. One theme of Buddhist meditation is to contemplate corpses in various succeeding stages of decomposition and to understand, to genuinely *know* at the Insight level, that there is no escape for any of us from such a condition.

Everybody accepts intellectually that the physical body will die and will be buried or burned. That intellectual acceptance of death is sometimes very shallow, though that's not entirely the point anyway. To reflect upon the impermanence and constantly changing nature of the physical body, dead or alive, can reduce our attachment to it. That lessens the mental suffering we inflict upon ourselves when the body becomes sick, old, no longer handsome or beautiful, or starts to let us down in various ways. That penetrative understanding can then help us to understand the impermanence of all other phenomena as well. It is our attachment and clinging to impermanent phenomena which is the main cause of our mental suffering. Impermanent phenomena means *everything*, since there are no phenomena with any permanence. With that Insight understanding about impermanence, we can change the way we view not only our own body, but also our reactions to other people, things, situations and everything around us. It can prompt a new way of evaluating ourselves and the way we live our life now, whilst we are still able to do something about it. That won't stop the physical body from dying of course, but it can greatly improve the quality of this life and lessen much of our self-inflicted suffering.

The Buddha recommended that his monks should meditate in charnel grounds about death and the impermanent nature of the body. He specified corpses in nine succeeding stages of decomposition as being suitable objects for meditation. In India in those days there were many places where corpses could be seen, but not in modern Thailand. Although I frequently see corpses during my normal duty at funerals, it isn't possible to spend much time with them – usually only a few moments and certainly not the several days needed to watch the changes that take place in a decomposing body. I thought that the nearest I could get to a charnel ground as an environment for that sort of meditation was the crematorium oven.

It was after one of the 'bake-ins' that I realised a couple of things. The monk in the other oven, Phra Perm, had been a monk for about eight years. He was a Dhamma teacher at the monastery school and was also a very serious and experienced meditator and worked hard to extend his understanding. At the end of two hours, our little alarm clocks rang to indicate the end of the sitting, though sometimes one or both of us would ignore the time and carry on until our own meditation reached a natural conclusion. On that occasion, we slowly and quietly climbed out of our respective ovens and adjusted our wet robes. We didn't look at each other, nor did we need to speak. There was no 'how was it for you?' type of chatter. We didn't need to analyse or compare notes. We walked slowly away from the crematorium to our kutis.

As I wearily climbed my kuti steps, I knew, without any doubt, that at some time in the last few months I had passed an important stage in my meditation practice. I believed there had come some point when I had built up a sufficiently solid foundation of understanding to carry me forward, each cautious new step seeming logical and natural. I had, in a sense, developed my own momentum, albeit a slow and sometimes faltering one.

That was nothing to do with meditating in the oven. I had quickly realised that the crematorium was just a place; a very hot and smelly place. Although my meditation there had been good, without a corpse the oven was a poor substitute for a charnel ground.

Soon after one of the 'bake-ins', I was in the meditation hall of Wat Kob's mango garden. Around the walls were posters of famous Thai meditation masters, as well as photographs of dead bodies. I'd seen such photographs frequently in other meditation halls in other monasteries. They are usually coloured pictures of men or women who have died violently or unnaturally; through murder, road accident, drowning, or something of that nature. Often they show the corpse lying on the road or on a floor with the body ripped open from throat to navel, revealing all the internal organs, which are sometimes pouring from the body. The head may be badly damaged, with the brain splattered about, that sort of thing.

One of the purposes of such photographs is apparently to help reduce sexual lust (obviously important for monks, who are supposed to be celibate), though I'm not sure if they are of any great value even in that. Anyway, I was looking at the photographs with no great curiosity when a young visiting monk, who could speak some English, approached me and said, 'They're horrible, aren't they?' I made no reply. He came closer and said, 'They are to make you understand how disgusting the body is, and that we should not think it is beautiful.'

I stared at the monk, feeling a physical tremor pass through me as an Insight, an absolute *knowing*, swept over me. What the monk had said was relatively obvious, relatively true and, I knew with total conviction, ultimately quite daft.

I must have been staring at him quite intently because he stepped away from me, looking uneasy. 'You should meditate on beauty and ugliness,' he advised, as he moved hurriedly to the other end of the hall.

Beauty and ugliness. Beauty *and* ugliness. But did either have any reality? Weren't they, ultimately, the same thing? Merely man-made concepts? I looked at the photographs again. They were not ugly and nor were they beautiful. They were just the way they were. We were putting names to states such as 'beauty' and 'ugliness' and trying to differentiate between them, thus conditioning ourselves even further to being averse to one and attracted to the other. To meditate on the 'ugliness' of the body was surely to reinforce that idea and, therefore, also to reinforce the idea that something else or some other condition was 'not ugly', or was 'beautiful'.

I had always understood that the whole point of meditation was to see all things in their Ultimate Truth, devoid of personal conditioned responses, concepts, cravings, aversions and delusions. It is only when we overcome all those that we achieve real freedom of mind. There was nothing ultimately ugly about a kidney or spleen. In the same way, there was nothing ultimately beautiful about a bunch of flowers; everything is just the way it is and any attraction or aversion we feel is a personal and relative truth. Of course, at the relative level, if I was a girl I'd much rather be given a bunch of flowers than a bunch of kidneys.

I decided to re-read the various translations I have of the *Maha Satipatthana Sutta*, the Buddha's most important teaching about meditation. Whilst doing so, I realised something which struck me as both very odd and very confusing.

The teaching is long and, in its printed form, the main sections are usually broken up by translators into smaller sub-sections, making it easier to read and the presentation more attractive.

The teaching gives guidance for meditation on all aspects of the body and mind. The sub-section which was of immediate interest to me recommends that the meditator should view the body as being composed of: 'hairs of the head, hairs of the body, nails, teeth, skin, flesh, sinews, bones, marrow, kidneys, heart, liver, pleura, spleen, lungs, intestines, mesentery, undigested food, excrement, brain, bile, phlegm, pus, blood, sweat, fat, tears, grease, saliva, mucus, synovial fluid and urine.' By contemplating the physical body in that way, we can learn to become less mentally attached to it.

What surprised and confused me, and what I had never noticed before in my many readings of the Sutta, was that in each of my four translations, the sub-section was headed, 'Repulsiveness of the body', or 'Loathsomeness of the body', or something similar. Repulsive? Loathsome? But surely those were relative concepts based on individual conditioning, our personal likes and dislikes, our cravings and aversions. Although most people would probably find the sight of a dissected body spread out on a table fairly repulsive, how we personally viewed it had nothing to do with what it ultimately *was*.

That all seemed very contradictory to me and I decided to seek scholarly advice.

Probably the most authoritative source in the world about the Pali language and the Buddhist scriptures is the Pali Text Society in England. The PTS was founded in 1881 and has published the entire Pali Canon in Roman script, as well as most of it in English. All the major commentaries have also been published and the society has compiled both a Pali-English and an English-Pali dictionary.

I wrote to the PTS asking whether the original Pali discourse contained the word 'repulsive', or 'loathsome' or any other word with a similar connotation. Their reply was unequivocal. According to the society, in the original text the Buddha taught only that the body should be seen to be a collection of various secretions and organs, just as it is and without adding relative concepts to it. So how did the misleading idea of meditating on the 'repulsiveness' of the body creep into the teaching? The PTS explained that modern translators have been influenced by the *Visuddhimagga* (The Path of Purification), which was written by a fifth-century commentator named Buddhaghosa. It was he who introduced the idea of the body being something nasty by using the word 'disgustingness' in his commentary. It was his own idea, introduced into the Buddha's teaching. In their letter to me, the PTS concluded, 'This shows the pitfalls of translators being too keen on using a fifth-century commentator to interpret the text.'

Buddhaghosa's commentaries have influenced the whole of modern Theravada Buddhism, not just the meditation practice, and I have since read criticism of some of his other commentaries by modern Thai scholars. I decided from that moment to be extremely cautious about taking anything I read at face value but, instead, to keep in mind the Buddha's own words: 'Do not be led by the authority of religious texts . . . but *know for yourself . . .*'

I decided that to really understand the Buddha's teaching about the physical body, I needed a corpse. I needed lots of them in fact, as well as living bodies. I gave all this great thought and decided to write myself a 'body meditation programme', to try to investigate this aspect of the teaching as thoroughly as I could. I discussed the programme with my abbot. He is not a meditative monk so he couldn't fully understand, but he was very supportive and said he would arrange with the local hospital for me to have access to unidentified, unclaimed corpses, as well as to attend autopsies.

It was to be a long and complex programme, involving a total of about fifteen bodies; individually, in comparative groups of different ages, in mixed groups of living and dead, as well as dissected and decomposed. I thought it might take several years to complete, partly at least because of the difficulty of finding suitably decomposed bodies. But I was in no hurry and, anyway, the programme was merely a part of my overall meditation practice. I am not going to write here in any detail about the programme, but even very soon after it started I discovered I was 'seeing' with totally different and clearer eyes. I realised it was something I should have done years before, at the very outset of my practice, though there are many practical difficulties in such meditation which would make it almost impossible to undertake in the West.

Despite that new impetus, there was still a niggling sense of dissatisfaction at the back of my mind. Not about the body meditation programme, but about my meditation as a whole. I was beginning to question where it was all leading. I knew where it should have been leading – but was it? It was all very well to read explanations in my meditation books of the expected *nimitta*, or visions, that can arise during meditation, but hallucinations, seeing lights, colours and feeling 'ripples of energy' seemed about as useful as fairy lights on a coffin. They didn't lead anywhere; they were just side-shows. I am not impatient in my meditation but

I was beginning to feel that in some ways my practice was in danger of becoming an end in itself, rather than the means to an end. I think that may be true for many meditators.

I decided I needed guidance. I was to find it, but in a most unexpected time and place.

Even before the start of the body meditation programme, I believe I was fairly dispassionate about bodies and did not think of them as beautiful, handsome, ugly, sexy, desirable etc., except at the shallowest relative level. But as the programme progressed, I realised it had prompted my thinking to spread wider. I found my clearer vision began to encompass not just bodies but *all* phenomena: every thing, every condition, every situation, every man-made and every *mind-made* concept.

A basic teaching of Buddhism is that 'nothing whatsoever should be clung to'. I had heard the phrase hundreds of times from meditation teachers and I had read it equally as often in meditation books. But it is natural for any meditator to work first towards letting go of those things, concepts and mental states which are generally thought of as 'bad', 'undesirable' or 'unwholesome' and, in consequence, to leave, cultivate and hence cling to their opposites; the 'good', the 'desirable' and the 'wholesome'. But while *any* concept of good or desirable existed, then automatically the opposite must exist also. This is good, therefore that is bad. But nothing whatsoever should be clung to, good or bad, desirable or undesirable. All such concepts had to be let go of. There could only be real progress when there was no clinging of any kind, when the mind was completely freed and stilled of conceptualisation and had reached a point where all such distinctions were seen to be without foundation.

I had always understood that intellectually. I found actually knowing it at the most fundamental level to be quite a different thing.

Beautiful, ugly, good, bad, happy, unhappy, clever, stupid, sane, insane, real, unreal, interesting, boring, past, future: they were all ultimately exactly the same, just mind-made concepts. By trying to differentiate between them, we were falling into a trap. What trap?

Dualism. That was the trap. And I was in it.

I had read something, some time . . . what was it . . . where was it? I searched through my bookshelves. There it was: a forty-year-old little volume, the book I had just finished reading when I met Dav, the Tibetan monk, in London. I had already read it several times but I had never understood it at the right level: the intuitive level.

The Zen teaching of Huang Po.

It is impossible to make my feelings clear as I re-read the little book. It is difficult even to use Huang Po's own words to try to explain. Both in and out of context, they seem to contain paradox within paradox.

For weeks, I grappled with the riddles that the teaching of this Chinese Zen master seemed to present. Every time I thought I had reached some understanding, I also realised that my understanding was shallow and based on more conceptual thinking. Slowly, his teaching began to make intellectual sense at least, though to understand Zen intellectually is hardly to understand it at all. Through Huang Po's words, I realised that although my meditation practice certainly hadn't been taking me in the wrong direction, it had been woefully incomplete. Suddenly, pieces of my meditation puzzle started to fall into place.

In our daily lives we all frequently need to make use of conceptual thinking to pass on relative truths. Even Huang Po was forced to do that in trying to explain things clearly to his students. But I wasn't interested in relative truths. Relative Truth does not lead to Insight-Wisdom.

Although all serious meditators should try to practise continuous mindfulness of thought, action and speech, I spent weeks watching everything I thought, did or said, while specifically looking out for dualistic and conceptual thinking. I was astonished at how deeply I was caught in the trap and how little relevance many of my thoughts had – to anything.

My meditation practice was perfectly sound, but by meditating on and deliberately trying to cultivate, 'good' qualities such as compassion, universal love, equanimity and all the rest, I was sidetracking myself. I might become a nobler, calmer person and the aim was in keeping with the Buddha's teaching, but it wouldn't take me, or anybody, a single step nearer the ultimate goal of all Buddhist meditation.

Even understanding how my unwholesome emotions arose and being able to recognise and control them ultimately had little value. It was a side issue. Without concepts of good, bad, desirable, undesirable and so on, those emotions could not arise in the first place.

Even if I meditated for a thousand years, whilst I retained the dualistic notion 'this is good', I must also have the idea 'and that is bad'. Both would continue to exist, both were equally conceptual and both were, ultimately, a hindrance.

Of course it was 'good' to do good. That was an essential teaching of Buddhism, but such activity had to be spontaneous and altruistic. There could be no thought of, 'if I do such and such it will be good, *therefore* I will do it.' Although the good deed would still be done, it would have entirely the wrong mental basis; one of attachment, clinging, or greed. It was clinging to the concept of 'doing good' – something else to be overcome and let go of.

In one of his more straightforward statements, Huang Po said: 'Away with your likes and dislikes, every single thing is just the one mind. When you have perceived this, you will have mounted the chariot of the Buddhas.'

I read the book again, and then again, trying to read it with a completely open mind, a mind empty of conceptual thinking, trying not to understand intellectually but rather just to let Huang Po's words flow into me. 'Begin to reason about it and you at once fall into error,' he said.

Many meditators follow Zen methods partly because Zen seems to offer faster results than Theravada, which is considered by many Zen masters to be a primitive and undeveloped form of Buddhism. With its riddles and paradoxes, its mystic dynamism and positive expression through painting, gardens, flower arrangement and martial arts, Zen seems to appeal much more to the enquiring Western mind than Theravada, which can seem dry, passive and downright dull by comparison.

But I wasn't looking for fast results. Right from the start, I had always been careful not to allow my mind to actively seek any results at all. That would be attachment and hence a hindrance to progress. I had already discovered for myself the truth and value of the Theravada teachings but after reading Huang Po's words I realised that although I had been travelling on the main road, I had become stuck in the left-hand lane. The wisdom of Zen seemed to offer a way of moving to the middle lane, though not necessarily the fast outside lane.

Was I becoming some sort of closet Zen monk? Would I eventually follow Dav and leave the saffron robes of the Theravadans for the purple and yellow of Tibetan Buddhism, or the grey of Korean Zen, or whatever? I didn't think so. I was a monk and I would be the same monk in my heart whether I was wearing orange robes, purple robes or blue Levis. I follow the Vinaya about such things but I actually couldn't care less what religious tradition or culture dictates I should wear. Theravada, Mahayana, Zen and all the rest were just labels – more concepts. I suppose I was becoming something a little different from a 'normal' Theravadan, certainly different from a normal Thai Theravadan, but

I wasn't about to undergo metamorphosis into a Mahayanist. I was still a Buddhist monk, following the teaching of the Buddha. I believe that teaching included what eventually came to be called Zen. Being a monk was about committing oneself to 'mind work' or 'mental cultivation': much better translations of the original word *bhavana* than 'meditation'.

The place of practice, whether it be a city temple, a forest, a mountain top or a crematorium oven; the robes, whether orange, brown or purple; the rites and rituals, both of Theravada and Mahayana, they were all just outward form of little real value. They had little or nothing to do with the real work: the personal realisation of Ultimate Truth.

Huang Po said, 'There is only the one mind and not a particle of anything else on which to lay hold, for this "Mind" is the Buddha. If you students of the way do not awake to this Mind substance, you will overlay Mind with conceptual thought, you will seek the Buddha outside yourselves, and you will remain attached to forms, pious practices and so on, all of which are harmful and not at all the way to Supreme Knowledge.'

'Awake to it, and it is there.'

And so I met my teacher, or at least a guide who may perhaps eventually lead me to my teacher. Huang Po died on a mountaintop in China more than a thousand years ago, but that doesn't matter. The Buddha has been dead for considerably longer. The Buddha originally pointed the way, Huang Po was another signpost on the same path.

It is only about five years since I ordained as a Buddhist monk and took my first step on the path. I have made many mistakes and there have been a few times when I have been discouraged. Maybe there are other such times to come. But I am still *trying*. Perhaps I have so far learned only a little, and I know I have a great deal more to learn. But already in my short life as a monk, through the Buddha's teaching, through practising that teaching and making it essential in my daily life, I have realised a profound happiness that goes far beyond the mundane meaning of the word. For me, the teaching of the Buddha *is* my daily life.

I believe that every day, every small step on the path, gives me a little more genuine understanding of what the Buddha taught. And I am happy, I am sabbai, to continue the journey.

Afterword

'*I am happy, I am sabbai, to continue the journey.*' Only a moment has passed since you read those words; for you, the turning of a page. For me, five years have gone by. I am now drawing to the end of my tenth Pansa as a monk. It will be my last. I will disrobe the day after the Pansa ends, in two days' time, on 11 October 2003.

This hasn't been an easy decision for me, nor has it been an impetuous one. I've thought about it for more than a year, examining the varied, complex and conflicting issues involved and trying to find some solution that doesn't necessitate leaving the monkhood, but which is also not a half-hearted compromise. There is nothing I dislike or can't handle about the life or discipline of a monk, nor is there anything that I miss about lay-life, but I had to make a choice.

A few years ago, if asked whether I would ever disrobe, I would have replied, 'No. I will remain in the robes for the rest of my life.' My words would have been sincere because my life as a monk has always been

371

satisfying and seemed to have purpose, but such a statement would only have shown my lack of understanding of the Dhamma. No phenomenon remains the same for two consecutive moments, including the working of our own minds. Any statement of permanence, no matter how sincere or well intended, cannot have any real meaning. I change – whether I like it or not – with the ever-changing circumstances and phenomena that surround me. I have learned that and I accept it. I tend anyway to think of 'change' as development and I am happy to embrace whatever developments occur in my life, whether they are apparently good or apparently not-so-good. If circumstances now dictate that I should disrobe and develop in a different direction, that's okay.

In my first year as a monk, I was concerned about my increasingly busy teaching schedule at the school near Wat Nahoob. I asked Ajahn Amara Thera how far my social responsibilities as a monk extended. He replied that really I had no such responsibilities at all. He said that my only duty as a monk was to increase my understanding of meditation and of Dhamma. He added, wisely, that by practising well and by being a good example for the lay-people, I would be helping them in their own practice of Dhamma and would increase their faith in the Sangha. I have tried to be that good example throughout my time in the robes.

Later, during a visit to Wat Buddhapadipa in London, I mentioned to Ajahn Amara Thera that my friends and I were supporting a few impoverished Thai students by raising money to help them study at university. He warned me to be cautious. He said that it was easy for a monk to become sidetracked from his own practice by the problems of the lay-people. I understood and accepted what he said but I thought that I could handle my developing dual role of monk and social worker. Perhaps I should have listened more intently or taken his warning more to heart. At the time – and I imply no disrespect for the Ajahn – his answer seemed to me to be somewhat lacking in compassion, at least in its ordinary sense. Despite the Ajahn's advice, I decided that I should continue to give whatever practical help I could to those who needed it. Soon after, I established the charity that became known as the Students' Education Trust.

SET is now more than ten years old. In its first few years, the charity was very small and I was able to maintain a comfortable balance between my life as a monk and my work with disadvantaged students. Then, I was a monk doing a little social work in my spare time. That changed in 1997 after the publication of the first edition of *Phra Farang*, in which I mentioned SET's work. Suddenly, SET had the support of many compassionate and generous people from all over the world. With increased funds, the charity rapidly expanded; it had no choice but to do so. The number of supported students rose dramatically each year and, as income increased further, other programmes were introduced. With SET's support, more than 1,000 students have since gained university degrees or vocational diplomas. Because I was becoming increasingly involved with my social work, I had correspondingly less time for my meditation practice or even for my everyday duties as a monk. Running the charity became like running a small business, with all the associated problems and petty worries. Instead of being a full-time monk doing a little social work in my free time, I became a full-time social worker dressed in robes. That wasn't why I originally ordained but SET had become so important to so many young people – and to me personally – that I could not, with good conscience, stop its development.

As I became busier with SET's work, so I also became criticised by some senior monks about my increasing social involvement, as well as my decreasing participation in the normal, ritualistic activities of the Thai Sangha. As Ajahn Amara Thera had explained, traditionally it isn't the job of a monk in Thailand to be so actively involved in society's problems. Monks are expected to develop compassion for others and to give leadership and advice on social issues, but without active involvement. That isn't really good enough for me any more, either as a monk or as a layman. Through my social work, I am in a position to offer practical help to disadvantaged people in the society in which I live. I consider I would be failing in my moral duty as a *person* – as a member of the human family – if I didn't offer that help. Even some Thai lay-people disapproved of my work with SET. Within the context of Thai Buddhism, their criticisms were probably justified. Although I never failed to walk on alms round and always attended morning and evening services in the monastery, I eventually had to stop accepting invitations to chant at house breakfasts or lunches, and at funerals, wedding blessings and other such functions. I simply didn't have time. I must admit, I also didn't have much inclination to participate anyway. I think that disappointed a few people because I was still very much 'on show' – still *Phra Farang Superstar* – and I was expected to appear and perform as required. Anyway, my monastery was full of Thai monks who were considerably more skilled at chanting than me and they had little else to do all day, so I let them get on with it. Since I'm hopeless at chanting and have never felt comfortable about giving 'blessings', I felt my own time was more productively spent doing what I *was* good at.

Besides running the charity, my life had become increasingly busy and complicated in other ways too. By then, I had written four books about various aspects of Buddhism. In a specialised sort of way, I'd become quite well known amongst Western Buddhists, though even that limited fame was never something I sought or wanted. As a result of my books, I began to be visited at my kuti by large numbers of people. I welcomed them all but many of them were experiencing spiritual uncertainties that they hoped and expected that I could resolve. Although I gave whatever advice I could, sometimes I didn't feel especially qualified to do so. On an average day I usually received two or three visitors but on one particularly memorable day, more than thirty dropped in, all unannounced. Although my time was being consumed by SET and my visitors, I was also teaching Ethics at a university, spending hours every day counselling people by email, running month-long meditation retreats, training foreign monks and novices and travelling frequently to Bangkok to give talks about Buddhism or to teach meditation. I did it all whole-heartedly but being monk, author, teacher, spiritual counsellor and social worker became too much for me to cope with. I was trying to be everything to everybody and was eventually forced to decide what my priorities were.

SET's work has become the driving force in my life. Helping disadvantaged students has become more important to me than my personal spiritual progress as a monk. I have no regrets about that. The charity is changing the lives of hundreds of young people, giving them the opportunity to rise above their impoverished backgrounds, to fully realise their potential and to achieve something for themselves. I find that wonderfully satisfying, more satisfying than anything I have ever done before. In fact, almost everything of importance that I have done before, including becoming a monk, has been entirely for my own benefit. Now, for a change, I am happy to work for the benefit of others.

Compared to living as a monk, running a charity may not seem like a very spiritual activity. I think it can be, depending on one's mental approach to the work. SET has become the vehicle through which I can practise and develop compassion for others in a very practical way. Without first developing compassion for others, there can be little personal spiritual advancement anyway, for any of us. Not many people ever have such an opportunity, so I consider myself very fortunate. In addition to helping to develop my own sense of compassion, SET is also the vehicle through which hundreds of young people can develop theirs. All SET's scholarship students are encouraged to voluntarily work with orphans, handicapped children, AIDS sufferers and old people.

So, in a couple of days' time, I'll go through that short ceremony in the Bote, chant a few simple Pali phrases and will suddenly cease to be a Buddhist monk. I'm not particularly looking forward to the ceremony and maybe I won't get through it without at least choking up, but I am already fairly well adjusted to the idea of being a layman rather than a monk. *Nothing whatsoever should be clung to.* Anyway, saying those Pali words can't change what I am *inside*. I will exchange my robes for a shirt and trousers, but that will be the only difference. For me, it will be a superficial one. Whether I am Phra Peter or Mr Peter, I will be the same person and I will try to live my life by the same code of ethics that has sustained and guided me for the past ten years. But I need closure on this chapter of my life.

When I ordained as a monk, I had the feeling that I was starting out on a great new journey. I wasn't. I understand now that I started my personal journey long, long before. Living as a monk was just one more step on the way. My journey continues and there is no end in sight, but I know it's leading me *somewhere*. I now travel with greater confidence, but I no longer need the props of religion to help me on my way. I will now perhaps take a slightly different route, but the destination remains the same. And I am happy, I am sabbai, to continue the journey . . .

An appeal from the Students' Education Trust

I n 1994, Phra Peter Pannapadipo and his friends established a small fund to help one impoverished Thai
student study at university. More than enough was
collected so the balance became the foundation of a
non-profit-making charity dedicated to helping other
students with similar difficulties. The charity – the Students'
Education Trust – has since grown and now receives
support from concerned people all around the world.

SET has a very specific aim: *to make a difference*.
That difference is between a disadvantaged student
being able to study at university or vocational college,
or instead being forced to labour in the rice paddies,
on a Bangkok building site, or in some other mundane,
dead-end job.

More than 1,000 students have already benefited
from SET's Scholarship Programme. That's 1,000
university degrees or vocational diplomas for students
who, without help, might never have been able to study
at all. Hundreds more have benefited from SET's

Student Welfare Programme, receiving grants to pay for their uniform and shoes, books and tools, bus fares or school lunches. Through its Educational Projects Programme, SET sponsors English Language Camps, Narcotic Drugs Awareness Camps and other projects with both short- and long-term benefits. The 'SET for Society' Programme encourages scholarship students to voluntarily work with orphans, handicapped children, AIDS patients and old people. Students also give thousands of hours of voluntary labour each year to renovate rural primary schools. Every year since 1994, SET has improved and expanded its programmes to reach increasing numbers of students. We do it voluntarily, cost-effectively and with great enthusiasm.

It costs very little to make a difference but there are thousands of students in Thailand who are prevented from achieving anything worthwhile simply because of their impoverished backgrounds. By supporting SET, you can make a positive difference to the lives of some of these deserving young men and women.

To find out more about SET and how you can help, please contact:

Peter S. Robinson, Director, The Students' Education Trust, Academic Resource Centre, Rajabhat University, Sawanwithi Road, Amphur Muang, Nakhon Sawan 60000, Thailand.

Email: SET_THAI@hotmail.com
Web site: www.thaistudentcharity.org.

Little Angels

Phra Peter Pannapadipo

The real-life stories of the novice monks in *Little Angels* reflect the lives of many youths in rural Thailand who are trapped in the vicious cycle of poverty, broken homes, illiteracy and drug abuse. When all else fails, Buddhism becomes their last resort: providing them with physical shelter and spiritual refuge. It heals their childhood traumas and gives them a moral framework for living and a better outlook on life. Each individual story, heartrending as it may be, subtly shows what Phra Peter sees and wishes others to appreciate: the 'human face' of Thai Buddhism.

arrow books